VIKING SOCIETY FOR NORTHERN RESEARCH
TEXT SERIES

GENERAL EDITORS
Anthony Faulkes and Alison Finlay

VOLUME XVIII

ÍSLENDINGABÓK — KRISTNI SAGA
THE BOOK OF THE ICELANDERS — THE STORY OF THE
CONVERSION

For Sunniva and Benjamin

ÍSLENDINGABÓK
KRISTNI SAGA

THE BOOK OF THE ICELANDERS
THE STORY OF THE CONVERSION

TRANSLATED BY

SIÂN GRØNLIE

VIKING SOCIETY FOR NORTHERN RESEARCH
UNIVERSITY COLLEGE LONDON
2006

© Siân Grønlie 2006
Reprinted 2015, 2020, 2025
ISBN-10: 0-903521-71-7
ISBN-13: 978-0-903521-71-0

The illustration on the cover is a detail from the aerial photograph of Þingvellir on the reverse of the map of Þingvellir published by Landmælingar Íslands in 1969, © National Land Survey of Iceland, Licence no. L06080007. The figures relate to the sites of booths (shelters used to accommodate chieftains who attended the Alþingi each summer and their followers). Many of these only date from the 18th or 19th centuries, and the identifications of the medieval booths are guesses from about 1700; there is no contemporary evidence for them. The supposed owners are listed below.

6	Gestr Oddleifsson	30	Gizurr hvíti (the White)
8	Snorri goði Þorgrímsson	31	Valgarðr grái (the Grey)
11	Víga-Skúta	32	Egill Skalla-Grímsson
12	Þorgeirr flatnefr Þórisson	33	Ásgrímr Elliða-Grímsson, Þórhallr Ásgrímsson
13	Hjalti Skeggjason		
17	Guðmundr ríki (the Powerful)	34	Mǫrðr gígja, Mǫrðr Valgarðsson
19	Skagfirðingar	35	Njálsbúð
23	Vatnsdœlingar	37	Flosi Þórðarson
24	Langdœlingar	38	Eyjólfr Bǫlverksson
25	Vatnsfirðingar	39	Skapti Þóroddsson
26	Hǫskuldr Dala-Kollsson	40	Sæmundr fróði
28	Geirr goði	41	Snorri Sturluson
	42	Þorgeirr Ljósvetningagoði	

Printed by Short Run Press Limited, Exeter

CONTENTS

ACKNOWLEDGMENTS vi
INTRODUCTION vii
  CONVERSION AND HISTORY-WRITING vii
  ARI'S *ÍSLENDINGABÓK* ix
    Ari's Life and Work x
    Íslendingabók as Family History xiv
    Íslendingabók as Ecclesiastical History xviii
    History and Myth-Making xxiv
    A Note on *Íslendingabók*, Prose Style and the Family Saga xxviii
  KRISTNI SAGA xxx
    Date, Authorship and Sources xxxii
    Kristni saga and Iceland's History xxxv
    Kristni saga as Missionary History xxxvii
    Conversion and Politics xlii
  CONCLUSION xlv
  NOTE ON THE TRANSLATIONS xlvi
  DATES IN THE HISTORY OF EARLY ICELAND xlvii
  LAWSPEAKERS OF THE EARLY COMMONWEALTH xlvii
  MAP OF ICELAND xlviii
THE BOOK OF THE ICELANDERS 3
  NOTES TO THE BOOK OF THE ICELANDERS 15
THE STORY OF THE CONVERSION 35
  NOTES TO THE STORY OF THE CONVERSION 57
BIBLIOGRAPHY 75
INDEX OF PERSONAL NAMES 86
INDEX OF PLACES AND PEOPLES 94

ACKNOWLEDGMENTS

During the years that I have been working on this book, I have received help and advice from many people. In particular, I would like to thank Thomas Charles-Edward, David Clark, Richard Dance, Alison Finlay, Judith Jesch and Carolyne Larrington (who first suggested this project to me), Sally Mapstone, Heather O'Donoghue, Ólafur Halldórsson, John McKinnell, Carl Phelpstead, Matthew Townend, and many others *þó at eigi sé ritaðir*. Thanks are also due to my colleagues at St Anne's, Matthew Reynolds and Ann Pasternak-Slater, for their encouragement and support. Finally, I owe an enormous debt of gratitude to Anthony Faulkes for his many helpful suggestions, meticulous corrections and editorial expertise. Any errors that remain are my own and, as Ari said about possible inaccuracies in his work, *þá es skylt at hafa þat heldr, es sannara reynisk*.

Siân Grønlie
Oxford
St Michael and All Angels, 2006

INTRODUCTION

CONVERSION AND HISTORY-WRITING

Christianity, it has been said, is 'a religion of historians', both because its sacred books are works of history and because it provides a historical framework—between creation and judgement—within which all human history unfolds.[1] For the Icelanders, as for the other Germanic peoples of early medieval Europe, Christianity was also a religion that made possible, for the first time, the writing down of oral history: it was the advent of Christianity to Iceland in the year 999/1000 which brought writing to that country and perhaps it is not surprising that, when the Icelanders began to write themselves, one of the first subjects they chose was their own conversion to Christianity. Ari's *Íslendingabók* is the oldest and most famous account of the moment of conversion in Iceland, accompanied by a brief description of the much longer process of Christianisation that followed it.[2] But the story of the conversion is retold in a number of later Icelandic texts written between the end of the twelfth and the fourteenth century, as well as being included in Norwegian synoptic histories, principally Theodoricus' *Historia de Antiquitate Regum Norwagiensium* and *Historia Norwegie*.[3] As is typical with conversion narratives, it appears in different contexts and genres and therefore in different guises: as a key moment in the history in the Icelandic people (in *Íslendingabók*), as a successful missionary effort on the part of the Norwegian king Óláfr Tryggvason (in both Oddr Snorrason's and Snorri Sturluson's *Óláfs saga Tryggvasonar* and in *Óláfs saga Tryggvasonar in mesta*) and as a focus for the 'historical fiction' of many of the family sagas, most famously *Njáls saga*.[4] *Kristni saga* is the only work in which

---

[1] Bloch 1992: 4.

[2] The terms 'conversion' and 'Christianisation' can be used in different ways, but the practice I follow here is to use 'conversion' for the 'moment and act' whereby a decision in favour of Christianity is made, and 'Christianisation' for the longer process of institutional change which follows it (Abrams 1996: 15); for uses that distinguish between the 'conversion' of an individual and the societal process of Christianisation/acculturation, see Sawyer, Sawyer and Wood 1987: 21–2; Russell 1994: 26–31; Muldoon 1997: 1–4.

[3] Theodoricus 1998: 15–16; *HN* 21.

[4] *Íslendingabók*, pp. 7–9 below (ch. 7); Oddr Snorrason 1932: 122–30; *ÍF* XXVI 319–20, 328–33, 347; *ÓTM* I 149–50, 168, 280–301, 308–11, 358–76, II 145–66, 177–98, 305; *ÍF* XII 255–72.

the missions to Iceland form the main subject of the narrative and the organisational principle of the whole; it shares with Bede's *Ecclesiastical History* the distinction of being one of the few works in the Middle Ages which can justly be described as 'missionary' history.[5]

Conversion had a central place in historical writing in the early Middle Ages, as the newly converted Germanic peoples sought to fit themselves into the new Christian world and to 'reinvent' their pasts on the model of biblical history, divided into two by the coming of Christ.[6] Bede, as is well known, modelled the pagan Anglo-Saxons on the Israelites of the Old Testament, God's chosen people with their own 'Promised Land', and it has been argued that Ari does the same for the Icelanders.[7] Yet what continues to astonish about early Icelandic histories is less their affinity with Latin European Christian literature than their resilient secularism, witness surely to a strong oral tradition which survived the conversion and passed into a new literate world, giving rise to literary genres not found elsewhere in medieval Europe. Although conversion to Christianity comes at the centre of Ari's *Íslendingabók* and is treated at most length, it is continuity rather than change which Ari emphasises as he describes the key stages in the development of a new and unique political system by the Icelanders. His avoidance of miracle, religious rhetoric and moral exempla can be contrasted with *Kristni saga*'s greater dependence on hagiography in its account of the early missionaries, and yet Ari's distinctive style and methods are still, arguably, the greatest inspiration for the author/editor/compiler of *Kristni saga* and possibly also a model for the larger historical compendium of which *Kristni saga* may have been part.[8] In this introduction, I would like to address the difficult question of what kinds of history *Íslendingabók* and *Kristni saga* represent, an issue often tied, rightly or wrongly, to their disputed reliability as historical sources. To what extent are they influenced by

---

[5] On the rarity of missionary histories in the Middle Ages, see Sawyer, Sawyer and Wood 1987: 17–18 and Wood 2001: 25, 42–3; on Bede, see especially Rollason 2001: 15–23.

[6] Smalley 1974: 55; Weber 1987: 98–100.

[7] See p. xxi below. On the Anglo-Saxon myth of origins, see Howe 1989. For Ari's adoption of the same migration myth, see Sverrir Tómasson 1988: 282–3.

[8] Because of the lack of consensus over whether *Kristni saga* is an original work or a compilation (on which, see pp. xxxi–xxxv), it is difficult to know what term to use for its author/editor/compiler. In what follows, I will use the term 'author' with the proviso that the exact nature of his 'authorship' remains in doubt and that editing or compiling may in fact be a more appropriate description of his activity.

histories along European lines, shaped by biblical and hagiographical models, or do they rather bear witness to a well-formed oral tradition and to the determinedly secular outlook of medieval Icelandic intellectuals? Ari's *Íslendingabók* is, undoubtedly, a unique source for early Icelandic history, both because of its closeness to the events it describes and because of Ari's careful citing of his sources, but the author of *Kristni saga*—I will argue—deserves more credit than he has hitherto been given. Together, the two works give us an insight into different modes of historical writing in medieval Iceland and allow us to trace the development over time of different ways of thinking about Iceland's conversion to Christianity.

ARI'S *ÍSLENDINGABÓK*

It has become common in accounts of Ari's work to describe him as the 'father' of Icelandic history, a pioneer and innovator (*brautryðjandi ok byrjandi*), whose work was a 'guiding star' (*leiðarstjarna*) in the history of the nation and laid the basis for Icelandic literature as a whole.[9] Ari's *Íslendingabók* is the first surviving written history of the Icelanders and the first work to be written in the vernacular. It contains one of the earliest uses of the term 'Icelanders', the earliest dating of the settlement and conversion, even the earliest occurrence in Old Norse of the term 'Vínland'. That Ari was as highly regarded by his contemporaries and successors as he is by contemporary scholars is clear from two witnesses, one from the mid-twelfth century and the other from the first half of the thirteenth: the *First Grammatical Treatise*, probably dating from *c*.1130–40, speaks of *þau in spakligu frœði, er Ari Þorgilsson hefir á bœkr sett af skynsamligu viti* 'those wise historical records, which Ari Þorgilsson has written down in books with his perceptive intellect', and Snorri Sturluson, in his prologue to *Heimskringla*, dated to *c*.1230, not only describes Ari as the first person to record *frœði* in the Norse tongue, but praises him highly as *sannfróðr at fornum tíðendum bæði hér ok útan lands . . . námgjarn ok minnigr* 'truly learned about past events both here and abroad . . . eager to learn and having a good memory'.[10]

At the same time, many scholars have perceived a disparity between Ari's high reputation—the breadth of the writings attributed to him in

---

[9] Einar Arnórsson 1942: 166; Björn Sigfússon 1944: 9; Einar Ól. Sveinsson 1948a: 48; Halldór Hermannsson 1948: 20, 29; Turville-Petre 1953: 88.
[10] Haugen 1972: 12–13, 32–3; *ÍF* XXVI 5–7.

the Middle Ages—and the comparatively narrow focus of the small history that is all we now possess. Eva Hagnell has suggested that the seventeenth-century copyist of his work, by labelling it as *schedae*, expressed *en viss besvikelse* ('a certain disappointment') about the meagre contents of *Íslendingabók* and, if so, he would have been the first but not the only person to do so.[11] Einar Arnórsson criticises Ari's style as *ónákvæmt* ('imprecise') and objects to his inclusion of *óþarft innskot* ('unnecessary interpolation') instead of vital information about, for example, the discovery and exploration of Iceland. He describes Ari's book as *safn minnisgreina* ('a collection of notes') rather than *samfelld saga Íslands eða Íslendinga* ('a continuous history of Iceland or the Icelanders').[12] Likewise, Gabriel Turville-Petre complains about how Ari 'selected his material so arbitrarily and treated it so disproportionately'; he concludes that *Íslendingabók* 'does not account for the great fame which Ari enjoyed among the scholars and saga-writers of the later Middle Ages'.[13]

The alleged 'narrowness' of Ari's extant work can be understood in different ways. On the one hand, it could be evidence of his meticulous gathering and careful recording of reliable information from truthful and well-informed individuals; on the other, his extreme 'selectivity' may demonstrate a bias towards the traditions of a small number of families and express a clear ideological stance.[14] In what follows, I wish to give particular attention to the ideological basis that lies behind Ari's representation of the history and conversion of his country.

Ari's Life and Work

Most of what we know about Ari's life comes from *Íslendingabók* (ch. 9, pp. 10–11 below) itself. Here he tells us that he was sent to live with Hallr Þórarinsson in Haukadalr one year after the death of his grandfather, Gellir Þorkelsson, when he was seven years old, and that he lived there for fourteen years. He says that he was present at the burial of Iceland's first bishop, Ísleifr, when he was twelve years old, and describes Ísleifr's son, Teitr, who was also brought up by Hallr, as his 'foster-father' (which probably includes the meaning 'tutor').[15] From the date of Ísleifr's death (1080), we can work out that Ari was born in 1068 (although his date of

---

[11] Hagnell 1938: 71. On the meaning of *schedae*, see note 34 below.
[12] Einar Arnórsson 1942: 24, 84, 170, 177, 183.
[13] Turville-Petre 1953: 91–2.
[14] Lindow 1997b: 460.
[15] Sverrir Tómasson 1988: 20.

birth is elsewhere given as 1067) and moved to Haukadalr in 1074/5, where he stayed until 1088/9.[16] At the end of his book (p. 14), he includes an account of his male ancestors, traced back through the kings of Norway and the legendary kings of Sweden to their mythical progenitor, Yngvi, king of the Turks. Some of the more recent members of his family line (for example, Þórðr gellir and Gellir Þorkelsson) are mentioned elsewhere in the book, either as participants in events or as Ari's informants.

From other sources we can fill in some of the blanks. Ari was descended from Eyvindr the Easterner, Auðr the Deep-Minded and Ósvífr the Wise on his father's side and from Hrollaugr and Hallr on Síða on his mother's side.[17] Ari's grandfather, Gellir Þorkelsson, lived at Helgafell in the west of Iceland and died in Denmark in 1073 on his return from a pilgrimage to Rome. Ari's father, Þorgils, had drowned at a young age in Breiðafjörður and Ari's uncle Þorkell took over the estate at Helgafell after his death.[18] Ari was probably sent to Haukadalr because Teitr's wife, Jórunn, was his mother's second cousin, and he was a pupil at the small school Teitr ran there—one of only four in Iceland at the time (the others were at Skálaholt, Oddi and Hólar).[19] *Kristni saga* tells us that he was ordained as a priest (ch. 17, p. 53). His son, Þorgils (d. 1170), also a priest, lived at Staðastaðr on Snæfellsnes in the west of Iceland and his grandson, Ari the Strong, was a chieftain there.[20] It therefore seems likely that Ari lived in the west after his education at Haukadalr, and perhaps also held a chieftaincy. Alternatively, it has been suggested that he remained in the south in the service of Bishop Gizurr, and perhaps even travelled around the country with him on episcopal visitations.[21] He died, according to Icelandic annals, on 9th November 1148.

Íslendingabók is Ari's only extant work, and the issue of what else he may have written has been much debated. The main problem is how to understand the wording of his prologue to the present *Íslendingabók*,

---

[16] All but two of the Icelandic annals give Ari's date of birth as 1067. This probably derives from the prologue to *Heimskringla*, where Snorri states that he was born 'the year after the fall of King Haraldr Sigurðarson' (in 1066; see *ÍF* XXVI 6).

[17] See *Íslendingabók* ch. 2, the genealogy on p. 14 and notes 22, 39, 61, 123–6. Eyvindr the Easterner's daughter was married to Þorsteinn the Red, Auðr was married to Óleifr the White and Ósvífr the Wise's daughter, Guðrún, was Ari's great-grandmother (her fourth husband was Gellir Þorkelsson).

[18] See *Íslendingabók* ch. 9 and notes 86 and 126.

[19] Jón Jóhannesson 1974: 158.

[20] *DI* I 186, 191; *Sturl* I 229–31, 241.

[21] *ÍF* I v–vii; Einar Arnórsson 1942: 7–13; Halldór Hermannsson 1948: 7.

where he states that he showed an earlier version to the Icelandic bishops and then reworked it: 'I wrote this on the same subject besides (*fyr útan*) the genealogies and regnal years of kings, and I added what has since become better known to me and is now more fully reported in this book than the other' (p. 3). It was not an uncommon procedure in the Middle Ages to submit one's work to a superior for correction, and Bede's Preface to his *Life of St Cuthbert* provides a close parallel.[22] The relationship between the two versions of Ari's *Íslendingabók*, however, is unclear. Some scholars have argued that Ari's first version contained genealogies of Icelanders and notices on the reigns of kings, and that these were excluded from his second version, perhaps to give it a more Icelandic emphasis.[23] On the other hand, it has been suggested that Ari wrote the genealogies and notices after his first version and appended them to his second, from which they were later separated.[24] Whichever is the case, it seems unlikely that Ari's first version, if it was ever more than just a draft, would have been copied for circulation after the composition of the second, corrected version. It has even been suggested that Ari's mention of two versions is nothing more than a literary cliché to emphasise his humility and subservience to a higher authority.[25] There is no good reason, then, to assume that there was ever a 'Book of the Icelanders' substantially different from the one we have now.

However, it is clear from references to Ari elsewhere that he did write more than just the extant *Íslendingabók*: several sources mention his 'books' (in the plural) and he is quoted widely in Old Icelandic literature as an authority on the kings of Norway and on the lives of early Icelanders, including his own ancestors and those of Icelandic bishops.[26] The most

---

[22] Sverrir Tómasson 1988: 155–7; Colgrave 1940: 142–7. Many critics have noted the similarity between Bede's prologue and Ari's own (*ÍF* I xxiv; Björn Sigfússon 1944: 78–80; Ellehøj 1965: 67).

[23] Hagnell 1938: 102–9; Turville-Petre 1953: 93–9 (where he calls the first version *liber* 'book' and the second *libellus* 'little book'). A full history of the differing views on Ari's literary output is given by Konrad Maurer (1870 and 1891), Halldór Hermannsson (1930: 26–36) and Eva Hagnell (1938: 5–26).

[24] This was first suggested by Árni Magnússon (1663–1730) in his unfinished work on Ari (1930 II 1, 85–8) and later revived by Johan Schreiner (1927: 60–65; further references can be found in Halldór Hermannsson 1930: 32–3 and Hagnell 1938: 5, 12–14, 23–25, 89–102). It was most recently argued by Else Mundal (1984).

[25] Sverrir Tómasson 1975: 268; 1988: 157.

[26] Haugen 1972: 12–13; *Flb* I 568; *ÍF* XXVI 5. Full lists of the places where Ari is cited are included in Hagnell (1938: 114–30, 142–44), Einar Arnórsson (1942: 36–39, 57–61), Björn Sigfússon (1944: 60–74), and Ellehøj (1965: 44–62).

important witness is Snorri Sturluson, who, after describing the contents of *Íslendingabók*, says that Ari also supplied 'many other facts, both lives of kings in Norway and Denmark, and also in England, and moreover important events that had taken place in this country'.[27] Snorri probably had his own reasons for wanting to set up Ari as an authority on the lives of Norwegian kings, not least as authentication for his own work in *Heimskringla*, but there is also reason to believe that he had first-hand access to Ari's works: he took over the farm at Reykholt in the west of Iceland from Magnús Pálsson, who was married to Ari's granddaughter Hallfríðr, and they lived with him there for a number of years.[28] It therefore seems likely that Ari wrote some kind of account of the kings of Norway, which Snorri at least had seen, and also that he had a hand in the compilation of the first *Landnámabók* ('The Book of Settlements'), as Haukr states in the epilogue to his later version.[29] Whether these were complete works or simply *minnisgreinir* ('collections of notes') will probably never be clear. Possibly the genealogy of Haraldr the Fine-Haired inserted before ch. 1 (p. 3) and the genealogy of Icelandic bishops and of Ari at the end of *Íslendingabók* (pp. 13–14) are extracts from Ari's other writings; they are certainly by Ari, whether or not they were inserted by a later copyist as parchment fillers.[30] A short life of Snorri goði (*Ævi Snorra goða*) and a list of priests from 1143 printed in *Diplomatarium Islandicum* are sometimes also attributed to Ari.[31]

Ari's *Íslendingabók* can be dated to 1122–33 because of the references to Bishops Þorlákr (1118–33) and Ketill (1122–45) in the prologue (p. 3).

The most important are: *Heimskringla* (*ÍF* XXVI 239, XXVII 326, 410, 431), *Landnámabók* (*ÍF* I 133), *Sturl* (I 57–58), *Laxdæla saga* (*ÍF* V 7), *Eyrbyggja saga* (*ÍF* IV 12) and *Páls saga biskups* (*ÍF* XVI 328). The use of Ari's name in *Jómsvíkinga þáttr* (*Flb* I 213), *Fríssbók* (1871: 3) and one manuscript of *Gunnlaugs saga Ormstungu* (*ÍF* III 51, note) probably only serves to lend credibility to the narrative.

[27] *ÍF* XXVI 6.

[28] Sverrir Tómasson 1975: 280–85; 1988: 279–80; *Sturl* I 241–2.

[29] *ÍF* I 395. Ari's works on the settlement of Iceland and on the lives of kings are usually considered to have been independent books or chapters appended to one of his versions of *Íslendingabók* (Hagnell 1938: 134, 149–58; Ellehøj 1965: 34–5, 53; *ÍF* I x–xiii, cix). Turville-Petre (1953: 98–102), among others, held the alternative view that the lives of kings and genealogies were scattered throughout the work, though he did believe that Ari had written a separate *Landnámabók*.

[30] *ÍF* I xv–vi; Hagnell 1938: 81, 84–86.

[31] *DI* I 180–94; *ÍF* I xiv; Hagnell 1938: 160–63, 165; *ÍF* IV 185–6.

It was probably written towards the beginning of this period, since it does not mention any events after 1118 (like the death of Bishop Jón in 1121), and the presence of Goðmundr Þorgeirsson (in ch. 10), who was lawspeaker 1123–34, is best interpreted as a later interpolation.[32] It is preserved in two paper manuscripts from the seventeenth century, AM 113 a fol. (B) and AM 113 b fol. (A), which has been used as the basis for all editions. They were copied by Jón Erlendsson in Villingaholt from the same exemplar, a medieval manuscript dating from *c*.1200, and B is dated 1651.[33] Both contain the heading *Schedæ Ara prests fröda*, and this title, which is probably neither authorial nor medieval, may suggest that *Íslendingabók* was written on loose leaves that had become separated from the rest of the manuscript, or it may refer just to the genealogies that follow it.[34] Two chapters of *Íslendingabók* are found elsewhere and were probably copied from an older manuscript than that used by Jón: ch. 4 is in GKS 1812 4to, this part of which dates from *c*.1200, and ch. 5 is in most manuscripts of *Hœnsa-Þóris saga*.[35]

Íslendingabók *as Family History*

What is immediately striking about the known details of Ari's life is how closely he is related to many of the main actors in his book. This is particularly evident in the section on the Conversion and the early Church, in which Ari is self-avowedly dependent on the report of his foster-father and tutor, Teitr, but it can be seen throughout his short book. His most important relationship is with the *Haukdœlir* family, which provided Iceland with its first two bishops, Ísleifr and Gizurr, donated its family estate at Skálaholt to be the first episcopal see and influenced the choice of subsequent bishops until the mid-twelfth century: Jón Ǫgmundarson

---

[32] *ÍF* I xvii–viii. Ari's second version is sometimes dated to 1134 because of the inclusion of Goðmundr (Hagnell 1938: 57–62; Einar Arnórsson 1942: 29–30; Sveinbjörn Rafnsson 2001: 158–59). However, the likelihood that this is a later interpolation (probably from a marginal note) is strengthened by its absence from sections based on ch. 10 elsewhere (*Sturl* I 59; *Kristni saga*, p. 53).

[33] Holtsmark 1967: 5, 8–9; Finnur Jónsson 1930: 59–60.

[34] Hagnell 1938: 69–71; Halldór Hermannsson 1948: 20–22; *ÍF* I xxviii; Mundal 1984: 267–8. A *scheda* is 'a piece of parchment on which were written notes or memoranda in preparation of a book' (Halldór Hermannsson 1930: 41–2). However, it seems that it could sometimes be used for whole works, as the diminutive *schedula* is used in Theodoricus (1998: 57, note 13).

[35] *Íslendingabók*, notes 41 and 51.

was educated by Ísleifr at Skálaholt; Þorlákr Runólfsson, the great-nephew of Hallr in Haukadalr, was nominated by Gizurr as his successor and Ketill Þorsteinsson was married to Gizurr's daughter.[36] In addition to his relationship with Teitr, Ari clearly knew Gizurr personally (see p. 11). He gives Teitr as his direct source for the date of Iceland's settlement, for the establishment of Úlfljótr's law, for his lengthy account of the conversion (on which Teitr had information from eyewitnesses), for the foreign bishops in Iceland and for the events of Ísleifr's episcopate, some of which Ari himself had also witnessed (pp. 3, 4, 9–11). Gizurr must be the source for the events of his own life, and Ari speaks glowingly of his achievements, especially the enforcement of the tithe law, which had caused many problems elsewhere in Scandinavia (pp. 11–12 and note 94). In his account of the conversion and the early Church, Ari is relating a family tradition and 'success' story, linking the first bishops of the Icelandic Church directly back to the men who converted Iceland, Gizurr the White and his son-in-law Hjalti Skeggjason.

Other central information can be traced back to Ari's own ancestors. Ari traced his lineage back to three of the four main settlers in ch. 2 as well as tracing Ísleifr and Gizurr directly back to Ketilbjǫrn at Mosfell.[37] Other than Teitr, Ari's two sources for the date of Iceland's settlement were his uncle Þorkell Gellisson and Þuríðr, daughter of Snorri goði and cousin to Ari's paternal grandmother Valgerðr.[38] Þorkell is also the source of Ari's information on the origins of land-dues (which probably came from his father Gellir) and the settlement of Greenland (which he himself had visited); and Ósvífr the Wise, who interprets Þorsteinn's dream about the changes to the Icelandic calendar, was Gellir Þorkelsson's maternal grandfather.[39] Likewise, the chapter on the division into Quarters revolves around a speech made by Þórðr gellir, Gellir's great-grandfather and fifth in a direct line above Ari (pp. 6–7). Hallr on Síða, from whom Ari was also directly descended, was one of the first Icelanders to be converted and, through his agreement with the lawspeaker Þorgeirr, key to the final successful outcome of the missions (pp. 7–9). Finally, Ari was third cousin once-removed to the lawspeaker Markús Skeggjason, who is his main

---

[36] *Íslendingabók*, pp. 10, 12 and notes 1 and 101. On the domination of the early Icelandic church by the *Haukdælir*, see Orri Vésteinsson 2000: 19–24, 146–47. The power of the *Haukdælir* in both the secular sphere and the Church is also discussed by Gísli Sigurðsson (2004: 60–66).

[37] *Íslendingabók*, pp. 4, 13 (and note 22).

[38] *Íslendingabók*, p. 3; Einar Arnórsson 1942: 5.

[39] *Íslendingabók*, pp. 4, 6, 7 (and notes 21, 39 and 58).

source of information on Iceland's lawspeakers, and Markús was himself related to one of the greatest of these, Skapti Þoróddsson.[40]

This web of family relationships is vital to an understanding of the nature of Ari's work, with regard both to his well-deserved reputation for reliability and to accusations of bias. There can be little doubt that Ari drew on a strong oral tradition in composing his history, and the transparency with which he lays bare his channels of information makes his work quite unique. His short biography of Hallr in Haukadalr is breathtaking in the direct link it gives us between the events of the past and Ari's present: 'And Hallr, who both had a reliable memory and was truthful, and remembered himself being baptised, told us that Þangbrandr had baptised him when he was three years old' (p. 11). Hallr died aged ninety-four. One could take other examples: Þuríðr, for example, whom Ari describes as 'wise in many things and reliably informed' (p. 3) and whose father, Snorri, appears as a literary character in *Eyrbyggja saga* as well as a historical figure here. According to *Kristni saga*, he was present at the conversion and Þuríðr herself was born only twenty-five or twenty-six years later; she lived to be eighty-eight.[41] Ari not only emphasises repeatedly where he and his informants have derived their information from, but also frequently comments on the desired qualities of those individuals acting as informants: 'wise' (*spakr, margspakr*), 'reliably informed' (*óljúgfróðr*), 'having a reliable memory' (*minnigr*), 'truthful' (*ólyginn*). This has inspired many to believe in his absolute reliability, to the extent that some have even described him as a 'modern' historian.[42] Since the distance between events around the year 1000 and Ari's own time

---

[40] On Markús Skeggjason, who was third cousin to Ari's father Þorgils, see *Íslendingabók*, p. 11 (and note 93). Ari's other named informants are the lawspeaker Úlfheðinn Gunnarson and Hallr Órœkjuson (see p. 5 and notes 32 and 33). Snorri Sturluson (*ÍF* XXVI 6) also mentions Oddr Kolsson, son of Hallr on Síða, but he is not known from elsewhere.

[41] *ÍF* XXVI 7. According to Snorri Sturluson, Snorri goði was 'about thirty-five' at the time of the conversion and both *Kristni saga* and *Eyrbyggja saga* mention his involvement (see p. 50 and note 88). Þuríðr's age at her death (in 1112/13) is recorded in many Icelandic annals.

[42] See *Íslendingabók*, pp. 3, 5, 11. Halldór Hermannsson (1948: 15) claims that *Hún fullnægir eiginlega vísindalegum kröfum nútímans til sagnaritunar* ('It actually satisfies the scholarly demands of the present with regard to history-writing'). Peter Foote (1993b: 107) concludes that it has 'unassailable authority' and Jón Hnefill Aðalsteinsson (1999: 55–57, 178) describes it as a 'first-class historical source'.

of writing could be covered by two generations, there is good reason to believe that some, at least, of Ari's information was accurate. It certainly seems to be no accident that he moves into fuller and more detailed narrative from the year 1000 on, as his sources expand.

At the same time, there is a strongly personal note throughout the work which raises questions about Ari's alleged objectivity: Ari begins his work with a personal statement of authorship ('I first wrote the book of the Icelanders', p. 3) and ends the last genealogy with his own name: 'and I am called Ari' (p. 14). He reserves his highest personal praise for his tutor Teitr ('the wisest man I have known', p. 3) and for Hallr in Haukadalr, who brought him up ('the most generous layman in the country and most eminent in good qualities'); indeed, the details about Hallr's household in Haukadalr included in ch. 9 (pp. 10–11) are surely there in part for personal reasons, since Ari never quotes Hallr directly as a source. All this marks out Ari's approach as unlike that of many later sagas, including *Kristni saga*, which present themselves more as records of a traditional knowledge that is common property. Ari, in fact, refers to commonly held views rather rarely, and then often uses them as a cover for subjective comments, on the quality of Gizurr and Hjalti's preaching, for example: 'it is said that it was extraordinary how well they spoke' (p. 8).[43] In contrast to *Landnámabók*, he draws only to a limited extent on place-names (like Ingólfshǫfði or Kolsgjá) or on features of the landscape (or, in the case of the *papar* and *Skrælingar*, archaeological remains) as witnesses to events.

Although it is possible that the short and extremely selective nature of his work is the result of a cautious desire for accuracy, it seems better explained by his narrow interest in a small number of leading families, including his own and that of Iceland's first bishops. Ari must have had more information than he tells us about events like the settlement and the conversion: it is clear from comparison of his work with the existing versions of *Landnámabók* and *Kristni saga* that lengthier traditions were available, although some may, of course, have originated much later. It is therefore hard to know exactly how to judge Ari's many omissions: he mentions the place-name *Minþakseyrr*, but did he know the tale in *Landnámabók* about the Irish slaves belonging to Ingólfr's travelling companion Hjǫrleifr, who threw their mouldy *menadach* (*minþak*)

---

[43] Another example is his comment on Hallr: 'a man whom everybody described (*sá maðr es þat vas almælt*) as the most generous layman in the country' (p. 10).

overboard there?[44] Even if Ari avoided this particular anecdote because of its strongly apocryphal and even parodic flavour, it is striking that he never mentions Hjǫrleifr, nor the presence of any Irish settlers in Iceland. *Kristni saga* offers us much fuller information about the missions to Iceland prior to the conversion; Ari mentions only Friðrekr 'who came here during the heathen period', but as early as c.1200, *Hungrvaka* tells us that stories (*sǫgur*) were current about Friðrekr, in oral if not in written form. Ari not only gives us no additional details about foreign bishops in Iceland—who would, like Ísleifr, have been missionary bishops without fixed sees—but actually creates the impression, through treating them separately before his chapter on Ísleifr, that they were not contemporary with the Icelandic bishop. It is clear from *Hungrvaka* that some of them were, and one suspects that Ari's apparent ignorance of this derives from a desire not to obscure the direct correspondence between Gizurr the White's prominent role in the conversion and his son Ísleifr's prominence as the Icelanders' first bishop.[45] This early history is as much family history as it is ecclesiastical history or national history: it provides an explanation of how the leading families of Ari's own day had got to where they were.[46]

Íslendingabók *as Ecclesiastical History*

As the first to compose a history of the Icelanders in the vernacular, Ari had no native models for how to put together a written work, and the extent to which he was dependent on foreign models for his endeavour has been the object of much scrutiny. Perhaps in reaction to the faith placed by some scholars in his 'unique' reliability, others have emphasised his dependence on European hagiographical and historical writing. Sverrir Tómasson, for example, describes him as writing *í anda guðfræðilegrar sagnaritunar miðalda* ('in the spirit of the religious history-writing of the Middle Ages') and stresses that *áhrif evrópskrar helgisagnaritunar á hana eru augljós* ('the influence of European hagiography on it is obvious').[47]

---

[44] *Íslendingabók*, p. 4 and note 15. The story reads like a parody of the throwing overboard of high seat pillars undertaken by so many more prominent settlers (with thanks to Heather O'Donoghue for this suggestion).

[45] On Friðrekr and the later bishops, see *Íslendingabók*, p. 10 and note 77 (which includes the reference to *Hungrvaka*).

[46] For the idea that missionary history is often family history, see Wood 2001: 91–2.

[47] Sverrir Tómasson 1988: 282–3.

The Book of the Icelanders

Both Bede's *Ecclesiastical History* and Adam of Bremen's *History of the Archbishops of Hamburg–Bremen* have been suggested as models for *Íslendingabók*, and Ari's practice of regularly citing his informants has been compared with that of Bede in his *Ecclesiastical History* and his *Life of Saint Cuthbert*. It has even been suggested that Ari's frequent use of *fróðr* ('learned') or *spakr* ('wise') to characterise his informants does not necessarily reflect a strong native oral tradition at all, but that this corresponds closely to the medieval European custom of describing informants as *doctus* or *sapiens*.[48] Ari thus creates Icelandic (oral) equivalents of European *auctores*—one of which he himself becomes for the Icelanders of the late twelfth and thirteenth centuries.

Clearly aspects of Ari's work are based on Latin models. His prologue and the division of his work into chapters with headings are obvious borrowings and various Latinisms, as one might expect at such an early stage, mark his vernacular style. Occasionally, he even uses a word in Latin like *obiit* (died) or *rex* (king), though these may just be used in the manuscript as abbreviations for Icelandic words.[49] What is most striking, given that Ari must have used some Latin sources, is the elusiveness of what these were: there are no library catalogues this early, and the *First Grammatical Treatise* mentions only that *þýðingar helgar* (literally 'holy translations', presumably homilies and perhaps also saints' lives) were in circulation.[50] We are dependent, therefore, on what Ari himself tells us, which is very little: he mentions a *saga* (probably a Latin life) of Saint Edmund, which has not been definitely identified,[51] and though Bede and Adam of Bremen seem obvious candidates for influence, it has proved hard to show for certain that Ari knew either of them. Concrete evidence that Ari knew Bede's *Ecclesiastical History* comes down to his reference at the end of the book to Pope Gregory's death in the second

---

[48] *ÍF* I xxii; Einar Arnórsson 1942: 167; Björn Sigfússon 1944: 77–80; Ellehøj 1965: 66–8; Benediktz 1976: 334–5; Sverrir Tómasson 1975: 278–80; 1988: 222–7; Mundal 1994; Würth 2005: 158. In fact, Bede cites oral informants most often to verify his miracle stories and emphasises their status as religious men, capable of understanding the true significance of events, rather than as detached observers (Ward 1976: 72). This is quite different from what Ari is doing.

[49] Bekker-Nielsen 1972. On Ari's Latinisms, see Hagnell 1938: 72–5; Björn Sigfússon 1944: 83–4; *ÍF* I xxvi.

[50] Haugen 1972: 12–13; Hermann Pálsson 1965: 164. For references to various kinds of books and their production in Iceland, see *Jóns saga helga* (*ÍF* XV 205–6, 219, 233) and *Hungrvaka* (*ÍF* XVI 26, 34).

[51] *Íslendingabók*, p. 3 and note 12.

year of Emperor Phocas' reign (604), which he could equally well have been taken from a life of St Gregory.[52] Attempts to show that Ari took the date of Óláfr Tryggvason's fall (1000) from Adam of Bremen have been equally inconclusive, and the difficulty of showing that Adam was known at all in Iceland in Ari's time led one scholar to the belief that Ari must have read it on a hypothetical trip to Lund.[53] If Ari did know Bede's works, one wonders why he did not in his account of the *papar* mention Bede's reference in *De temporum ratione* to travels between Thile and Britain, as *Landnámabók* does.[54] If he knew Adam's work, one is left with the problem of why he does not mention the account there of Ísleifr's consecration at the hands of Archbishop Adaldag.[55]

Ari's main debt to European learning must be in the area of chronology, and he would certainly have learned about European time-reckoning through the works of Bede. One of Ari's greatest achievements in his work is to set the events of Icelandic history within a coherent chronological framework, which is one of the pre-requisites for writing European-style history at all. The way in which Ari achieves this, using absolute and relative dating, has been much studied.[56] His first and one of his three central dates is that of Iceland's settlement, which he connects, intriguingly, with a key event in English religious history, the killing of St Edmund of East Anglia at the hands of the Vikings in 870 (869 by modern reckoning; see *Íslendingabók*, p. 3 and note 11). With this established, he is able to calculate later developments in Iceland in relation to this date—'sixty years after the killing of St Edmund', '130 years after the killing of St Edmund', '250 years after the killing of Edmund' (pp. 5, 9, 13). He also gives absolute dates for the fall of Óláfr Tryggvason in the year 1000 (p. 9) and for the change of lunar cycle in 1120, two years after Gizurr's death. At the end

---

[52] *Íslendingabók*, p. 13; *ÍF* I xxiv; Ólafia Einarsdóttir 1964: 24–29; Ellehøj 1965: 76–77; Louis-Jensen 1976. There was an Icelandic translation of John the Deacon's life of St Gregory from *c*.1200 (see *Kristni saga*, p. 72, note 115).

[53] *Íslendingabók*, p. 9; *ÍF* I xxiv–v; Ólafia Einarsdóttir 1964: 22–3, 73–4; Ellehøj 1965: 66–7, 78, 80; Christiansen 1975. Ari's own wording ('according to Sæmundr') implies that he used Sæmundr's dating.

[54] *Íslendingabók*, p. 4 (and references in note 18).

[55] *Íslendingabók*, p. 10 (and reference in note 82). One theory is that Ari was deliberately countering Adam's line on Iceland's conversion: the difference between the two men's views of Óláfr Tryggvason and Óláfr Haraldsson is quite striking (Sveinbjörn Rafnsson 1999).

[56] The most thorough study is still Ólafia Einarsdóttir 1964: 37–90, but see also *ÍF* I xxix–xlii and Ellehøj 1965: 68–80. On Ari's probable use of an Easter table, see note 105 to *Íslendingabók* (p. 30 below).

of his book, he brings all these dates together in one great sweep along with with his final absolute date, 604, for the death of Pope Gregory I (p. 13). This chronological framework is cleverly integrated with others, principally the terms of office of the Icelandic lawspeakers, but occasionally also the reigns of Norwegian kings. Ingólfr's first trip to Iceland, for example, takes place when King Haraldr is sixteen years old (p. 4). The practical value of Ari's three round numbers (870, 1000, 1120) should not be underestimated in an age that still used Roman numerals for calculation; but the ideological value of dates for the settlement and conversion is also important and will be discussed below (pp. xxiv–xxvii).

Some scholars have also brought forward evidence that Ari's *Íslendingabók* was conceived as an ecclesiastical history or even as a chronicle of the bishops of Skálaholt, not least the facts that it was submitted to—if not commissioned by—Bishops Þorlákr and Ketill and corrected by Sæmundr, the most learned cleric of his day. It has been suggested that, like Bede, Ari envisaged the pre-Christian history of his people as parallel to that of the Israelites: Iceland, wooded and fertile, is the promised land, consecrated by the presence of Christian people there—the *papar*—before the arrival of the Norsemen.[57] As Ari himself does not conceal, the main settler in each Quarter of the land provides an ancestor for each of the first four Icelandic bishops, making these appropriate representatives for the whole country.[58] The mythical role of Úlfljótr as the first law-giver has been connected with that of Moses in the Old Testament, and the chapter on the calendar is of obvious interest to the Church, as the accurate calculation of time was crucial for the correct dating of Easter as well as for the celebration of other feasts central to Christian worship.[59] The discovery of Greenland, which may have been under the jurisdiction of the Icelandic bishops in Ari's time, had opened up an arena for missionary work, and Ari's long account of Iceland's conversion, as has often been noted, is the thematic centre of his book.[60] Ari certainly uses the biographical form suitable for a bishops' chronicle for his last two chapters, which give brief accounts of the lives of Bishops Ísleifr and Gizurr, with

[57] Clunies Ross 1997: 21–2; Lindow 1997b: 456; Mundal 1994: 71; cf. p. viii above.

[58] *Íslendingabók*, p. 4 and 13. Halldór Hermannsson (1930: 75) claimed that 'nothing shows more clearly the clerical bent of Ari's book'.

[59] Halldór Hermannsson 1930: 81; Líndal 1969: 21–3; Mundal 1994: 70.

[60] Halldór Hermannsson 1930: 82–3; Lindow 1997b: 460; Mundal 1994: 68. The likelihood that settlers in Greenland were under the jurisdiction of the Icelandic bishops is based on Adam IV.xxxvi, xxxvii (2002: 216–18).

a particular emphasis on Gizurr's role in establishing tithe laws and integrating Iceland into the diocesan structure of the wider Church.

However, if Ari is writing a Church history, he does not—as Bede does—see his own Church as a localised component of the Universal Church: the absence of information about events in the Church outside of Iceland is quite striking.[61] Although Ari mentions the popes at the time of Ísleifr's and Gizurr's consecration and gives a list of international fatalities to mark the occasion of Gizurr's death (pp. 10, 11, 13), there is very little sense in his book of how the Icelandic Church is part of a wider international community. He tells us nothing about the role of Hamburg–Bremen in missions to the north, despite the fact that Ísleifr was consecrated in Bremen; nor does he say anything about the investiture conflict, which led to Gizurr travelling to Rome to receive orders from the Pope, because the archbishop of Hamburg–Bremen, Liemar, had been excommunicated.[62] While some scholars have interpreted his silence about Hamburg–Bremen as a sign of hostility (Hamburg–Bremen and Lund were in competition for archiepiscopal jurisdiction over Scandinavia in the early twelfth century), it is equally true that Ari says nothing about the establishment of a Nordic archiepiscopal see in Lund in 1102–3, where Bishops Jón, Þorlákr and Ketill were consecrated.[63] The fact that Ari is silent about events relevant not just to the international Church but specifically to the Church in Scandinavia (and events which are considered worthy of inclusion in other Icelandic chronicles/lives of bishops) suggests that his interest in Church history derives from the importance of the Church as a secular institution within Icelandic society rather than as an autonomous entity. Indeed, it is noteworthy that the qualities Ari admires in his bishops are social rather than religious: he praises Gizurr for his popularity and persuasiveness, but tells us nothing about his piety and humility.[64] As Orri Vésteinsson has shown, the Icelandic Church at this early date had no 'corporate identity'. Dominated by secular interests, it was a cohesive part of the social fabric,

---

[61] On the genre of ecclesiastical history and Bede's distinctive contribution to it, see Barnard 1976, Markus 1975 and Tugéne 1982.

[62] See notes 82 and 91 to *Íslendingabók*, and note 102 to *Kristni saga*. On the wider history of the Church in Scandinavia, see Orrman 2003.

[63] Orrman 2003, 429–30. The first archbishop, Asser, received the pallium in 1104, but the see was abolished for a brief period in the 1130s and again in 1150. See notes 100 and 101 to *Íslendingabók* and, on the conflict between Hamburg–Bremen and Lund, Sveinbjörn Rafnsson 1997: 130–32; 1999: 113; 2001: 157–60.

[64] On the image of the Icelandic bishop as an ideal chieftain, see Orri Vésteinsson 2000: 161–6.

and not until the episcopates of St Þorlákr (1178–93) and Bishop Guðmundr (1203–37) was there any attempt to create a separation between secular and ecclesiastical power.[65] It seems unlikely, then, that Ari would have distinguished the history of the Church from the history of secular Icelandic institutions. They were too closely enmeshed to be separated from one another. Even for a historian like Bede, who was explicitly committed to writing 'ecclesiastical' history on the model of Eusebius, the separation of ecclesiastical from secular history was not always easy to enforce.[66]

This brings us to perhaps the most remarkable difference between Ari's work and European historiography and hagiography, which is Ari's consistently secular attitude towards the events he describes, even when these are of a religious or spiritual nature. His interest in conversion is clearly focussed on the process of Christianisation in its legal and institutional aspects; he is not interested in it as a change of religious belief. Ari tells us nothing about Icelandic heathenism, although he does throw in a tantalising reference to temples in ch. 2 (p. 5) and quotes Hjalti's verse attack on Freyja to explain why he was outlawed (p. 8). This is our one glimpse of any religious conflict other than the aborted battle at the Althing. Indeed, Ari begins to use the word 'heathen' only when he tells us in ch. 9 about Gizurr and Hjalti's mission to Iceland, which effectively divides the Icelanders into two separate groups under separate laws. It is the very real danger of civil war posed by this division, rather than the spiritual danger of heathenism, which forms the centre-piece of the speech by which Þorgeirr, himself a heathen, persuades the Icelanders to accept conversion to Christianity. He gives a warning to those on both sides—heathens and Christians—who are prone to religious extremism ('do not let those who most wish to oppose each other prevail'; p. 9) and proposes a solution that will be in the interest of the Icelanders' unity as a people rather than specifically for the benefit of their souls. Ari does not even describe the baptism of the Icelanders following the legal assembly, but tells us only that 'it was then proclaimed *in the laws* that all people should be Christian and that those in this country who had not yet been baptised should receive baptism' (my emphasis). Despite various attempts to draw a parallel between Ari and the well-known conversion narratives of European literature—Bede's account of King Edwin for example—Ari's depiction of the conversion as a legal compromise between two parties is surely highly unusual, and it is not surprising that later writers felt the need to 'embroider' the received

---

[65] Orri Vésteinsson 2000: 3–4, 167–78.
[66] See Smalley 1974: 55; Markus 1975: 8–10; Brooks 1999: 2.

story with the religious rhetoric and miracles so noticeably lacking from Ari's version.[67] Perhaps the only place where Ari gives any sense of a spiritual dimension is Þorgeirr's long meditation under the cloak before addressing the Althing, but even this may indicate only the complete concentration required for the formulation of such an important speech.[68]

History and Myth-Making

Central to an understanding of what lies behind Ari's composition of a history for the Icelanders is the emergent sense of Icelandic identity in the early twelfth-century.[69] The title of Ari's *Íslendingabók*, as noted above (p. ix), includes one of the earliest recorded uses of the term 'Icelander' and other twelfth-century writings show a similar consciousness of a separate Icelandic identity: it was in 1117–18, as Ari tells us, that the laws were first written down, and the *First Grammatical Treatise* speaks of providing *oss Íslendingum* 'us Icelanders' with a written language, something especially important, of course, to the correct understanding and interpretation of the written law.[70] Like the author of the *First Grammatical Treatise*, Ari clearly addresses an Icelandic audience and assumes an Icelandic perspective: he talks about 'our bishops', 'our reckoning', 'our countrymen' in Norway and describes movement between Norway and Iceland as 'out here' (to Iceland) and 'from out here' (to Norway).[71] Indeed, his decision to write in Icelandic rather than in Latin, which was probably not obvious at the time, restricted his audience to Icelanders—and perhaps to a lesser extent Norwegians—rather than opening it to a more international audience of Latinists.

The necessary conditions for the development of ethnic identity—now understood not as a biological but as a historical and cultural construct—have been much studied of late. Chief among them are the identification

---

[67] For the conversion of King Edwin, see *Bede's Ecclesiastical History* 1969: 182–7. For parallels with European literature, see Sveinbjörn Rafnsson 1979; Pizarro 1985: 822–3; and Weber 1987: 115–23. Contrast these with the emphasis on Ari's unconventionality and strong political concerns in Foote 1984a: 62–4; 1993b: 107; and Jochens 1999: 649–52. Knirk (1981: 33) stresses that Þorgeirr's speech is not a 'religious sermon intended to convert the heathen but an address of political deliberative nature'.

[68] On the different interpretations of this event, see *Íslendingabók*, p. 25, note 72.

[69] For an anthropological study of this phenomenon, see Hastrup 1990: 69–82, 83–102, 123–5.

[70] *Íslendingabók*, p. 12 and note 98. Haugen 1972: 12–13.

[71] *Íslendingabók*, pp. 3, 4, 6, 8 and notes 13 and 63.

of a particular group of people with a territory or homeland, the acceptance for a whole people of a common history or 'myth of origin' which is often that of the dominant group or family, the adoption of a common language or other 'cultural' symbols (in the case of the Normans, it was hairstyle) and, interestingly, a 'collective amnesia' concerning variant traditions or older/subject peoples.[72] History-writing, it is clear, can play a central role in this process and the contribution of Bede's *Ecclesiastical History* to the formation of the concept of a single 'English' people is a well-known example. As Brooks has shown, Bede's work 'not only recorded a history of that people, but was also helping to create it': he provided the English with an ethnic terminology, a shared history narrated within a single chronological sequence and also, in his treatment of the Britons, an 'other' against whom the English could define themselves.[73] This idea that the creation of ethnic identity involves interaction with other peoples and ultimately the creation of 'outsiders' through 'ethnic closure' is an important one.[74]

Like the so-called 'historians of barbarian peoples'—Bede, Gregory of Tours, Jordanes and Paul the Lombard—Ari creates a myth of origins for the Icelanders involving migration over the sea and settlement in a 'promised' land. It is important to note that he emphasises the Norwegian ancestry of the Icelanders over and above any other possible provenances (Swedish or Celtic, for example). His reiteration of the Icelanders' Norwegian origins is striking in comparison with the more disparate origins of the settlers in *Landnámabók*. After giving a genealogy for the Norwegian king Haraldr the Fine-Haired, Ari states that Iceland was 'first settled from Norway', mentions only the journeys of 'a Norwegian named Ingólfr' (*Landnámabók* also tells of two earlier voyages, one by a Swede), and specifies that 'a great many people began to move out here from Norway' (pp. 3–4). In the case of all four of his main settlers, he specifies Norwegian descent: Hrollaugr is the son of Rǫgnvaldr 'earl in Mœrr' (in western Norway), Ketilbjǫrn is 'a Norwegian', Auðr is the daughter of Ketill Flatnose 'a Norwegian lord', and Helgi the Lean, again, is 'a Norwegian' (p. 4). This is particularly noteworthy given that Ari's own ancestor, Auðr, travelled in Scotland, Ireland and the Hebrides before coming to Norway, something which Ari must have known from his mention of Þorsteinn the Red (see notes 22 and 124). The first laws are brought 'from Norway'

[72] Davis 1976: 19–69; Heather 1996: 3–6; Pohl 1997: 7–10; Brooks 1999: 5.
[73] Brooks 1999: 22; see also Wormald 1983; Foot 1996; Howe 1989: 49–71, 108–25.
[74] Moreland 2000: 40.

and Christianity is introduced by a Norwegian king (pp. 4, 7). There is no hint of any continuity with Celtic Christianity and thê *papar* conveniently leave when the Norwegians arrive, even though *Landnámabók* and *Kristni saga* say that there had been Christians at Kirkjubœr in the south continuously from the time of settlement (pp. 41–2 and note 47). In the main, however, Ari's disregard of Celtic Christians colours all later sources: when *Óláfs saga Tryggvasonar in mesta* introduces the Icelandic missionary Stefnir, a descendant of Helgi bjóla, it assumes that he was converted abroad, despite that the fact that Helgi was a Celtic Christian (p. 39 and note 36). Ari's silence about the mass of conflicting traditions recorded in *Landnámabók* suggests that he is deliberately simplifying and streamlining to provide a distinct people with a distinct geographical origin— Norway. The privileging of this particular origin is likely to reflect contemporary power relationships and Iceland's dependence on a political relationship with Norway; it may also reflect the ancestry of the *Haukdœlir* family, since Bishop Ísleifr's father, Gizurr, was second cousin to Óláfr Tryggvason (see p. 46 and note 69).

At several points, we see Ari negotiating the Icelanders' relationship with other countries, principally Norway, but also Greenland. The first occurs during his account of the migration from Norway, which is initially forbidden by Haraldr the Fine-Haired and finally permitted upon the payment of land-dues. This reflects contemporary agreements about the status of Icelanders in Norway and the rights of the king of Norway over Icelanders, the most recent of which had been witnessed by Bishop Gizurr as well as by the lawspeaker Markús Skeggjason (see p. 4 and note 21). The account of Greenland's settlement, which has striking verbal parallels with the settlement of Iceland (including the archaeological signs of earlier habitation) establishes Iceland as no longer a periphery of Norway ('out here'), but a centre for migration elsewhere: Eiríkr the Red travels 'out there from here' (p. 7 and note 57). The most important moment, however, is the conversion itself, when Þangbrandr returns to Norway to report to Óláfr Tryggvason that 'it was beyond all expectation that Christianity might yet be accepted here' (p. 8). Óláfr's angry and violent reaction towards 'our countrymen who were there in the east' ('our' countrymen is, in the context, strongly partisan) is averted only by the diplomacy of Gizurr and Hjalti, who themselves agree to plead the cause of Christianity on his behalf. From this point on, Óláfr disappears from the narrative and there is little sense of his agency in the scenes at the Althing. The last we hear is that he 'fell the same summer' that Christianity was proclaimed in the laws (p. 9). This contrasts with, for example, the account of the A-text of

Oddr Snorrason's *Óláfs saga Tryggvasonar*, where Óláfr's physical absence at the conversion of Iceland is amply compensated for by the sense of his spiritual presence there.

Ari's attitude towards the kings of Norway is conveyed even more clearly in the speech in which Þorgeirr persuades the Icelanders to accept his judgement on which religion Iceland is to observe: he gives an exemplum about how the kings of Norway and Denmark had 'kept up warfare and battles against each other for a long time, until the peoples of those countries (*landsmenn*) had made peace between them, even though they did not wish it'. There is a telling contrast between the unreasonable kings, who resist peace at their peoples' cost, and the wise *landsmenn*, who are able to impose peace in spite of them; the term *landsmenn* is used repeatedly of the Icelanders in *Íslendingabók*. Attention is drawn to Iceland's own unique position as a kingless state, upheld and legitimised by the way in which its people peacefully accept conversion, not through royal power, but through the legal process of arbitrated resolution.[75]

In the absence of an executive power, the law is central to Ari's understanding of Icelandic identity. In *Njáls saga*, Njáll famously declares that 'by laws shall our country be built up and by lawlessness laid waste', and it may be partly thanks to the ideology of Ari's short history that such a statement rings true.[76] Ari describes the stages by which a new society is created in a virgin land and the process, for him, is primarily a legal one. The first event after the settlement is the bringing of laws or law (the Icelandic *lǫg* is plural) from Norway, laws which are carefully adjusted to meet the demands of a new situation. After the land has been explored, the Althing is established and, in a mythical patterning, held on the confiscated land of a murderer: order is imposed against a background of lawlessness and feud. The ever-present danger of social disintegration is averted again and again through the counsel of *spakir menn* 'wise men' with the cooperation of *landsmenn* 'countrymen': the disorder of the seasons results in an improved reckoning of time, fighting at the Althing leads to the division of the country into Quarters and, in each case, speeches at the Althing are decisive. At the climax of Þorgeirr's speech, he identifies the law as the single most important source of social unity: 'It will prove true that if we tear apart the law, we will also tear apart the peace' (p. 9). The hint of the numinous in his night under the cloak, rather like Þorsteinn Black's mysterious dream about the calendar, serves

---

[75] Jochens 1999: 647–54.
[76] *Njáls saga*, *ÍF* XII 172: 'Með lǫgum skal land várt byggja, en með ólǫgum eyða'.

as 'mythical underpinning' for the entire system.[77] Christianity is proclaimed 'in the laws', and brings with it the dissolution of old laws and the passing of new ones. Ari depicts bishops, clerics, lawspeakers and chieftains as working together on this: Gizurr, Markús and Sæmundr on the tithe law, and Gizurr, Hafliði and Bergþórr on the first written law code. Ari emphasises how strong leaders, wise men and social consensus preserve the laws of the land, hold back feuds and strengthen social order for the good of all; if he was writing, as is sometimes suggested, against the background of the feud between Hafliði and Þorgils (which also involved fighting at the Althing), this message—a call for law and unity to prevail—would have been particularly apt.[78]

Perhaps the best way to understand Ari's history is as a new literary genre, created to meet the needs of a new people with a distinctive political system unrivalled in early medieval Europe. His book of 'the Icelanders' is not quite Church history or national history, though it includes both: it is a history of the Icelandic constitution, which Ari and subsequent Icelanders closely identified with the law, and changes to this constitution form its main structuring device, alongside the biographies of bishops in chs 9 and 10.[79] As Bede does for the English, Ari provides for the Icelanders a shared history based on the key moments of settlement and conversion but, despite his loans from European Latin literature, his freedom from religious ideology and rhetoric and his emphasis on social, legal and political processes make his work unique among early medieval histories. As Snorri Sturluson declared in the prologue to *Heimskringla*, though perhaps for different reasons, *þykkir mér hans sǫgn ǫll merkiligust* 'all his account seems to me most remarkable'.[80]

A Note on Íslendingabók, Prose Style and the Family Saga

As far as we know, Ari was the first Icelander to write an original prose composition in Icelandic: according to the *First Grammatical Treatise*, only *lǫg* (laws), *frœði* (historical information, probably genealogies) and *þýðingar helgar* (see p. xix) had previously been written down.[81] As one might expect, the innovatory character of his work inevitably results in

---

[77] On the mythic undercurrent in *Íslendingabók*, see further Lindow 1997b.

[78] Björn Sigfússon 1944: 40; Ellehøj 1965: 82–4.

[79] On the importance of settlement and a sense of 'standing at the beginning' for the origins of written literature in Iceland, see further Schier 1975 and Clunies Ross 1997.

[80] *ÍF* XXVI 6.

[81] Haugen 1972: 12–13, 32–3.

some clumsiness of style: Ari has trouble with complex subordination (in the first sentences of chs 1 and 4, for example) and includes in his work various Latinisms, as noted on p. xix). Although both temporal and causal subordination are found, long stretches of prose are mainly paratactic with 'and', 'but' and 'then' as the most frequent connectives. Among the stylistic devices used, the most important are repetition and parallelism, in the account of Ingólfr's exploration in ch. 1, for example ('for the first time . . . for the second time . . . The place to the east . . . the place to the west') or in the genealogies of ch. 2 ('settled in the east . . . settled in the south . . . settled in the west . . . settled in the north'). Sometimes, verbal parallels create deliberate symmetries between chapters, as for the paired accounts of the settlement of Iceland and Greenland, or the mini-biographies of Ísleifr and Gizurr. Many of Ari's sentences include carefully balanced clauses: 'where things should be added, or removed, or set up differently' (p. 4), 'and tithes paid on it, and laws laid down' (p. 12, with alliteration in the etymologically related words *lǫg á lǫgð*). Ari also frequently uses word-pairs and parallel phrases: 'according to the belief and reckoning' (p. 3), 'for killings or injuries' (p. 6), 'their kinsmen and friends' (p. 8), 'the same law and the same religion' (p. 9), 'killings or fighting', 'authority and governance' (p. 10). In ch. 4, there is a nice example of chiasmus with the repetition of different forms of the same two verbs: 'awake . . . asleep . . . asleep . . . wake up'. The awakening of Þorsteinn's dream audience is connected with the approval from his real audience through a play on the literal and metaphorical meanings of the verb phrases *vakna* and *vakna við* 'to wake up' and 'to recognise' (the second translated on p. 6 as 'welcomed'). As well as these more 'learned' features, Ari makes some use of alliteration, most noticeably in Þorgeirr's speech to the Althing.[82]

Although Ari's *Íslendingabók* is not a saga and differs from this genre by, among other things, its relatively frequent use of the first-person singular referring to the author, it does presage in some interesting ways aspects of later saga tradition. In a few cases, it seems clear enough that the saga-writers have inherited traditions from Ari: the close connection between migration to Iceland and King Haraldr Fine-Haired, for example (compare *Egils saga* chs 1–27), or the depiction of the conversion as a legal and political process (compare *Njáls saga* chs 100–05). In other cases, however, shared similarities perhaps go back to an oral tradition of prose narrative which pre-existed the conversion: Ari and the family

[82] On Ari's prose style, see further Björn Sigfússon 1944: 84 and Þórir Óskarsson 2005: 363.

sagas both adopt a secular outlook and style most striking for its detachment from Christian ideology and rhetoric and both use oral tradition, based around genealogy and topography, as a source.[83] Above all, many of the stories which Ari tells read like miniature versions of later saga narrative: the feuds, burnings and battles in chs 3 and 5, the dream which heralds Þorsteinn Black's success in ch. 4 and the citation of a skaldic strophe in ch. 9 are all motifs which can be easily paralleled in the best-known family sagas. In his account of Iceland's conversion, Ari shows himself more than capable of masterful narrative: events in Norway are deftly drawn, with Þangbrandr's complaint, Óláfr's anger and Gizurr and Hjalti's hasty reassurances tersely expressed in indirect speech. As the scene moves to Iceland, the tension builds: Hjalti, left behind because of his recent outlawry, comes 'riding' (this is also a present participle in the Icelandic) to join Gizurr at the Assembly and it comes so close to fighting, Ari tells us, that 'no one could foresee which way it would go' (*eigi of sá á milli*). In the midst of the tumult caused by the abandonment of legal procedure, Ari describes a period of tense silence: the lawspeaker Þorgeirr lies under his cloak 'all that day and following night, and did not speak a word'. The speech he makes upon awakening is carefully structured and shows a concentration of the stylistic devices described above, while the move from indirect to direct discourse at its climax is characteristic of saga style: it gains impact from being the only direct speech in the whole book.[84] Ari's skill and the 'strong saga flavour' of the scene suggest that native models were available to him for the composition of narrative prose; if so, these models must have been oral.

KRISTNI SAGA

Kristni saga ('The Story of the Conversion') offers the possibility of direct comparison with Ari when it comes to those sections of his work concerned with Iceland's conversion and the growth of the early Church, just as *Landnámabók* offers comparable material on the settlement. Both *Landnámabók* and *Kristni saga* were, in fact, connected with *Íslendingabók* from an early date in the study of the sagas: one of the first theories about their origin was that *Landnámabók* was compiled from the first version of *Íslendingabók*, and that the material left over was fashioned into a *Kristni saga*.[85]

---

[83] Foote 1974.
[84] Knirk 1981: 32–5.
[85] Brenner 1878: 7–10, 156; Maurer 1870: 318–9; 1891: 86–96.

Kristni saga xxxi

The author of *Kristni saga* clearly had Ari's *Íslendingabók* in mind (if not in front of him) when he wrote chs 14 to 16 on Ísleifr and Gizurr, and he states himself in ch. 14 that Ari 'has said most about the events written down here' (p. 52). He may also have used *Íslendingabók* for his account of the legal prodecure of conversion, which is in places very close to Ari, and he appears to cite Ari as his authority for Stefnir's death (p. 51, but see note 97). Even the longer account of Friðrekr's mission probably has its origins in Ari's mention of 'Friðrekr, who came here during the heathen period' (p. 10).

One's immediate impression upon reading the two together, however, is that *Kristni saga* is a very different sort of work. On the one hand, it is more like the family sagas than *Íslendingabók*: it is anonymous, with a self-effacing narrator, and presents itself as an account of shared, traditional, knowledge. Although it may have some basis in the reports of individual oral informants, it rarely cites its oral sources other than in impersonal formulas ('it is said' in ch. 1, p. 35, 'as far as is known' in ch. 2, p. 37). Apart from one reference to a saga of Óláfr Tryggvason, it is equally reticent about any written sources. Like the kings' sagas, it includes a number of skaldic verses as substantiation for the narrative and the slight differences between verse and prose suggest that the former do pre-date the saga and that some may even be contemporary with the events described. On the other hand, *Kristni saga* is more in tune with the Latin European hagiographical tradition than either *Íslendingabók* or the family sagas, and provides more of what one expects from a 'missionary' history: fierce conflict between heathens and Christians, miracles, exempla and Christian symbolism. This has resulted in different attitudes towards what kind of text it is and therefore towards its historical reliability: while early scholars praised its basis in *historiske principer* ('historical principles') and its *stræng kronologisk tendens* ('strong chronological tendency'), it has more recently been described as a 'religious tract', more concerned with *undri og stórmerkjum en raunverulegum atburðum* ('marvels and miracles than real events'), drawing on *táknmáli kirkjunnar og frásögnum Biblíunnar eða annarra helgirita sem á henni byggja* ('the symbolism of the Church and stories from the Bible or other religious texts based on it').[86] In the following analysis, I want to look at different theories about the origins of *Kristni saga* and evaluate its relationship to *Íslendingabók* and its status as a medieval history.

---

[86] These quotations are from the following works (in this order): Ólsen 1893:332–33; Finnur Jónsson 1920–24, II 570; Jón Hnefill Aðalsteinsson 1999: 59–60; Líndal 1974: 248; *ÍF* XV cxli–ii.

Date, Authorship and Sources

Kristni saga is preserved in one medieval manuscript, *Hauksbók*, dated to c.1306–10, where it is written in Haukr's own hand immediately after his version of *Landnámabók* (also known as *Hauksbók*). The part of the manuscript that contains the two works (AM 371 4to) is fragmentary, comprising only eighteen leaves, and the text of *Kristni saga* runs from 'shortly afterwards' (*síðarr*) in ch. 5 to 'the lawspeaker Markús and' (*Markúss lǫgsǫgumanns ok*) in ch. 15. For the beginning and end of the saga, we are dependent on a copy made by Jón Erlendsson in the mid-seventeenth century (AM 105 fol.).[87]

Most attempts to establish the authorship and date of *Kristni saga* have involved some sort of interpretation of the relationship between *Landnámabók* and *Kristni saga* in the only surviving medieval manuscript. At some stage, the two have clearly become linked, as is clear from a comparison of *Kristni saga* with two (related) versions of *Landnámabók*: *Sturlubók*, which is associated with Sturla Þórðarson (d. 1284) and *Hauksbók*, which is associated with Haukr Erlendsson (1260–1334). *Sturlubók* and *Hauksbók* both end with an account of how Iceland 'was completely heathen for about one hundred years' and *Kristni saga* begins with '*Now* [the story of] how Christianity came to Iceland begins . . . ' (p. 35, my emphasis).[88] *Sturlubók* and *Hauksbók* date the settlement to 874 and *Kristni saga* says that, upon the arrival of Friðrekr and Þorvaldr, 'the land had been inhabited for one hundred and seven years'. This assumes that a date for the settlement has already been given and coincides with the dating of *Landnámabók* if we agree, on the basis of the internal sequence of events in the saga, that the missionaries arrived in 981 (cf. p. 35 and note 5). The same goes for the saga's later, more approximate, statement that, upon Gizurr's death in 1118, Iceland had been inhabited for 'two hundred and forty years, the first half in heathendom and the second in Christianity' (p. 53). Finally, *Sturlubók* and *Hauksbók* both contain lists of the most important settlers for each quarter of Iceland and, at the end, a list of the most important chieftains in 930. *Kristni saga* contains related lists of the most important chieftains in 981 and 1118, as well as including a list of chieftains who were priests in ch. 17 (see p. 35 and note 6; pp. 53–4).

On the basis of these connections, some of the earliest editors and critics of *Kristni saga* assumed that it was written by Haukr Erlendsson in the early fourteenth century, and Guðbrandur Vigfússon was the first to challenge

---

[87] *Hauksbók* 1960: xii, xxviii–xxix, xxxiii.
[88] *ÍF* I 396.

Kristni saga xxxiii

this view: he showed that the saga must predate Haukr's copy and concluded that it was present in one of Haukr's sources, probably Styrmir Kárason's (lost) version of *Landnámabók*, known as *Styrmisbók*. He also suggested, however, that it may have been written even earlier, perhaps by Oddr Snorrason in the second half of the twelfth century, which is when the genealogies in ch. 18 end.[89] Later scholars agreed that the saga predated Haukr's version, but disagreed on the originality of the link with *Landnámabók*: whereas Maurer and Brenner saw both works as one in scope and purpose, originating in Ari's older *Íslendingabók*, Björn M. Ólsen argued persuasively that *Kristni saga* represented an original work appended to *Landnámabók* only in Haukr's version. He dated it to the mid-thirteenth century on the basis of its reference in ch. 3 to Bishop Bótólfr, who left Iceland in 1243 and died in 1246 (see p. 37 and note 25).[90] Finnur Jónsson and Bernhard Kahle, on the other hand, thought that Sturla Þórðarson had first appended the saga to *Landnámabók* and that he had interpolated some of the genealogies and chronological notices. They conjectured that he had reworked the saga to provide a bridge between his version of *Landnámabók* and the collection of sagas of contemporaries included in *Sturlunga saga*.[91] In his *Gerðir Landnámabókar*, Jón Jóhannesson took this argument further: he suggested that *Kristni saga* had never existed in independent form, but was composed by Sturla from different sources as a continuation to his *Landnámabók*. It formed one link in a chain of sagas documenting the history of Iceland from its beginnings to Sturla's own day, perhaps on the model of what Snorri Sturluson had done for Norway in *Heimskringla*.[92] However, although many scholars have accepted Jón Jóhannesson's attribution of the saga to Sturla, this has not gone unquestioned, and the most recent editor of the saga, Sigurgeir Steingrímsson, is content to label its author *óþekktur* ('unknown')—he thinks that it dates from *c*.1237–50 on the basis of its relationship to other sagas. Other scholars (including one within the same volume) disagree with his view on these relationships, but there seems to be a tentative agreement that *Kristni saga* does date from the mid-thirteenth century.[93]

---

[89] *Kristni-saga* 1773, 'Ad lectorem'; *BS* I xix–xxiii; see also Brenner 1878: 3–5.
[90] Ólsen 1893: 263–349.
[91] *Hauksbók* 1892–6: lxv–lxxiv; Finnur Jónsson 1920–24, II 571–2; Kahle 1905: ix–x. Sturla's involvement was first suggested by Brenner 1878: 10, 155.
[92] Jón Jóhannesson 1941: 16–19, 69–72, 224–5.
[93] *ÍF* XV cliv–clv. Ólafur Halldórsson (1990: 461–4) and Sveinbjörn Rafnsson (2001: 25–32, 154, 164) have both questioned Sturla's authorship of *Kristni saga*, but on different (and mutually incompatible) grounds; Sveinbjörn's view

In the absence of any final consensus as to date and authorship, it is hard to say much about the written sources of the saga: other than Ari, only the 'saga' of Óláfr Tryggvason is explicitly referred to, and this could be either that of Oddr Snorrason or the lost saga of Gunnlaugr Leifsson (it is not Snorri Sturluson's; see p. 39 and note 34). There is a close relationship between chs 1–13 of *Kristni saga* and a series of short stories about the missions to Iceland in *Óláfs saga Tryggvasonar in mesta* (known as *Kristni þættir*), and Ólsen suggested that the common source for these was Gunnlaugr's lost *Óláfs saga Tryggvasonar*—Gunnlaugr, a monk at Þingeyrar who died in 1218, is explicitly cited as a source of *Þorvalds þáttr víðfǫrla* in *Óláfs saga Tryggvasonar in mesta*.[94] Ólsen's views are accepted with a few reservations by the most recent editor of *Kristni þættir*, but rejected by Sigurgeir Steingrímsson in the same volume: he asserts instead that *Kristni saga* was an original work and a source for the stories in *Óláfs saga Tryggvasonar in mesta*.[95] The same lack of consensus prevails with regard to other sources: Jón Jóhannesson suggested *Vatnsdœla saga*, *Laxdœla saga* and 'various annals' and I myself think it likely that *Heimskringla* was also a source—but Sigurgeir Steingrímsson rejects all of these except *Heimskringla*, while Óláfur Halldórsson accepts *Vatnsdœla* saga and (in places) *Heimskringla*, but thinks that Gunnlaugr's lost saga is the source of the material that *Kristni saga* and *Laxdœla saga* have in common.[96] Chs 14 to 18 of *Kristni saga* contain passages also shared by *Hungrvaka* and *Jóns saga helga*, which may go back to a different redaction of Ari's *Íslendingabók*, although not necessarily the 'first' one mentioned by Ari.[97] Ch. 18, which has verbal parallels with the longer account of the same events in *Þorgils saga ok Hafliða*, is also found in the appendix to the version of *Landnámabók* in *Skarðsárbók*, where it is copied from a different (and probably more original) text of *Kristni saga* than that of *Hauksbók* (see p. 72, note 109). Sources other than written include skaldic verse (Brandr's verse in

---

of its sources differs from Sigurgeir's, but he dates it to a similar time-period on the basis of its reference to Bishop Bótólfr.

[94] *ÓTM* I 290; Ólsen 1893: 309–33.

[95] *ÍF* XV cxxix–xxxi, clxiii–iv.

[96] Jón Jóhannesson 1941: 70–71; Óláfur Halldórsson 1978: 382–89; Duke [Grønlie] 1998–2001; *ÍF* XV lxxix, cxv, cxxx, clxxv, cci–ccii.

[97] Sveinbjörn Rafnsson 2001: 148–54; *ÍF* XV ccxliv–v. The view that other redactions of *Íslendingabók* were in circulation may be supported by Knirk's observation (1981: 129) that the versions of Þorgeirr's speech in Oddr's *Óláfs saga Tryggvasonar* and *Kristni saga* share variants which suggest a 'mutual relationship' between their originals against the preserved redaction of *Íslendingabók*.

ch. 13 is not found elsewhere) and oral traditions surrounding place-names and physical features of the landscape. These are most prominent in the saga's account of Þangbrandr's enforced stay in the west of Iceland (p. 43 and note 55), which must be based on local tradition.

Kristni saga *and Iceland's History*

The idea that *Kristni saga* may have been part of a projected history of Iceland from settlement down to the time of the sagas of contemporaries is suggestive, and would explain some of the peculiarities in the form of the extant saga, not only its abrupt beginning, chronological notices and its inclusion of lists of chieftains, but also its more puzzling conclusion with the offspring of Hafliði Másson. These are listed after a brief retelling of the conflict between Hafliði and Þorgils, which follows a chronological summary at the end of ch. 17 and a list of chieftains halfway through ch. 18, either of which would seem to be a more fitting conclusion for the saga. The second part of ch. 18, although clearly leading on from the natural catastrophes that follow Gizurr's death, shifts markedly from a fairly narrow focus on ecclesiastical history (the author omits most of Ari's comments on lawspeakers and events unrelated to the Church in previous chapters) to secular history (the feud between Þorgils and Hafliði) with only a sprinkling of ecclesiastical history (the death of Bishop Jón and the election of Ketill Þorsteinsson as bishop). Another church history, *Hungrvaka*, which mentions the feud between Þorgils and Hafliði only in a list of secular events within the episcopate of Bishop Þorlákr, provides a telling contrast.[98] The end of *Kristni saga* is best understood, therefore, to my mind, as a transitional episode leading on to the sagas of contemporaries, or at the least as a 'miscellany' following the saga proper; that the whole of ch. 18 was considered separable from the saga by some early scholars is clear from its inclusion on its own in the appendix to *Skarðsárbók*.

If *Kristni saga* was intended as part of a projected history of Iceland, this would explain both its dependence on Ari's *Íslendingabók* (which is a more appropriate model for such a history than *Heimskringla*) and some of the ways in which it diverges from it. Whereas Ari's account of the conversion is based on family history and focuses primarily on the south of Iceland, *Kristni saga* deliberately widens its focus to embrace the whole country: Friðrekr and Þorvaldr's mission to the north and Stefnir's mission to the west are added to those of Þangbrandr, Gizurr and Hjalti, and Þangbrandr travels almost the whole way around the country, to Skjálfanda-

[98] *ÍF* XVI 27.

fljót in the north-east and as far as Barðastrǫnd in the west. In place of Ari's narrow focus on Gizurr and Hjalti, there is a host of different missionaries and converts: Þorvaldr the Far-Traveller, the German bishop Friðrekr, Stefnir Þorgilsson (who, like Þangbrandr, is an envoy of Óláfr Tryggvason), Koðrán, Síðu-Hallr and Kjartan. Even in the case of Gizurr and Hjalti there is a different emphasis, showing much more interest in stories about Hjalti than Ari does: the fact that the two crosses at the Althing mark the height of Óláfr and Hjalti respectively (p. 48) suggests that in some traditions about the conversion he—rather than Gizurr— was the main Icelandic figure.[99] It seems likely that some of these traditions were local and originated in different areas of Iceland. They are certainly closely attached to the landscape and to place-names, especially in the north and west. The church built by Þorvarðr 'was still standing' in the first half of the thirteenth century (p. 37), and the burial cairns of Skeggbjǫrn and his men 'can still be clearly seen' (p. 43). Some of the stories about Þorvaldr and Stefnir in particular may have been modelled on earlier traditions about Þangbrandr. The events of Þorvaldr's mission recall those of Þangbrandr's (battles with berserks, libel, killings) and Stefnir's shipwreck may also be in imitation of Þangbrandr's. Occasionally, the joining of these disparate traditions is still visible: when Stefnir arrives in Iceland, we are told that 'all people were then heathen in this country' (p. 39), yet we have just heard of the many converts made during the mission of Þorvaldr and Friðrekr.[100]

As well as bringing together traditions from different parts of the country, *Kristni saga* also makes an effort to show the cooperation of each of the four Quarters of Iceland in its legal conversion.[101] This once again suggests a link between *Kristni saga* and *Sturlubók/Hauksbók*, both of which trace the settlement in each of Iceland's four Quarters and provide Christian settlers for each one (Helgi the Lean for the north, Jǫrundr, Helgi bjóla and Ǫrlygr for the south, Auðr the Deep-Minded for the west, and Ketill the Foolish for the east).[102] As well as listing chieftains

---

[99] Sveinbjörn Rafnsson 2001: 139; *ÍF* XV cxxxiii. Hjalti's greater prominence in *Kristni saga* was first recognised by Vigfússon and Powell (1905: I 370–71, 375), who were also first to point out that his comments to Narfi and Runólfr could be construed as verse (see chs 10 and 12 and notes 62 and 87). Together with his famous verse from the Law-Rock, these may have formed the nucleus of later stories about Hjalti.

[100] Sveinbjörn Rafnsson 1977; *ÍF* XV cxxxii.

[101] *ÍF* XV cxxxiii; Sveinbjörn Rafnsson 2001: 139.

[102] *ÍF* I 396.

from each Quarter, *Kristni saga* records missions to each Quarter and conversions within each Quarter. When King Óláfr takes hostages in Norway, he takes one from each Quarter: Kjartan from the west, Halldórr from the north, Kolbeinn from the east, and Svertingr from the south (p. 47 and note 70). Most interesting is the little anecdote about what happened at the Althing among the Christians while Þorgeirr was lying under his cloak. In order to counter the pagans' sacrifice, Gizurr and Hjalti request 'victory offerings' of two men from each Quarter of Iceland: they themselves step forward for the south, Síðu-Hallr and Þorleifr for the east, Hlenni the Old and Þorvarðr Spak-Bǫðvarsson for the north, and Gestr and Ormr Koðránsson from the west (p. 49). This neatly recalls to our minds the key converts from each Quarter, and Ormr's on-the-spot baptism, so as to participate on behalf of his absent brother Þorvaldr the Far-Traveller, completes the circle of countrywide conversion. After Þorgeirr has proclaimed the Christian laws, we are told that the peoples of the Northern and Southern Quarters were baptised in Reykjalaug in Laugardalr on their way home; the 'whole assembly was baptised', and 'most of the westerners were baptised in Reykjalaug in southern Reykjadalr' (p. 50). This is a history that consciously involves Icelanders from all parts of the country, with a particular emphasis on the north and west, which perhaps indicates the author's own provenance.

Kristni saga *as Missionary History*

Apart from the occasional reservation, most scholars would agree that *Kristni saga* is missionary history or Church history—and it certainly has more claim than *Íslendingabók* to be considered as such.[103] The missions to Iceland form the organisational principle of the whole work which, as Sigurgeir Steingrímsson has shown, is threefold: first, the three missions to Iceland of Þorvaldr, Stefnir and Þangbrandr, then the story of the legal conversion, covering events in Norway and Iceland, and finally the history of the early church from Ísleifr's consecration to the events following Gizurr's death.[104] *Kristni saga* is the only source to join these three strands together: Ari lacks a full account of the missions and *Kristni þættir* in *Óláfs saga Tryggvasonar in mesta* lack the history of the early Church.

---

[103] Brenner (1878: 8, 14) argued on the basis of various omissions (specifically, its failure to mention the names of foreign priests in Iceland) that *Kristni saga* was not conceived as a Church history but as an appendix of miscellaneous information relating to *Landnámabók*.

[104] *ÍF* XV lx–lxii.

In contrast to the continuity in Icelandic history that marks Ari's work, this saga clearly divides Icelandic history into two, 'the first half in heathendom and the second in Christianity' (p. 53). It is explicitly stated in the opening sentence that the work will focus on the mission and conversion that brought about this momentous change. Against the background of the Icelanders' heathenism, this is the story of 'how Christianity came to Iceland' (p. 35).

In many ways, this story is told in a manner closer to European hagiography than Ari's narrowly legal and political focus permits. Most noticeable are the signs of Christian rhetoric so lacking in Ari: Þorvaldr accepts 'the true faith' and preaches 'God's message', Friðrekr is 'truly a saint', Stefnir travels 'boldly', Þangbrandr preaches 'outstandingly', as do Gizurr and Hjalti (pp. 35, 38, 40, 42). The missionaries' opponents, on the other hand, are derided: Heðinn opposes Þorvaldr 'with many evil words', many people at the Assembly where Hjalti is prosecuted 'blasphemed greatly', and Runólfr shows 'his tyranny and intransigence more than justice' (pp. 37, 44–5). The heathens are often treated as an indiscriminate group: 'those people who were heathen' dislike the church Arngeirr has built, 'the heathens' attack the missionaries at Hegranes, 'the heathens' are 'displeased' when Kjartan accepts a gift from King Óláfr (pp. 37–8, 46). The conflict between heathens and Christians is much more sharply drawn than in *Íslendingabók* and considerably more violent: there is a total of eighteen killings, two attempted killings and several other threats—a higher body count than in any other source. Stefnir and Þangbrandr both meet resistance as soon as it is known that they are Christians, and families are divided by the new faith: Klaufi enlists Arngeirr's own brother to help destroy his church and Stefnir is outlawed by his own kinsmen (pp. 37, 39–40). This is all very different from Ari's account of the conversion, where the only potential battle is avoided and the imagined dangers of religious violence form the keynote of Þorgeirr's speech.

Like European lives of missionaries, *Kristni saga* also includes miracles that fall into two main types: those connected with the conversion of individuals and those that show God's protection of his messengers.[105] Þorvaldr's father, Koðrán, is converted after Friðrekr drives the guardian spirit away from his farm; the rock in which it dwells bursts apart after Friðrekr chants over it, convincing Koðrán that 'the spirit had been overcome' (p. 36). Both Friðrekr and Þangbrandr bring about conversions by defeating pagan berserks: by consecrating the fire they stride through,

[105] Wood 2001: 262–4.

they destroy the berserks' immunity to it, and Þangbrandr also uses the sign of the cross (pp. 36, 44). The illusion of fire and supernatural arrows protect the church at Áss from the attacks of pagans, and Þorvaldr and Friðrekr are kept safe from an ambush by the miraculous flight of a flock of birds, which scares away the pagans' horses (pp. 37–8). The incense at the Althing is smelt upwind as well as down and the pagans are unable to reply to Gizurr and Hjalti's speech there on account of the 'great fear' that 'came with their words' (p. 48). It is striking how many of these miracles are centred on the power of Christian rites—ecclesiastical chant, the sign of the cross and the use of incense. This connection between rite and conversion is implied in the case of Kjartan's conversion in Norway and made explicit in the case of Síðu-Hallr's. Both are converted following the services for Michaelmas, and Hallr's household are particularly impressed by the external trappings of Christian worship, 'the sound of bells', 'the scent of incense' and 'men clothed in costly material and fine cloth' (p. 41 and note 45). The saga also specifies that Þormóðr sang mass before the meeting at the Althing with other men 'wearing vestments', an event not mentioned by Ari despite the fact that he was a priest himself (p. 48). The sign of the cross is important throughout: it is marked on Þangbrandr's shield, which first arouses King Óláfr's interest in Christianity, Þangbrandr raises crosses during his mission, and the two crosses later raised at the Althing measure the 'height', either literally or metaphorically, of King Óláfr and Hjalti (p. 48 and note 80).

In places, it is clear that there is a moral and spiritual dimension to the narrative lacking in Ari's terse account. Hallr responds deeply to Þangbrandr's sermon about 'the glory of God's angels' and Þangbrandr describes his conversion explicitly as the result of divine revelation: 'God has given you this understanding' (p. 41). Kjartan's swimming competition with Óláfr involves three dips in the sea followed by the gift of a cloak and it is likely that this is figural: it presages the threefold immersion of baptism and the donning of baptismal garments (pp. 45–6).[106] Likewise, the church built by Gizurr and Hjalti on the site of 'heathen places of worship' symbolises the conversion of the landscape: like Friðrekr's driving out of Koðrán's spirit, it shows the physical cleansing of the land and its re-consecration to Christianity (pp. 47–8).[107] The scene among

---

[106] See note 66 to *Kristni saga* and, on the extensive symbolism of water, cloak and ships, see Lindow's excellent study (1997a) of the related account of Hallfreðr's conversion in *Hallfreðar saga*.

[107] On the conversion of non-Christian sacred space, see Howe 1997.

the Christians at the Althing is carefully designed to draw out the differences between pagan sacrifice and the meaning of sacrifice in a Christian context. It is one of the few places in the Icelandic conversion narratives where an emphasis is placed on moral living ('we must therefore live better lives and be more careful to avoid sin than before', p. 49), a theme which is much more central in European histories and lives of missionaries.[108]

Most interesting are those exemplary passages dealing with revenge and forgiveness which involve Hjalti and the enemies who outlaw him, and in which Runólfr's 'tyranny and intransigence' are contrasted with Hjalti's forgiveness of the man who tries to murder him, Narfi (p. 45). Narfi is commissioned by Runólfr to kill Hjalti 'to free himself from outlawry' and, when Hjalti suggests 'a better plan' (*betra ráð*) for his reprieve, he perhaps implies spiritual release from sin, as well as temporal release from the status of outlaw; he offers Narfi not only a different means of reprieve, but a whole new way of life (cf. *at betra ráð sitt* 'to amend one's way of life').[109] At the court of King Óláfr in Norway, Hjalti speaks up on behalf of Runólfr's son, Svertingr, and this is explicitly commended by Þangbrandr; he contrasts Hjalti's behaviour with that of men 'given to passionate anger' and emphasises, in an echo of Romans xii, that Hjalti and Gizurr 'often repay evil with good' (p. 47). This is made manifest again when Hjalti stands sponsor to Runólfr at his baptism, though his verse about 'teaching the old chieftain to nibble on the salt' is not unaffected by a sense of personal vindictiveness (p. 50). Hjalti is significantly different in his approach to opposition from Þorvaldr, described by Friðrekr as 'eager to take revenge' (p. 38), and from Þangbrandr, notorious for his revenge killings; in the midst of the insults, killings and outlawries, Hjalti provides a reminder of the spirit of the Christian faith. At the same time, there is an echo of the moral of *Íslendingabók* in the condemnation of 'passionate anger' among both parties, a reminder of Þorgeirr's warning against 'those who most wish to oppose each other' (p. 9; *Kristni saga* adds 'with most vehemence', p. 50). Christian virtue, in this saga, joins seamlessly with social morality.

There is one aspect of *Kristni saga* that is distinctly different from European conversion narratives, however: the presence of pagan verses embedded in the Christian prose. While the prose tends to deal with pagans as a force to be overcome, giving very few details about the specifics of

---

[108] See, for example, *Bede's Ecclesiastical History* 1969: 76–7.
[109] See also the symbolic interpretation of this scene in *ÍF* XVI cxlviii–cxlix.

paganism (even the existence of Koðrán's 'guardian spirit' is never endorsed by the author), the poetry offers a counterpoint to the prevailing Christian ideology: we find complex kennings based on pagan mythology and strong attacks on Christ and the Christian God, highly unusual in a missionary history and, if they are authentic, unparalleled in European literature. The verse about Stefnir triumphantly proclaims that the power of the 'bonds' or Æsir lies behind his shipwreck, and the idea of the 'bonds' as a cohesive force in the cosmos contrasts nicely with their effective dissolution of Stefnir's 'hollow' ship (p. 40). Steinunn's verses on Þangbrandr's shipwreck are particularly accomplished: she makes Þórr the active, dominating force—drawing, shaking, hitting, hurling, hewing into splinters—while 'the bell's keeper', Þangbrandr, watches helpless, and God and Christ fail to intervene (pp. 43–4). The contrast between her assertion that Christ 'was not watching' and the emphasis in the prose narrative on how God miraculously protects his messengers is striking. Finally, the *níð* verses provide an insight into possible contemporary perspectives on Christianity: the perceived 'effeminacy' of the missionaries, the misunderstanding of baptism in the verse about Friðrekr 'bearing children' (the apostle Paul describes himself as 'in the pains of childbirth' in Galatians iv), the description of Þangbrandr as a 'spineless wolf of God', whom the warrior-poet, the 'wielder of steel', must drive from the land (p. 38 and note 27, p. 42 and note 51). While Steinunn calls on Þórr, two other verses connect the poets with the god Óðinn through his role in poetry's myth of origins: Úlfr addresses Þorvaldr as 'a well-tried swimmer | in Hárbarðr's (Óðinn's) sanctuary's fjord', by which he means the mead of poetry, and the same image is found in the verse about Guðleifr, which describes the poet Vetrliði's breast as 'the smithy of the vessel of poetry' (pp. 42–3, notes 52 and 54). These verses are forceful enough to need watering down within the Christian prose: when describing the shipwrecks, the author feels compelled to add that the Stefnir's ship was 'not much damaged' and that Þangbrandr's was later 'repaired' (pp. 40, 44). The voice given to paganism here, perhaps even its own voice, is unique to Old Icelandic literature. The relative sympathy it implies is found to a greater extent in secular genres like the family saga and in Snorri's *Edda*, especially *Gylfaginning* and the Prologue (cf. Snorri Sturluson 2005).

Conversion and Politics

Although *Kristni saga* is evidently more influenced by hagiography than Ari's *Íslendingabók*, it would be wrong to describe it in a derogatory fashion as a 'religious tract' or as 'uncritical history writing'—as wrong, perhaps, as to assume uncritically that missionary hagiography is unconcerned with history or politics.[110] *Kristni saga* is different from saints' lives in several ways, not least in giving a voice to the pagans it represents, and although it proclaims of Friðrekr that he 'is truly a saint' (*sannheilagr*), it does not show any particular interest in sanctity. Indeed, the author is clearly ambivalent about any claim to sainthood on Þorvaldr's part (he cautiously asserts that 'they call him a saint' without specifying who 'they' are) and the death of Stefnir at the hands of Earl Sigvaldi, about whom he has composed an insulting verse, is hardly a martyrdom.[111] When *Kristni saga* is compared with the more explicitly exemplary stories about conversion in *Óláfs saga Tryggvasonar in mesta*, it becomes clear that the author consistently passes over opportunities to point up the moral and spiritual dimensions of events. In good saga style, he avoids homiletic speeches and interpretive comments, and even seems to attenuate the presence of the supernatural, which is in any case, with a few exceptions, mainly confined to Þorvaldr's mission. As Peter Foote has shown, not all the author's anecdotes can be considered edifying in a Christian sense: Snorri goði's quip when the heathens attribute a volcanic eruption to the gods (p. 49: 'What were the gods enraged by when the lava we are standing on here and now was burning?') inclines towards scepticism rather than belief.[112] What, likewise, are we meant to make of the fact that Digr-Ketill dropped his religiously inspired lawsuit against Þorleifr in exchange for some good food and a warm fire?—or the comment that some Icelanders chose to be baptised in warm springs 'because they did not want to be immersed in cold water' (pp. 49–50)? Even the polarisation of Christian and heathen noted above is not consistent throughout: there are 'good men' among the heathens, who rejoice when Þangbrandr kills a berserk (a social menace more than a representative of heathenism) and at the Althing, battle is avoided because some 'wished to prevent trouble, even though they were not Christians' (pp. 44, 48). Perhaps we are not so far from Ari's 'secular' attitudes after all.

Also in line with Ari is the emphasis throughout the saga on legal and political processes, both in the early missions to Iceland and in those parts of the saga based directly on *Íslendingabók*. Unlike *Óláfs saga*

---

[110] It is a common misconception that hagiography is a homogenous genre characterised by a total disregard for historical facts; it is in reality much more flexible and wide-ranging. On the various 'agenda' that can lie behind missionary hagiography in particular, see Wood 1999 and 2001: 248–50.

[111] *ÍF* XV cxxxiv; see also *Kristni saga*, note 36 (p. 62).

[112] Foote 1993a: 142–3; Grønlie 2005: 151–4.

Tryggvasonar in mesta, Kristni saga presents the conflict between heathens and Christians as a legal battle rather than as evil and unmotivated persecution: Þorvaldr and Þangbrandr are libelled, kill in response to that libel (a legally justifiable, if not 'Christian', response) and are outlawed not because of their faith, but because of these killings. Attacks on the missionaries occur after their outlawry rather than before it, and both are forced to go abroad as a result. Stefnir and Hjalti, on the other hand, are both outlawed for blasphemy: Stefnir 'for being a Christian' (but more probably for his destruction of shrines and temples) and Hjalti for his insulting verse about the goddess Freyja.[113] Indeed, the law passed during Stefnir's mission, which designates Christianity as 'a disgrace to one's family' (*frændaskǫmm*) may be included in part to explain the grounds on which Stefnir and Hjalti were sentenced: it seems unlikely in fact that paganism, which was neither a universal nor an institutional religion, had any monopoly on what people should believe. In the passage on Kolr, who refuses food to Þangbrandr, the author's sympathies seem divided: on the one hand Kolr has no good reason for his refusal (he has 'so much food he hardly knew what to do with it'), but on the other Þangbrandr 'flatly' refuses a legal request for compensation. In the second half of the saga, the author focuses, as does Ari, on early Christian legislation, with an additional emphasis on the 'Golden Age' during Gizurr's episcopate: Gizurr, he tells us, 'made the land so peaceful that no great conflicts arose between chieftains and the carrying of weapons almost ceased' (p. 53). As well as preparing for the conflict and litigations of the sagas of contemporaries, this emphasises the role of the bishops in peace-making, something which is also a concern of the version of ch. 18 preserved in *Skarðsárbók*: Ketill's election as bishop is here a direct result of his successful resolution of the feud between Hafliði and Þorgils.[114] The social unrest at the end of the saga ties in with the author's earlier preoccupation with violence and killings during the missions themselves: it is a preoccupation with the law's frequent failure to regulate violence both before and after the conversion.

It would have been no revelation to a medieval Christian, hagiographer or not, that conversion had political consequences and, if anything, the author of *Kristni saga* is more alert than Ari to the difficulties posed by Norway's role in Iceland's conversion to Christianity. The tension is

---

[113] Foote (1984a: 62) suggests that *Kristni saga* has misunderstood the grounds for Stefnir's outlawy. On the concept of blasphemy in pagan times, see p. 24, note 68.

[114] See p. 73 note 118 and, on the role of clerics as peacemakers, Orri Vésteinsson 2000: 219–34.

palpable in the scenes that depict Kjartan's conversion in Norway and Þangbrandr's return from Iceland, where pagan and Christian Icelanders come face to face with the Norwegian king Óláfr Tryggvason. Kjartan's response to Óláfr's offer of baptism is interesting: although predisposed towards Christianity, he demands 'no less honour here than I can expect in Iceland' (p. 46), protecting himself against any loss of face associated with submission to the Norwegian king. Þangbrandr's return from Iceland leads to a more sinister turn of events: Óláfr immediately seizes the Icelanders in Norway (it is not specified that the Christians are spared) and threatens to repay them 'for how disrespectfully their fathers in Iceland had received his communications'. It takes Gizurr and Hjalti to remind him of the 'pardon' or 'peace' promised to those who accept baptism and, even then, hostages (including Christians) are taken 'until it is found out which way this matter will go' (p. 47). Óláfr's royal power, as much as the souls of the Icelanders, hangs in the balance. Likewise, Gizurr and Hjalti's criticism of Þangbrandr betrays deep-seated concerns about Icelandic identity and foreign intervention: 'he killed several men there', they tell Óláfr, 'and people thought it hard to take that from a foreigner' (p. 46).

This anxiety about Norwegian intervention may explain why the author of *Kristni saga* has chosen to dissociate the missions to Iceland from the life of King Óláfr Tryggvason, starting his mission with an Icelandic—not a Norwegian—initiative and framing it with lists of chieftains that place it firmly within the sphere of Icelandic—not Norwegian—history. It may also be why he ends the account of the missions with the deaths of the Icelandic missionaries Þorvaldr and Stefnir (we never hear what became of Þangbrandr) and omits Ari's list of foreign bishops in order to move seamlessly from Gizurr the White's role in the conversion to the consecration of his son Ísleifr as bishop at the unanimous request of 'the people of the country' (p. 51). The conversion effort is firmly attributed to Icelandic chieftains: they are among the first to be converted and the first church-builders, they provide the first two bishops of Iceland and 'most men of high rank', the author tells us, 'were educated and ordained priests, even though they were chieftains' (p. 53 and note 106). At the time he was writing, due to the influence of the Gregorian reform movement, those holding secular office were no longer permitted to be ordained.[115] Yet it appears that the author admires rather than condemns this short-lived

---

[115] On this reform movement and its influence in Iceland, see Jón Jóhannesson 1974: 179–86, 200–14, 216–18; Magnús Stefánsson 1975: 92–104, 119–41; Orri Vésteinsson 2000: 167–78.

unity of secular and ecclesiastical power: it is a fitting tribute to the success of those chieftains who negotiated the political threat from Norway and brought Iceland into the Christian world.

CONCLUSION

Both Ari's *Íslendingabók* and *Kristni saga* are centrally concerned with Christianity and the Church, yet what the above analysis has shown is that neither can straightforwardly be described as hagiography: they are marked by the specific cultural and social circumstances of medieval Iceland and by the close integration of secular and ecclesiastical power that continued right up until the mid-thirteenth century.[116] The two works have much in common, despite their obvious differences: oral tradition, genealogy and law are central to both, although Ari is the pioneer in this, while *Kristni saga* rests on an already established tradition of saga-writing. Ari's account of Icelandic history has a more personal (or familial) slant, while *Kristni saga* is more of a compilation, drawing together traditions from around the country and extending Ari's account of the missions in time and space. In both, evaluative comment and religious rhetoric are avoided in favour of an apparently objective style, although Ari has touching words of praise for those who fostered him, and *Kristni saga* is much more open to the moral and spiritual dimension of events. It is too simple to set Ari up as the only reliable source on Iceland's conversion and to dismiss *Kristni saga* as later fabrication: this introduction has shown that there are a number of reasons to distrust what Ari has to say and that, conversely, more attention should be paid to *Kristni saga*. It certainly seems to be the case that Ari's narrowness of vision is deliberate, and that *Kristni saga* may be more representative of how heterogeneous historical traditions about the conversion really were. However, the issue of historical reliability is not, perhaps, the most important: what is interesting from a literary point of view is how flexible and versatile the conversion narrative proves itself to be, how the representation of conversion varies in different contexts, and how the same events can be viewed in different ways even within the same text, as is the case with the verse and prose in *Kristni saga*. Conversion, for medieval Icelanders as for other medieval peoples, was not just about the saving of individual souls: it was an ideological issue, a legal issue, a political issue—an issue

---

[116] See Orri Vésteinsson 2000: 200–201 and Lönnroth, Vésteinn Ólason and Piltz 2003: 490–92.

that brought to the fore the uniqueness of the Icelandic constitution and the Icelanders' difficult relationship with the kings of Norway. Through their depiction of the process of conversion and Christianisation in medieval Iceland, these writers address the legal and political consequences of the arrival of a new faith and they emphasise the Church's importance as a cohesive part of Icelandic society. The greater pessimism in *Kristni saga* about the capacity of the law—celebrated by Ari—to contain violence probably has much to do with the turbulent one hundred or so years that separate the two texts chronologically. Finally, Ari's notably secular perspective on conversion and the inclusion of pagan skaldic verse in *Kristni saga* are witnesses to something quite unique about Icelandic literature: they show how a strong oral tradition and a distinctively Icelandic outlook came together with European Latin literacy to create a secular literature unparalleled in medieval Europe.

NOTE ON THE TRANSLATIONS

The translations of *Íslendingabók* ('The Book of the Icelanders') and *Kristni saga* ('The Story of the Conversion') are based on the editions in *ÍF* I and XV (*Biskupa sögur* I). My aim has been to remain as faithful as possible to the original Icelandic text within the limits of what constitutes readable English prose. Unfortunately, it has not been possible to achieve complete consistency with regard to names. All Icelandic personal names and place-names have been put into the Old Icelandic nominative form, but some variant manuscript spellings have been preserved as evidence of date (both forms, when more than one occurs, can be found in the index). Names given in a Latin form in the manuscripts have been anglicised wherever possible and occasionally replaced with a widely accepted alternative (e.g. Arnulf for manuscript Arnaldus). Nicknames have been translated when it is clear what they mean (e.g. Þorsteinn the Red), but have otherwise been left in Old Icelandic with explanations in the notes. Names of countries and places outside Iceland (e.g. Canterbury) are sometimes anglicised, but where there is no exact modern equivalent or where the Old Norse form itself is well known (as in the case of Old Norse place-names in Russia), they have been left in Old Icelandic with English equivalents in the index.

DATES IN THE HISTORY OF EARLY ICELAND

c.870	Discovery and settlement of Iceland
c.927	Úlfljótr's laws
c.930	Iceland fully settled; establishment of the Althing
c.960	Amendment to the Icelandic calendar
c.965	Division of Iceland into quarters
981–5	Friðrekr and Þorvaldr's mission
983/4	First church built at Áss in Hjaltadalr
985/6	Discovery and settlement of Greenland
995/6	Stefnir's mission
998/9	Þangbrandr's mission
999/1000	Conversion of Iceland and fall of Óláfr Tryggvason
c.1000	Leifr discovers Vínland
c.1004	Institution of Fifth Court
c.1016	Last heathen provisions removed from the laws
c.1020	Land-dues agreement
1056	Bishop Ísleifr consecrated
1067/8	Ari the Learned born
1082	Bishop Gizurr consecrated to see at Skálaholt
1096/7	Tithe law passed
1106	Bishop Jón consecrated to see at Hólar
1117–18	Writing down of laws
1118	Bishop Þorlákr consecrated. Gizurr dies.
1121	Legal settlement between Þorgils and Hafliði.
1122	Bishop Ketill consecrated.

LAWSPEAKERS OF THE EARLY ICELANDIC COMMONWEALTH

Úlfljótr (?)	?–c.930
Hrafn Hœngsson	930–949
Þórarinn Ragi's Brother	950–969
Þorkell Moon	970–984
Þorgeirr Þorkelsson	985–1001
Grímr Svertingsson	1002–1003
Skapti Þóroddsson	1004–1030
Steinn Þorgestsson	1031–1033
Þorkell Tjǫrvason	1034–1053
Gellir Bǫlverksson	1054–1062, 1072–1074
Gunnarr the Wise	1063–1065, 1075
Kolbeinn Flosason	1066–1071
Sighvatr Surtsson	1076–1083
Markús Skeggason	1084–1107
Úlfheðinn Gunnarsson	1108–1116
Bergþórr Hrafnsson	1117–1122
Goðmundr Þorgeirsson	1123–1134

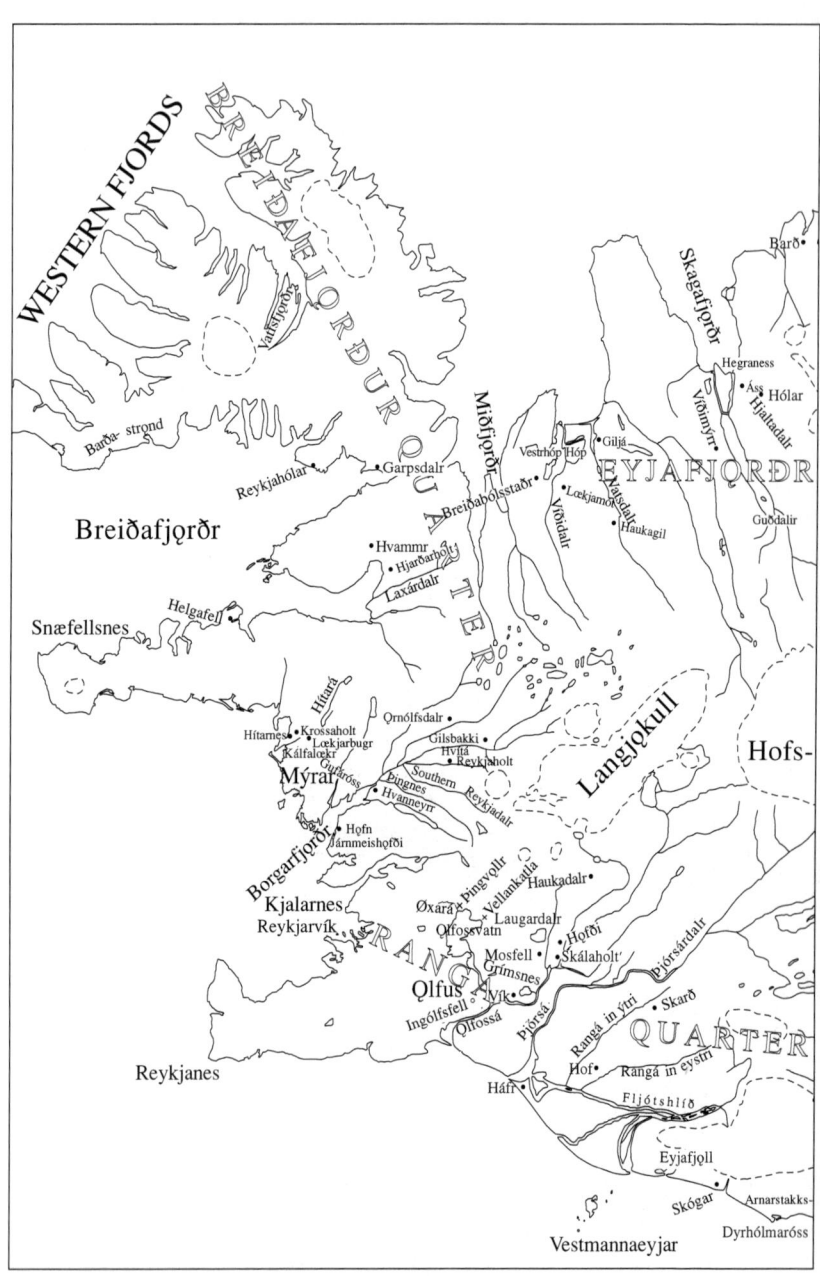

WEST ICELAND

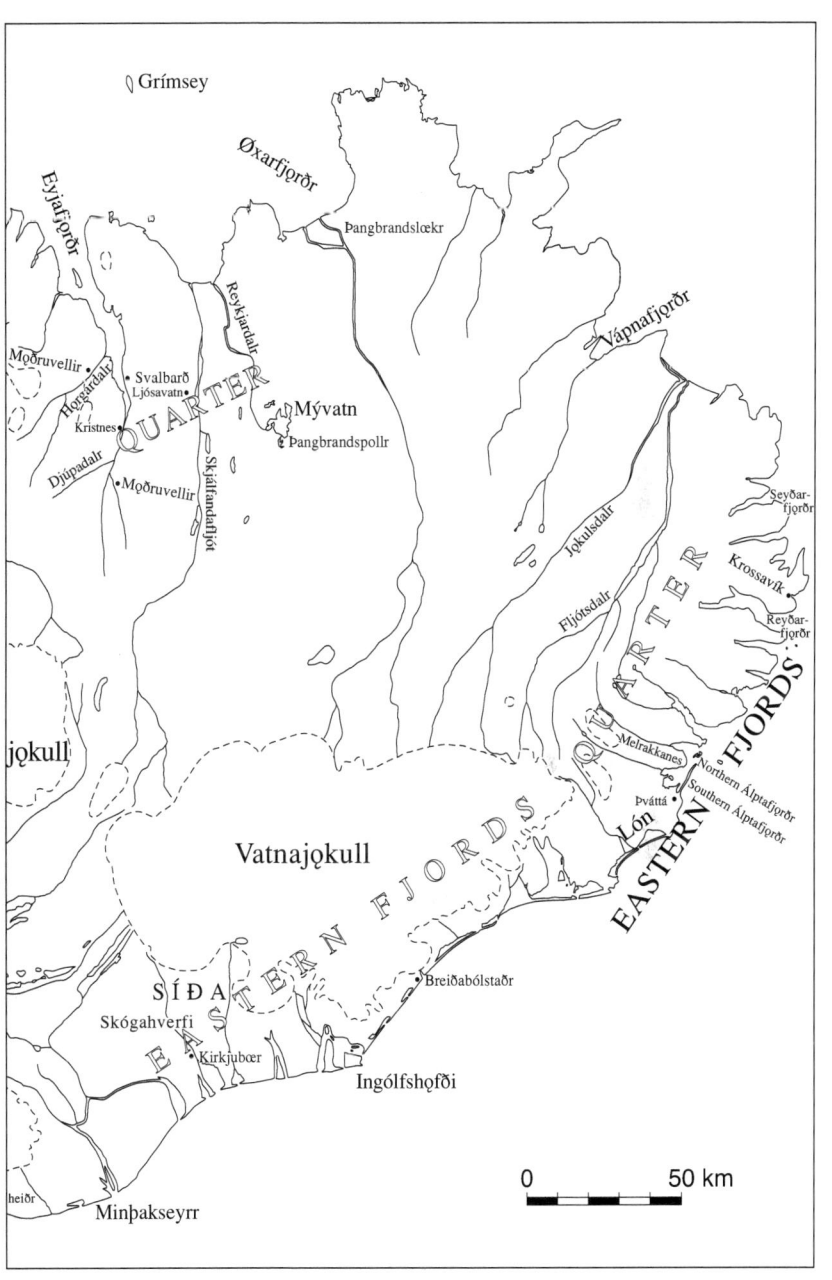

EAST ICELAND

ÍSLENDINGABÓK

THE BOOK OF THE ICELANDERS

I FIRST WROTE the Book of the Icelanders for our bishops Þorlákr and Ketill,[1] and I showed it both to them and to the priest Sæmundr.[2] And in so far as it pleased them to keep it as it was or to add to it, I wrote this on the same subject, besides the genealogies and regnal years of kings,[3] and I added what has since become better known to me and is now more fully reported in this book than in the other. But whatever is incorrectly stated in these records, it is one's duty to prefer what proves to be more accurate.[4]

Hálfdan Whiteleg, king of the Upplanders, son of Óláfr Treefeller, king of the Swedes,[5] was the father of Eysteinn Fart, father of Hálfdan the Bounteous but Stingy-with-Food,[6] father of Goðrøðr the Hunter-King,[7] father of Hálfdan the Black, father of Haraldr the Fine-Haired, who was the first of that family line to become sole king over the whole of Norway.[8]

THESE CHAPTERS ARE CONTAINED IN THIS BOOK

I. On the settlement of Iceland.
II. On the settlers and the establishment of laws.
III. On the establishment of the Althing.
IV. On the calendar.
V. On the division into Quarters.
VI. On the settlement of Greenland.
VII. On how Christianity came to Iceland.
VIII. On foreign bishops.
IX. On Bishop Ísleifr.
X. On Bishop Gizurr.

HERE THE BOOK OF THE ICELANDERS BEGINS

CHAPTER I

Iceland was first settled from Norway in the days of Haraldr the Fine-Haired, son of Hálfdan the Black, at the time (according to the estimate and reckoning of my foster-father Teitr, son of Bishop Ísleifr and the wisest man I have known, and of my paternal uncle Þorkell Gellisson, who remembered a long way back, and of Þóríðr daughter of Snorri goði, who was both wise in many things and reliably informed)[9] when Ívarr, son of Ragnarr loðbrók,[10] had St Edmund, king of the Angles, killed;[11] and that was 870 years after the birth of Christ, according to what is written in his [Edmund's] saga.[12]

It is said with accuracy that a Norwegian called Ingólfr travelled from there [Norway] to Iceland[13] for the first time when Haraldr the Fine-Haired was sixteen years old, and a second time a few years later; he settled in the south in Reykjarvík.[14] The place to the east of Minþakseyrr[15] where he first came ashore is called Ingólfshǫfði, and the place to the west of Ǫlfossá which he later took possession of is called Ingólfsfell.[16]

At that time Iceland was covered with woods between the mountains and the seashore.[17] There were then Christians here, whom the Northmen call *papar*,[18] but they later went away, because they did not wish to stay here with heathens; and they left behind them Irish books and bells and staffs.[19] From this it could be seen that they were Irishmen.

And then a great many people began to move out here from Norway, until King Haraldr forbade it, because he thought it would lead to depopulation of the land. They then came to the agreement that everyone who was not exempt and travelled here from there should pay the king five ounces of silver. And it is said that Haraldr was king for seventy years and lived into his eighties. These were the origins of the tax which is now called land-dues, and sometimes more was paid for it and sometimes less, until Óláfr the Stout[20] made it clear that everyone who travelled between Norway and Iceland should pay the king half a mark, except for women and those men whom he exempted.[21] Þorkell Gellisson told us so.

CHAPTER II

Hrollaugr, son of Rǫgnvaldr earl in Mœrr, settled in the east on Síða; from him the people of Síða are descended.

Ketilbjǫrn Ketilsson, a Norwegian, settled in the south at upper Mosfell; from him the people of Mosfell are descended.

Auðr, daughter of Ketill Flatnose, a Norwegian lord, settled in the west in Breiðafjǫrðr; from her the people of Breiðafjǫrðr are descended.

Helgi the Lean, a Norwegian, son of Eyvindr the Easterner, settled in the north in Eyjafjǫrðr; from him the people of Eyjafjǫrðr are descended.[22]

And when Iceland had been settled widely, an Easterner[23] called Úlfljótr first brought laws out here from Norway (Teitr told us so) and they were subsequently called Úlfljótr's laws; he was the father of Gunnarr, from whom the people of Djúpadalr are descended in Eyjafjǫrðr.[24] They were for the most part modelled on how the laws of Gulaþing[25] were at the time, or how the advice of Þorleifr the Wise, son of Hǫrða-Kári, indicated where things should be added, or removed, or set up differently.[26] Úlfljótr lived in the east in Lón. And it is said that his foster-brother was Grímr geitskor,[27] who explored the whole of Iceland on Úlfljótr's recommendation before the Althing was held. And everyone in this country gave him a penny for that, and he later gave the money to the temples.[28]

CHAPTER III

The Althing was established where it now is by the decision of Úlfljótr and everyone in the country;[29] but before that there was an assembly at Kjalarnes, which Þorsteinn, son of Ingólfr the settler, father of the lawspeaker Þorkell Moon, held there together with those chieftains who attended it.[30] And a man who owned land in Bláskógar had been outlawed for the murder of a slave or freedman; he was called Þórir kroppinskeggi,[31] and his daughter's son was called Þorvaldr kroppinskeggi, who later went to the Eastern Fjords and there burned his brother Gunnarr to death in his home. Hallr Órœkjuson said so.[32] And the man who was murdered was called Kolr. The gorge that has since been called Kolsgjá, where the remains were found, is named after him. The land afterwards became public property, and the people of the country set it apart for the use of the Althing. Because of that, there is common land there to provide the Althing with wood from the forests and pasture for grazing horses on the heaths. Úlfheðinn told us this.[33]

Wise men have also said that Iceland was fully settled in sixty years, so that no further settlement was made after that. At about that time Hrafn, son of Hœngr the settler, took up the office of lawspeaker after Úlfljótr, and held it for twenty summers;[34] he was from the Rangá district. That was sixty years after the killing of King Edmund, and one or two years before Haraldr the Fine-Haired died, according to the reckoning of wise men. Þórarinn Ragi's brother, son of Óleifr hjalti,[35] took up the office of lawspeaker after Hrafn and held it for another twenty summers; he was from Borgarfjǫrðr.

CHAPTER IV

It was also at that time, when the wisest men in this country had reckoned 364 days in the two seasons of the year[36] (which makes 52 weeks, or twelve months of thirty days each and four days left over), that they noticed from the course of the sun that summer was moving backwards into spring; but no one could tell them that there was one day more in two seasons than was equal to the number of full weeks, and that was what was causing it.[37] But there was a man called Þorsteinn Black, he was from Breiðafjǫrðr, son of Hallsteinn, son of Þórólfr Mostrarskeggi the settler and of Ósk, daughter of Þorsteinn the Red.[38] He dreamed that he seemed to be at the Law-Rock when a crowd was assembled there and he was awake, but all the other people seemed to him to be asleep. And after that it seemed to him that he fell asleep, but all the others then seemed to wake up. Ósvífr Helgason, maternal grandfather of Gellir Þorkelsson, interpreted the dream to mean that everyone would remain silent while he spoke at the Law-Rock, but that when he fell silent, everyone would applaud what he had said.[39] And they were both very wise men. And later, when people came to the assembly, Þorsteinn Black put forward the proposal at the Law-Rock that they should extend every seventh summer by a week, and see how that would work.[40] And in accordance with how Ósvífr had interpreted the dream, everyone then welcomed the proposal warmly, and it was immediately made law with the consent of Þorkell Moon and other wise men.[41]

By the correct reckoning, there are 365 days in each year if it is not a leap year, and then there is one more; but by our reckoning there are 364. And when every seventh year is extended by a week in our reckoning, but no extension is made in the other, then seven consecutive years will be equally long in both. But if there are two leap years between the years that are to be extended, then the sixth year needs to be extended instead.[42]

CHAPTER V

A great lawsuit arose at the assembly between Þórðr gellir, son of Óleifr feilan from Breiðafjǫrðr, and Oddr, who was called Tungu-Oddr;[43] he was from Borgarfjǫrðr. His son Þorvaldr was with Hœsna-Þórir at the burning of Þorkell Blund-Ketilsson[44] in Ǫrnólfsdalr. And Þórðr gellir was the leader of the prosecution, because Hersteinn, son of Þorkell Blund-Ketilsson, was married to Þórunn, his sister's daughter.[45] She was the daughter of Helga and Gunnarr, and the sister of Jófríðr, who was married to Þorsteinn Egilsson.[46]

And the burners were prosecuted at the assembly in Borgarfjǫrðr at the place that has since been called Þingnes. It was then law that cases of homicide should be prosecuted at the assembly that was nearest to the scene of the event. But they fought there, and the assembly could not be conducted according to the laws. Þórólfr Fox, brother of Álfr in the Dales, fell there on Þórðr gellir's side.[47] And then the lawsuits were referred to the Althing, and there they fought again. Then men fell on Oddr's side and, furthermore, Hœsna-Þórir was outlawed and later killed, together with others who had been at the burning. Then Þórðr gellir made a speech at the Law-Rock[48] about how disadvantageous it was for men to go to an unknown assembly to prosecute for killings or injuries done to them, and told what had hindered him, before he could obtain legal redress in this case, and said that difficulties would arise one after another, if things were not put right. Then the country was divided into Quarters, so that there were three assemblies in each Quarter; and in each place the members of the assembly had to conduct the prosecution of lawsuits together, except that there were four assemblies in the Northern Quarter, because the Northerners would not accept anything else.[49] Those who lived north of Eyjafjǫrðr were not willing to attend the assembly there, and those who lived west of Skagafjǫrðr were not willing to go there. However, the same number of judges had to be nominated and there had to be the same number of members of the Law Council[50] from that Quarter as from each of the others. And later the Quarter Assemblies were established.[51] The lawspeaker Úlfheðinn Gunnarsson told us so.

Þorkell Moon, son of Þorsteinn Ingólfsson, took up the office of lawspeaker after Þórarinn Ragi's brother and held it for fifteen summers; then Þorgeirr Þorkelsson of Ljósavatn held it for seventeen summers.[52]

CHAPTER VI

The country called Greenland was discovered and settled from Iceland.[53] A man from Breiðafjǫrðr called Eiríkr the Red went out there from here,[54] and took possession of land in a place that has since been called Eiríksfjǫrðr. He gave a name to the country and called it Greenland, and said that it would encourage people to go there that the country had a good name.[55] They found signs of human habitation there both in the east and west of the country, fragments of skin-boats and stone implements, from which it may be deduced that the same kind of people had passed through there as had settled Vínland[56] and the Greenlanders call *Skrælingar*.[57] And Eiríkr began to settle the country fourteen or fifteen years before Christianity came here to Iceland, according to what a man who had himself accompanied Eiríkr the Red there told Þorkell Gellisson in Greenland.[58]

CHAPTER VII

King Óláfr, son of Tryggvi, son of Óláfr, son of Haraldr the Fine-Haired, brought Christianity to Norway and to Iceland.[59] He sent to this country a priest called Þangbrandr,[60] who preached Christianity to people here and baptised all those who accepted the faith. And Hallr Þorsteinsson on Síða had himself baptised early on, as did Hjalti Skeggjason from Þjórsárdalr and Gizurr the White, son of Teitr, son of Ketilbjǫrn from Mosfell,[61] and many other chieftains; but those who spoke against Christianity and rejected it were, even so, in the majority. And when he had been here for one or two years, Þangbrandr left, and had killed two or three men here who had libelled him.[62] And when he arrived in the east, he told King

Óláfr everything that had happened to him here, and said that it was beyond all expectation that Christianity might yet be accepted here. And Óláfr became very angry at this, and determined to have those of our countrymen who were there in the east maimed or killed for it.[63] But that same summer, Gizurr and Hjalti travelled there from out here and got the king to release them, and promised him their help afresh so that Christianity might yet be accepted here, and said they expected nothing other than that this would work.[64]

And the next summer, they left the east together with a priest called Þormóðr,[65] and arrived in the Vestmannaeyjar when ten weeks of the summer had passed, and their journey had gone smoothly in every way. Teitr said a man who was there himself had said so. Now the previous summer it had been proclaimed in the laws that people should come to the Althing when ten weeks of the summer had passed, but up until then they had come a week earlier.[66] And they crossed to the mainland at once and then proceeded to the Althing, and managed to persuade Hjalti to stay behind at Laugardalr with eleven men, because the previous summer he had been convicted as a lesser outlaw[67] at the Althing for blasphemy.[68] And the reason given for this was that he had uttered this little verse at the Law-Rock:

> I don't wish to bark at the gods:
> It seems to me Freyja's a bitch.[69]

But Gizurr and his men travelled on until they came to a place beside Ǫlfossvatn called Vellankatla; and from there they sent word to the assembly that all their supporters should come to meet them, because they had heard that their adversaries intended to keep them from the assembly field by force. But before they set off from there, Hjalti came riding there together with those who had stayed behind with him. And then they rode to the assembly, and their kinsmen and friends had come to meet them beforehand as they had requested. And the heathens thronged together fully armed, and it came so close to them fighting that no one could foresee which way it would go.[70] And the next day, Gizurr and Hjalti went to the Law-Rock, and announced their mission, and it is said that it was extraordinary how well they spoke. But what happened as a result was that one man after another named witnesses, and each side, the Christians and the heathens, declared itself under separate laws from the other, and they then left the Law-Rock.

Then the Christians asked Hallr on Síða to speak the law, the one that was to go with Christianity. But he freed himself from this responsibility towards them by agreeing[71] with the lawspeaker, Þorgeirr, that he should speak it, although he was still heathen at the time. And later, when everyone had returned to their booths, Þorgeirr lay down and spread his cloak over himself, and rested all that day and the following night, and did not speak a word.[72] And the next morning, he got up and sent word that people should go to the Law-Rock. And once people had arrived there, he began his speech, and said that he thought people's affairs had come to a bad pass, if they were not all to have the same law in this country, and tried to persuade them in many ways that they should not let this happen, and said it would give rise to such discord that it was certainly to be expected that fights would take place between people by which the land would be laid waste. He spoke about how the kings of Norway and Denmark had kept up warfare and battles against each other for a long time, until the people of those countries had made peace between them, even though they did not wish it. And that policy had worked out in such a way that they were soon sending gifts to each other and, moreover, this peace lasted for as long as they lived.

'And it now seems advisable to me,' he said, 'that we too do not let those who most wish to oppose each other prevail, and let us arbitrate between them, so that each side has its own way in something, and let us all have the same law and the same religion. It will prove true that if we tear apart the law, we will also tear apart the peace.'

And he brought his speech to a close in such a way that both sides agreed that everyone should have the same law, the one he decided to proclaim. It was then proclaimed in the laws that all people should be Christian, and that those in this country who had not yet been baptised should receive baptism; but the old laws should stand as regards the exposure of children and the eating of horse-flesh.[73] People had the right to sacrifice in secret, if they wished, but it would be punishable by the lesser outlawry if witnesses were produced.[74] And a few years later, these heathen provisions were abolished, like the others.[75]

Teitr gave us this account of how Christianity came to Iceland. And Óláfr Tryggvason fell the same summer according to the priest Sæmundr. He [Óláfr] was then fighting the king of the Danes, Sveinn Haraldsson, and the Swedish Óláfr, son of Eiríkr at Uppsala, king of the Swedes, and Eiríkr Hákonarson, who was later earl in Norway. That was 130 years after the killing of Edmund, and 1000 after the birth of Christ by the common method of reckoning.[76]

CHAPTER VIII

These are the names of the foreign bishops who have been in Iceland according to Teitr's account. Friðrekr came here during the heathen period, and these were later: Bjarnharðr the Book-Learned for five years, Kolr for a few years, Hróðólfr for nineteen years, Jóhan the Irishman for a few years, Bjarnharðr for nineteen years, Heinrekr for two years.[77] In addition, five others came here who called themselves bishops: Ǫrnólfr and Goðiskálkr and three from Ermland,[78] Peter and Abraham and Stephen.

Grímr Svertingsson at Mosfell took up the office of lawspeaker after Þorgeirr and held it for two summers, but then he got permission for his sister's son, Skapti Þóroddsson, to hold it, because he himself was hoarse.[79] Skapti held the office of lawspeaker for twenty-seven summers. He instituted the Fifth Court,[80] and the legal provision that no killer should pronounce anyone other than himself legally responsible for a killing, whereas before there were the same laws about that here as in Norway.[81] In his days many chieftains and powerful men were outlawed or driven from the land for killings or fighting on account of his authority and governance. And he died in the same year that Óláfr the Stout fell, son of Haraldr, son of Goðrøðr, son of Bjǫrn, son of Haraldr the Fine-Haired, thirty years after Óláfr Tryggvason fell. Then Steinn Þorgestsson took up the office of lawspeaker and held it for three summers; then Þorkell Tjǫrvason held it for twenty summers; then Gellir Bǫlverksson for nine summers.

CHAPTER IX

Ísleifr, son of Gizurr the White, was consecrated bishop in the days of King Haraldr of Norway, son of Sigurðr, son of Hálfdan, son of Sigurðr Bastard, son of Haraldr the Fine-Haired.[82] And when chieftains and good men perceived that Ísleifr was far abler than other clerics who could then be obtained in this country, many sent him their sons to be educated and had them ordained priests. Two of them were later consecrated bishops: Kolr, who was in Vík in Norway, and Jóan at Hólar.[83] Ísleifr had three sons, who all became able chieftains: Bishop Gizurr and the priest Teitr, father of Hallr, and Þorvaldr.[84] Teitr was brought up by Hallr in Haukadalr, a man whom everyone described as the most generous layman in this country and the most eminent in good qualities.[85] I also came to Hallr when I was seven years old, one year after Gellir Þorkelsson, my paternal grandfather and my foster-father, died; and I stayed there for fourteen years.[86]

Gunnarr the Wise had taken up the office of lawspeaker when Gellir left off, and he held it for three summers. Then Kolbeinn Flosason held it for six; the summer he took up the office of lawspeaker, King Haraldr fell in England.[87] Then Gellir held it a second time for three summers; then Gunnarr held it a second time for one summer; then Sighvatr Surtsson, Kolbeinn's sister's son, held it for eight. In those days, Sæmundr Sigfússon came to this country from Frakkland in the south and later had himself ordained priest.[88]

Ísleifr was consecrated bishop when he was fifty; Leo VII was then pope.[89] And he spent the next winter in Norway and then came out here. And he died at Skálaholt, when he had been bishop for twenty-four years in all. Teitr told us so. That was on a Sunday, six nights after the feast of Peter and Paul, eighty years after the fall of Óláfr Tryggvason.[90] I was there with Teitr my foster-father at the time, and I was twelve years old. And Hallr, who both had a reliable memory and was truthful, and remembered himself being baptised, told us that Þangbrandr had baptised him when he was three years old, and that was one year before Christianity was made law here. And he set up house when he was thirty, and lived at Haukadalr for sixty-four years, and was ninety-four when he died; and that was on the feast of Bishop Martin, the tenth year after the death of Bishop Ísleifr.

CHAPTER X

Bishop Gizurr, son of Ísleifr, was consecrated bishop at the request of his countrymen in the days of King Óláfr Haraldsson, two years after Ísleifr died.[91] One he spent in this country and the other in Gautland. And then his name was altered so that he was called Gisrøðr; he told us so.[92]

Markús Skeggjason held the office of lawspeaker after Sighvatr, and took it up the summer that Bishop Gizurr had been in this country for one year, and he carried out his duties for twenty-four summers.[93] The terms of office of all those lawspeakers who came earlier than my memory extends are written down in this book according to his account, and his brother Þórarinn and their father Skeggi and other wise men told him about the terms of those who came earlier than his memory extends, in accordance with what Bjarni the Wise, their paternal grandfather, had said, who remembered Þórarinn the lawspeaker and six of his successors.

Bishop Gizurr was more popular with all his countrymen than any other person we know to have been in this country. Through his popularity and his and Sæmundr's persuasions, with the guidance of the lawspeaker Markús, it was made law that everyone should reckon up and value all their property and swear an oath that it was correctly valued, whether it was in land or in movable possessions, and pay a tithe on it afterwards.[94] It is a great sign of how obedient the people of the country were to that man, that he brought it about that all property in Iceland was valued under oath, including the land itself, and tithes paid on it, and laws laid down that it should be so as long as Iceland is inhabited. Bishop Gizurr also had it laid down as law that the episcopal see in Iceland should be at Skálaholt, whereas before it had had no fixed location, and he endowed the see with the estate at Skálaholt and many other forms of wealth both in land and in movable possessions.[95] And when he thought that the see had increased sufficiently in wealth, then he gave more than a quarter of his diocese to the end that there should be two episcopal sees in this country rather than one, just as the Northerners had asked him. And he had first had the householders in this country counted, and at that time there were a full 840 in the Eastern Fjords Quarter, and 1200 in the Rangá Quarter, and 1080 in the Breiðafjǫrðr Quarter, and 1440 in the Eyjafjǫrðr Quarter;[96] but those who did not have to pay assembly attendance dues were not counted throughout the whole of Iceland.[97]

Úlfheðinn, son of Gunnarr the Wise, took up the office of lawspeaker after Markús and held it for nine summers, then Bergþórr Hrafnsson held it for six, and then Goðmundr Þorgeirsson held it for twelve summers. The first summer that Bergþórr spoke the law, a new pronouncement was made that our laws should be written down in a book at the home of Hafliði Másson the following winter, at the dictation and with the guidance of Hafliði and Bergþórr, as well as of other wise men appointed for this task.[98] They were to make new provisions in the law in all cases where these seemed to them better than the old laws. These were to be proclaimed the next summer in the Law Council, and all those were to be kept which a majority of people did not oppose. And it happened as a result that the Treatment of Homicide Law and many other things in the laws were then written down and proclaimed in the Law Council by clerics the next summer.[99] And everyone was very pleased with this, and no one opposed it. The same summer that Bergþórr spoke the law for the first time, Bishop Gizurr was unable to come to the assembly because of illness. He then sent word to his friends and the chieftains at the Althing that they should ask Þorlákr, son of Runólfr, son of Hallr in Haukadalr's brother Þorleikr, to have himself consecrated bishop.[100] And everyone acted in accordance with his instructions, and this was obtained because Gizurr himself had urged it so strongly; and Þorlákr went abroad that summer and returned out here the next, and had then been consecrated bishop.

Gizurr was consecrated bishop when he was forty. Gregory VII was then pope. And he spent the following winter in Denmark and came to this country the summer after that. And when he had been bishop for twenty-four years, just like his father, Jóan Qgmundarson was consecrated bishop, the first to the see at Hólar; he was then fifty-four.[101] And twelve years later, when Gizurr had been bishop for thirty-six years in all, Þorlákr was consecrated bishop; Gizurr had him consecrated to the see in Skálaholt during his lifetime.[102] Þorlákr was then thirty-two, and Bishop Gizurr died thirty nights later in Skálaholt on the third day of the week, the fifth [day] before the calends of June.[103]

In the same year Pope Paschal II died before Bishop Gizurr, as did Baldwin king of Jerusalem and Arnulf patriarch in Jerusalem, and Philip king of the Swedes and, later the same summer, Alexius king of the Greeks; he had then sat on the throne in Miklagarðr for thirty-eight years.[104] And two years later a new lunar cycle began.[105] Eysteinn and Sigurðr had then been kings in Norway for seventeen years after their father Magnús, son of Óláfr Haraldsson. That was 120 years after the fall of Óláfr Tryggvason, and 250 years after the killing of Edmund, king of the Angles, and 516 years after the death of Pope Gregory, who brought Christianity to England, according to what has been reckoned. And he died in the second year of the reign of the Emperor Phocas, 604 years after the birth of Christ by the common method of reckoning. That makes 1120 years altogether.

Here this book ends.

This is the ancestry of the bishops of the Icelanders and their genealogy[106]

Ketilbjǫrn the settler, who settled in the south at upper Mosfell, was the father of Teitr, father of Gizurr the White, father of Ísleifr, who was the first bishop in Skálaholt, father of Bishop Gizurr.

Hrollaugr the settler, who settled in the east on Síða at Breiðabólstaðr, was the father of Qzurr, father of Þórdís, mother of Hallr on Síða, father of Egill, father of Þorgerðr, mother of Jóan, who was the first bishop at Hólar.

Auðr the female settler, who settled in the west in Breiðafjǫrðr at Hvammr, was the mother of Þorsteinn the Red, father of Óleifr feilan, father of Þórðr gellir, father of Þórhildr Ptarmigan, mother of Þórðr Horsehead, father of Karlsefni,[107] father of Snorri, father of Hallfríðr, mother of Þorlákr, who is now bishop in Skálaholt after Gizurr.

Helgi the Lean, the settler, who settled in the north in Eyjafjǫrðr at Kristnes, was the father of Helga, mother of Einarr, father of Eyjólfr Valgerðarson,[108] father of Goðmundr, father of Eyjólfr, father of Þorsteinn, father of Ketill, who is now bishop at Hólar after Jóan.

THESE ARE THE NAMES OF THE MALE ANCESTORS OF THE YNGLINGS AND THE PEOPLE OF BREIÐAFJǪRÐR[109]

I. Yngvi[110] king of the Turks.[111] II. Njǫrðr king of the Swedes.[112] III Freyr. IIII. Fjǫlnir, who died at Frið-Fróði's.[113] V. Svegðir. VI. Vanlandi. VII. Vísburr. VIII. Dómaldr.[114] IX. Dómarr. X. Dyggvi. XI. Dagr. XII. Alrekr. XIII. Agni.[115] XIIII. Yngvi. XV. Jǫrundr. XVI. Aun the Old.[116] XVII. Egill Crow of Vendill.[117] XVIII. Óttarr. XIX. Aðils at Uppsala.[118] XX. Eysteinn. XXI. Yngvarr. XXII. Braut-Ǫnundr.[119] XXIII. Ingjaldr the Evil.[120] XXIIII. Óláfr Treefeller. XXV. Hálfdan Whiteleg, king of the Upplanders.[121] XXVI. Goðrøðr. XXVII. Óláfr. XXVIII Helgi. XXIX. Ingjaldr, son of the daughter of Sigurðr, son of Ragnarr loðbrók.[122] XXX. Óleifr the White.[123] XXXI. Þorsteinn the Red.[124] XXXII. Óleifr feilan, who was the first of them to settle in Iceland. XXXIII. Þórðr gellir. XXXIIII Eyjólfr, who was baptised in his old age, when Christianity came to Iceland.[125] XXXV. Þorkell. XXXVI. Gellir, father of Þorkell—father of Brandr—and of Þorgils, my father; and I am called Ari.[126]

NOTES TO THE BOOK OF THE ICELANDERS

[1] Þorlákr was bishop of Skálaholt 1118–33 and Ketill was bishop of Hólar 1122–45; both men's genealogies are given in the genealogy of bishops (p. 13). Þorlákr's consecration is related in ch. 10, and an account of his life is given in *Hungrvaka* (*ÍF* XVI 22–28); he was the great-nephew of Hallr in Haukadalr and educated by Teitr Ísleifsson. On Ketill, an important chieftain from the north of Iceland who was married to the daughter of Bishop Gizurr, see *Hungrvaka* (*ÍF* XVI 19, 24–5, 30–31), ch. 18 of *Kristni saga* below and note 118. The two men are best known for compiling the first Christian law in 1125 in cooperation with Sæmundr, who was Ketill's cousin (*Grágás* 1980–2000: I 50).

[2] Sæmundr inn fróði 'the Learned' (1056–1133) was a priest and chieftain of distinguished family from Oddi in the south of Iceland. He was the great-grandson of Guðmundr the Powerful and Síðu-Hallr and could trace his ancestry back to Rǫgnvaldr earl in Mœrr (*ÍF* I 229, 318; see notes 22, 61 and 108 below). His grandson, Jón Loptsson, fostered the historian Snorri Sturluson (*Sturl* I 113–14). Sæmundr is frequently cited as an authority in the sagas and, although none of his works has survived, he probably wrote a Latin chronicle of the kings of Norway down to Magnús the Good (Halldór Hermannsson 1932: 33–36). On his studies abroad, which became legendary, see note 88 below.

[3] Ari's phrasing here is ambiguous and, although most have understood it that he omitted genealogies and regnal lists from his revision (e.g. Ellehøj 1965: 27–34, 62), it has also been suggested that these were independent sections or chapters written alongside it and perhaps collected in the same manuscript (Mundal 1984). The exact meaning of *konunga ævi* (here translated 'regnal years of kings') is also disputed, but it probably signifies short notices accompanying names and regnal dates rather than lengthy biographies. See further Introduction, pp. xi–xiii above.

[4] Ari's submission to ecclesiastical authority, concern for accuracy and authorial modesty are typical topoi in medieval prefaces (Sverrir Tómasson 1988: 68, 155–7).

[5] Ari, like the author of *Historia Norwegie* (*HN* 13) assumes that Óláfr remained king of the Swedes; but Snorri (*ÍF* XXVI 73; cf. *Hauksbók* 1892–6: 456) tells that he was driven out of central Sweden to Värmland, bordering on eastern Norway, where he obtained his nickname by clearing the woodland to build settlements. This neatly explains why the son of a Swedish king might have become king in Norway.

[6] According to Snorri, Hálfdan was 'as generous with gold coins as other kings were with silver coins, but he starved men of food' (*ÍF* XXVI 78; cf. *Hauksbók* 1892–6: 457).

[7] *HN* 14 and *Flb* I 28 follow Ari in calling Goðrøðr 'the Hunter-King', a nickname appropriate to Upplǫnd (Oppland in eastern Norway), but *Ynglingatal* (where he is king in Vestfold) gives his nickname as *inn gǫfugláti* 'the munificent' (cf. *Hauksbók* 1892–6: 457). Snorri plays safe and records both traditions (*ÍF* XXVI 79).

[8] This genealogy (sometimes considered a later addition) provides a prehistory for the king with whom the settlement of Iceland is most closely linked, Haraldr the Fine-Haired, so called after he had fulfilled a vow not to cut his hair until he had conquered the whole of Norway (*ÍF* XXVI 97, 122). The first five names come from Þjóðólfr of Hvinir's *Ynglingatal*, a dynastic poem probably composed

c.890 in honour of a king of Vestfold (but see Krag 1991 for a later dating). The connection with Hálfdan, Haraldr and Upplǫnd, however, appears to be a later Icelandic innovation, serving to link Norwegian royalty with the legendary Swedish dynasty of the Ynglings (Turville-Petre 1978–81: 7–8, 14–15).

⁹ Teitr was fostered by Hallr in Haukadalr and inherited his estate, where he held a small school. He was married to Jórunn Einarsdóttir, great-granddaughter of Hallr on Síða, and numbered among his pupils Ari, Bishop Þorlákr and Bishop Bjǫrn Gilsson. On Þorkell Gellisson (Ari's uncle), see Ari's genealogy (p. 14) and note 126. Þuríðr is mentioned in *Eyrbyggja saga* (*ÍF* IV 182), in which her father Snorri (died 1031) plays a central role; she was born in 1025/6, and lived to the age of 88.

¹⁰ The historical Ragnarr (probably identical with the Reginheri who sacked Paris in 845) was active in Viking raids in France and Ireland in the mid-ninth century, but in later tradition he became a legendary hero and ancestor of kings (Smyth 1977: 98–100). On the origin of his nickname, which means 'hairy breeches', see McTurk 1991: 6–39. His son Ívarr is the In(g)wære/Iwere of English sources who led the Great Army to England in 865.

¹¹ It is striking that Ari chooses to date the settlement of Iceland from the martyrdom of an English saint by Vikings in 870 (or 869 by modern reckoning, since it took place in November and the new year seems at that period to have begun in September; see further note 76 on the date of the conversion). The connection may have been made because some Icelanders (including Ari's three informants) claimed descent from King Edmund (see *ÍF* I 49, 312) or because of the official recognition of Edmund's sanctity at a Church council in Oxford in 1122 (de Vries 1942: 28), but it has also been suggested that the link with Ragnarr loðbrók, from whom Ari and other Icelanders claimed descent, is more significant (Ólafia Einarsdóttir 1964: 62–8).

¹² Ari is probably referring here to a Latin life of St Edmund, but it is not clear whether this is Abbo of Fleury's *Passio Sancti Eadmundi* (which does not contain a date), Hermannus' *De miraculis Sancti Eadmundi* (which does), or some kind of composite version (Maurer 1867: 531; Ellehøj 1965: 64–65). It is unlikely to refer, as Hermann Pálsson (1957) argued, to a saga in Old Norse.

¹³ Ari often refers to Norway simply as 'there' and to Iceland as 'here' or 'out here'.

¹⁴ The exact dating of Ingólfr's settlement is problematic. It has convincingly been argued that Ari dated Haraldr's birth to 848/9 (and no later than 851/2), which would place Ingólfr's first journey in 864/5 (and no later than 867/8). However, since Ari's chronology of Haraldr's reign seems to fall over a decade too early, his age is not a reliable indicator of the real date of settlement. In *Landnámabók*, the settlement is dated to 874, but this is probably based on later calculations (*ÍF* I xxxv–xxxviii, cxxxv–cxxxvii; XXVI lxxi–lxxxi).

¹⁵ From Irish *menadach* 'gruel' < *men* 'meal, flour'. *Landnámabók* (*ÍF* I 42–43) tells how Irish slaves who came to Iceland with Ingólfr's companion Hjǫrleifr made a mixture of flour and butter to quench their thirst, but threw it overboard when it went mouldy.

¹⁶ A fuller account of Ingólfr's travels is given in *Landnámabók* (*ÍF* I 38–45).

¹⁷ Research into the history of Icelandic vegetation supports Ari in suggesting that at the time of settlement a much larger area of Iceland was covered with birch

and willow woods, but from c.900, woodland began to disappear as a result of climate change, volcanic activity and settlement. The cutting down of trees by settlers and the grazing of pasture animals were major factors contributing to soil erosion and the disappearance of vegetation (Sigurður Þórarinsson 1974: 49–54).

[18] The term *papar* (sg. *papi*) probably derives from Old Irish *papa* 'pope, anchorite', from ecclesiastical Latin *papa* 'father, pope' (cf. also the related Old Irish forms *papa* 'master, sir' and *pupu* 'priest'). Ari's *papar* appear to have been Irish monks following the practice of *peregrinatio*—renouncing their homeland to live in foreign countries for the love of God. This practice reached its peak in the Celtic Church in the seventh and eighth centuries (Charles Edwards 1976; Hughes 1960) and there is some independent literary evidence that Irish monks reached as far as the Faeroes and Iceland during this period: in his *Liber de mensura orbis terrae*, the Carolingian historian Dicuil (1967: 75–7) reports the recent presence of Irish monks on islands which must, from their description, be the Faeroes and Iceland (which he calls Thule). Bede also mentions travels between England and Thule (*BVO* 317) and Irish sources describe journeys in search of a desert place that may be Iceland, but this is less certain (*VSH* I 61; Adomnán 1991: 28–31, 46–7, 166–71). The *papar* are also mentioned in *Landnámabók* (*ÍF* I 31–2) and *Historia Norwegie* (*HN* 8) and place-names incorporating the element *pap-* have been documented in south-eastern Iceland, as in the Hebrides, Caithness, Isle of Man, Orkney, Shetland, Faeroes and Norway. These may not always indicate Irish settlements: in Iceland and the Faeroes, they may perhaps reflect a naming tradition formed in other Norse colonies (Fellows-Jensen 1996: 116–17). There is as yet no archaeological evidence to support Ari's account. It has recently been suggested that, in some areas, the *papar* lived alongside the Norsemen for extended periods and that their activity was missionary rather than monastic (Morris 2004: 181–4): Lamb (1992; 1993) argues that the term in *Historia Norwegie* is used not for Celtic monks, but for the hierarchy of the Roman Church. It is not clear how this would apply to *papar* in uninhabited countries like Iceland.

[19] Books, bells and staffs are characteristic emblems of Irish Christianity. The books would have been gospels, psalters and service-books, all carried by travelling monks. Small bells of iron or bronze were used to summon monks to worship and were often treasured as relics. The staffs could be either abbots' staffs or simply walking sticks, which monks regularly carried with them on their journeys; these could be credited with miraculous powers or handed down in hereditary succession (Gougaud 1932: 351–59). Small bronze bells similar to the Irish ones have been discovered in two graves in Iceland and, although they are probably of Norse workmanship, it is tempting to link them with Ari's comment (Eldjárn 1956: 330–32). Many have felt it unlikely that the monks would have left behind their sacred objects and suspect they may instead have been robbed, killed or enslaved (Hermann Pálsson 1997: 37).

[20] St Óláfr Haraldsson, king of Norway 1015/16–30, canonised shortly after his death in 1031. The nickname *(inn) digri* 'the Stout' also occurs in *Heimskringla* (*ÍF* XXVII 39) and other kings' sagas (e.g. *Ágrip* 1995: 38–9).

[21] This tax on travellers to Iceland from Norway later became a tax on Icelanders travelling to Norway, and in a treaty with St Óláfr dated to c.1020, was fixed at

six ells of homespun or half a mark of silver (*Grágás* 1980–2000, II 210–13; *DI* I 65–7). This treaty, known as *Óláfslǫg*, was later confirmed by Bishop Ísleifr, probably towards the end of his life, and by Bishop Gizurr in 1083; also present on this occasion were Gizurr's son, Teitr, and the lawspeaker Markús Skeggjason. The payment of land-dues is mentioned twice in *Óláfs saga helga* in *Heimskringla* (*ÍF* XXVII 55–6, 95), and Gellir Þorkelsson, who travelled to Norway during the reign of Óláfr Haraldsson (*ÍF* XXVII 220), may have been Ari's ultimate source of information. According to *Ágrip* (1995: 42–3, 70–71) and *Heimskringla* (*ÍF* XXVII 400, XXVIII 256), King Sveinn Alfífuson (reigned 1030–35) issued a new law to the effect that travellers to Iceland also had to pay land-dues, but this was later abolished by Sigurðr Crusader (reigned 1103–30). The tax on Icelanders travelling to Norway was abolished in 1262–4 (see *Grágás* 1980–2000, II 211, note 100).

[22] On these settlers, see *Landnámabók* (*ÍF* I 136–47, 248–53, 314–18, 384–6), *Eyrbyggja saga* and *Eiríks saga rauða* (*ÍF* IV 3–11, 195–7), *Laxdœla saga* (*ÍF* V 3–9), *Orkneyinga saga* (*ÍF* XXIV 7, 10) and *Sturl* I 57. Ari begins in the east, traditionally the first quarter of Iceland to be settled (*ÍF* I 288), and moves clockwise round the country; he himself could trace his ancestry from Hrollaugr, Auðr and Helgi, and Ketilbjǫrn is an ancestor of his foster-father, Teitr. Ari emphasises the Norwegian origins of these settlers, and is strikingly silent about their links to the British Isles: Hrollaugr's family were earls in Shetland and Orkney (and his brother Hrólfr conquered Normandy); Auðr lived in Dublin and Caithness before travelling to Iceland via the Hebrides, Orkney and Faeroes; and Helgi, whose mother was the daughter of an Irish king, was brought up in the Hebrides and Ireland.

[23] The term 'easterner' (*maðr austrœnn*) can be used synonymously with 'Norwegian', but it has also been suggested that it may indicate an East Norwegian or even Swedish origin; Eyvindr was called *austmaðr* because he came from Gautland, and Bjǫrn the Easterner in *Eyrbyggja saga* was fostered in Jamtaland (*ÍF* I 249, IV 5, 10; see Einar Ól. Sveinsson 1948b: 122; Barði Guðmundsson 1967: 17).

[24] Ari's account of how Iceland's first laws were established has been questioned by Sigurður Líndal (1969: 14–24), who compares it to other legitimising myths about first law-givers (for example, Moses). According to *Hauksbók* (*ÍF* I 313), Úlfljótr was 60 when he travelled to Norway, and remained there for three years; Icelandic annals give the date of his return as 926, 927 or 928, but these are most likely guesses. The initial clauses of Úlfljótr's laws are cited in *Hauksbók* (*ÍF* I 313–15) and *Þorsteins þáttr uxafóts* (*Flb* I 274–5), in *Skarðsárbók* 1958: 146–7 and in the appendix to *Þórðarbók*, and in *Brot af Þórðar saga hreðu* (*ÍF* XIV 230–32), but are probably a learned reconstruction dating from no earlier than c.1200 (Olsen 1966: 34–49; but see Jón Hnefill Aðalsteinsson 1997: 163–87). Úlfljótr's son, Gunnarr, who was married to the daughter of Helgi the Lean, is mentioned in *Landnámabók* and *Þórðar saga hreðu* (*ÍF* I 266; XIV 232).

[25] Many settlers came from the Gulaþing area in the west of Norway. However, since laws in Norway would at this time have consisted of orally transmitted customs rather than codified wholes, it is more likely that Úlfljótr was sent to Norway to collect information about what was or was not valid custom than that he imported any kind of unified law-code to Iceland (Líndal 1969: 6–9). Indeed, it is not entirely clear whether the Gulaþing laws existed as early as 930; according

to Snorri (*ÍF* XXVI 163), they were set up by Hákon the Good, who reigned 933–60.

[26] Þorleifr is mentioned in *Heimskringla* as Hákon's advisor on the laws of Gulaþing, as well as advisor to Hálfdan and Haraldr (*ÍF* XXVI 90–91, 126–7). His life therefore spans three generations, and it is unclear how historical his role is in the establishment of Iceland's laws (Jakob Benediktsson 1974: 170–71). According to *Hauksbók* (*ÍF* I 313), Úlfljótr was son of Hǫrða-Kári's daughter Þóra, and therefore Þorleifr's nephew.

[27] It is not clear from the manuscript whether this is *geitskǫr* 'Goatbeard' or *geitskór* 'Fireweed' (rose-bay willowherb); cf. dialect Norwegian *geitskor*.

[28] Grímr's journey may have been either to select a suitable meeting-place for the Althing, or to gather support for it (Einar Ól. Sveinsson 1948b: 167; Jón Jóhannesson 1974: 38–9). His gift to the temples is perhaps parallel to the medieval Christian practice of giving a sum of money to the Church for the salvation of one's soul (Jakob Benediktsson 1974: 171).

[29] The Althing (or General Assembly) was a national assembly of free men held each year, the main seat of judicial and legislative activity for the whole of Iceland. It was probably based on regional assemblies held in Norway and elsewhere in Scandinavia, but differed from these in being countrywide and independent of any executive power. It was held at Þingvellir (Assembly Fields) on Øxará in the southwest of Iceland, a site easily accessed from all parts of the country; it lasted two weeks and, after 999, was convened on the Thursday after ten weeks of the summer had passed (between 18 and 24 June). All chieftains and one-ninth of their assembly men were required to attend (*Grágás* 1980–2000: I 51, 57–8, 108; Jón Jóhannesson 1974: 41–5). It is difficult to reconstruct its organisation prior to the reforms in the 960s (on which see ch. 5), as the law-codes and sagas mostly reflect these.

[30] This was probably a local judicial assembly attended by Þorsteinn and his relatives; another local assembly at Þórsnes that predated the Althing is mentioned in *Landnámabók* (*ÍF* I 125–6) and *Eyrbyggja saga* (*ÍF* IV 10), but the reliability of this information is uncertain. It seems likely that the foundation of the Althing originated with the assembly at Kjalarnes and that the descendants of Bjǫrn buna played a central role: the appendix to *Þórðarbók* (in *Skarðsárbók* 1958: 157–8) specifies that Þorsteinn established it together with Bjǫrn's grandsons Helgi and Ǫrlygr, and Þorsteinn would have known Úlfljótr through another grandson, Þórðr skeggi, who sold his land in Lón to Úlfljótr (*ÍF* I 312–13). The holder of the chieftaincy belonging to Þorsteinn was allotted the position of *allsherjargoði* (priest/chieftain of the whole host) and was responsible for hallowing the assembly at its official opening (Nordal 1990: 63–73).

[31] Either 'curly beard' or (more probably) 'bent (bearded) man'.

[32] Hallr Órœkjuson is not otherwise known, but is perhaps son of the Órœkja mentioned in *Landnámabók* (*ÍF* I 296, 297 note 5) and father of Þuríðr, by whom Snorri Sturluson had his son Órœkja (*Sturl* I 242).

[33] Úlfheðinn Gunnarson, a kinsman of Hafliði Másson, was lawspeaker 1108–16 (cf. *ÍF* I 226 note 4); see also ch. 10.

[34] The lawspeaker was Iceland's only paid secular official. He was elected for a three-year term (which was renewable) and had several duties: he presided over the Althing, declared the rules of procedure every year, made other official

pronouncements, and was required to speak the whole law from memory in the course of his term of office. He was also responsible for giving advice to anyone who asked on what was valid law. In return, he received a fee of 240 ells of homespun and half of the fines imposed during lawsuits (*Grágás* 1980–2000: I 187–8, 193; Jón Jóhannesson 1974: 47–9). It is not clear whether Ari understood Úlfljótr or Hrafn to be the first lawspeaker, nor how long before Hrafn's appointment in *c*.930 the Althing was established (Jón Jóhannesson 1974: 40).

[35] On Óleifr, Þórarinn and Ragi, see *Landnámabók*, *Egils saga* and *Njáls saga* (*ÍF* I 73; II 76–7; XII 40–41). Þórarinn was married to the sister of Þórðr gellir, and Bishop Þorlákr Rúnólfsson was a direct descendant of Ragi. Hjalti (also a personal name) probably comes from *hjalt*, which usually means the hand-guard between sword-hilt and blade.

[36] On the pre-eminence of the week and the season in Icelandic time-reckoning, see Hastrup 1985: 24–7. The Icelandic year consisted of two seasons (summer and winter) of twenty-six weeks each, and lengths of time were usually calculated in terms of winters passed. The need for a reliable calendar probably arose in conjunction with the establishment of regular meetings at the Althing as well as being important for agricultural activities (Thorsteinn Vilhjálmsson 1993: 70–71).

[37] The Icelandic year was just under $1\,^1/_4$ days shorter than the solar year (the interval between two successive occurrences of the vernal equinox), which would have resulted in a noticeable loss within a short time period, e.g. 30 days after 24 years.

[38] Þorsteinn and his parentage are also mentioned in *Landnámabók*, *Eyrbyggja saga* and *Laxdœla saga* (*ÍF* I 126, 164; IV 13; V 11). The nickname *Mostrarskeggi* 'bearded man, i.e. male inhabitant, of Mostr' is sometimes given as *Mostrarskegg* 'beard from Mostr' (*ÍF* IV 6; synecdoche), though the author of *Eyrbyggja saga* seems to take it as the equivalent of *mostrskegg* 'huge beard'.

[39] Ósvífr was a descendant of Ketill Flatnose and father of Guðrún, the heroine of *Laxdœla* saga. His wisdom is alluded to in *Landnámabók* and a number of sagas, including *Egils saga*, *Eyrbyggja saga* and *Laxdœla saga* (*ÍF* I 122–3; II 268; IV 12; V 85–6, 159).

[40] Þorsteinn's invention of the *sumarauki* 'summer-extension' presupposes a year of $365\,^1/_6$ days, which is remarkably close to the length of the solar year. There are different views as to how Þorsteinn could have calculated this so accurately. On the one hand, knowledge of a year with 365 days could have come from the British Isles; Þorsteinn the Red, Þorsteinn's maternal grandfather, was a king in Scotland (see note 124 below). On the other hand, reference points for sunrise and sunset (such as mountain ranges) change so quickly at high latitudes that Þorsteinn may well have been able to calculate the length of a year for himself; his proximity to the assembly place at Þórsnes would certainly have given him an incentive to follow the calendar closely (Trausti Einarsson 1968; Thorsteinn Vilhjálmsson 1993: 72).

[41] This probably took place shortly before Þorsteinn's death by drowning in *c*.960 (*ÍF* V lix, 40–41). Þorkell Moon, however, was lawspeaker in 970–84. There is a slightly abbreviated version of this chapter up to this point in GKS 1812 4to (*AÍ* II 65–6).

[42] Shortly after the conversion, it became necessary to adjust the Icelandic

calendar so that it matched the Julian calendar and ecclesiastical festivals could be celebrated on the same days as elsewhere. This involved adding five weeks in a period of 28 years rather than four, because of the leap years in the Julian calendar. Although this paragraph has been understood differently and even dismissed as an interpolation, it seems most likely that in it Ari is counting inclusively after the Roman practice, so that 'every seventh year' and 'every sixth year' mean 'every sixth year' and 'every fifth year'; this would reflect the practice of intercalation in Ari's time as recorded in contemporary Easter tables and align the two calendars exactly (Magnús Már Lárusson 1962; Thorsteinn Vilhjálmsson 1993: 72). The same rule is found in GKS 1812 4to (AÍ II 78), also with inclusive counting.

[43] Gellir: 'Loud man', cf. *gjalla* 'to scream, shriek'. Feilan: from the common Irish name *Fáelán* 'little wolf' (Hermann Pálsson 1997: 170–71). Tungu-Oddr: 'Oddr of Tunga', the tongue of land between Reykjadalsá and Hvítá settled by Oddr's father, Ǫnundr (*ÍF* I 74; III 46).

[44] Hœsna-(or Hœnsa-)Þórir: 'Þórir of the hens', so-called because he spent one summer selling hens (*ÍF* III 6); *blundr*: 'Doze, nap', cf. *blunda* 'to sleep, shut the eyes'.

[45] In *Hænsa-Þóris saga* (*ÍF* III 24–42), *Sturlubók* (*ÍF* I 75, 85) and Icelandic annals (which date the event to 962), it is Blund-Ketill who is burned, and Hersteinn is his son. *Þórðarbók* (in *Skarðsárbók* 1958: 28), however, agrees with Ari that Þorkell, son of Blund-Ketill, was burned, and *Laxdœla saga* (*ÍF* V 14) calls Hersteinn son of Þorkell, son of Blund-Ketill. Either there is confusion between two different men called Blund-Ketill or, more likely, there were divergent traditions about the event (*ÍF* III xvi–xviii; Jónas Kristjánsson 1980: 299–300).

[46] On Óleifr feilan, Þórðr gellir and his descendants, see *Landnámabók*, *Egils saga*, *Laxdœla saga* (*ÍF* I 145–6; II 275; V 11–14) and the genealogy of bishops (p. 13 above). Þórðr gellir is mentioned in a number of sagas as a powerful chieftain (e.g. *ÍF* I 396; XXVI 271) and appears in the role of legal mediator in *Eyrbyggja saga* (*ÍF* IV 16–18). Þorsteinn Egilsson is mentioned in *Kristni saga* ch. 1 (see note 6) below.

[47] The death of Þórólfr Fox is also mentioned in *Landnámabók* (*ÍF* I 145).

[48] The Law-Rock was on the eastern side of Almannagjá. It was there that the lawspeaker had his seat, the assembly was inaugurated and concluded, the courts started out, the law was spoken, and all official announcements were made (*Grágás* 1980–2000: I 51, 59, 187; Jón Jóhannesson 1974: 43–4). In Ari's account, important constitutional events are all marked by speeches at the Law-Rock. It thus becomes the symbolic centre of the Icelandic law and constitution.

[49] A number of changes followed upon this reform, which is usually dated to *c*.965. First, the number of spring assemblies (*várþing*) in each Quarter was fixed and, as a result, the number of chieftains was increased from thirty-six to forty-eight. Each assembly was convened by three chieftains, and nine new chieftains from the Southern, Western and Eastern Quarters sat in the Law Council to redress the imbalance caused by the fourth assembly in the Northern Quarter. Spring assemblies met when four to six weeks of the summer had passed (i.e. in May) for four to seven days and had a primarily judicial function. Second, four quarter courts (*fjórðungsdómar*) were established at the Althing, each with a panel of thirty-six judges, which acted as courts of first instance except for matters of

minor significance, and courts of appeal from the spring assemblies (*Grágás* 1980–2000: I 53–4, 98–109; Jón Jóhannesson 1974: 49–52, 66–70, 74–82).

[50] The Law Council (*Lǫgrétta*) consisted of the thirty-six (later forty-eight) chieftains, each of whom was allowed two advisors, the lawspeaker, and later the two Icelandic bishops. It met yearly at the Althing and was responsible for passing new laws, amending old ones, interpreting the laws when their meaning was disputed and granting exemptions. It also elected the lawspeaker and acted on behalf of the Icelanders in foreign affairs (*Grágás* 1980–2000: I 189–93; Jón Jóhannesson 1974: 63–5).

[51] The quarter assemblies were judicial courts presumably intended to serve as neutral ground for disputes between men from different spring assemblies; but little is known about them. They are mentioned only once in *Grágás* (1980–2000: I 222) and they do not appear to have been held regularly (Ólafur Lárusson 1958: 100–118). A version of this chapter up to this point is interpolated in most manuscripts of *Hœnsa-Þóris saga* (*ÍF* I 12–13, note 4; III 39–40).

[52] *Landnámabók* says about Þorkell Moon that he 'lived as pure a life as the best of Christians' and entrusted himself on his deathbed to 'the god who created the sun'; his son Þormóðr was *allsherjargoði* at the time of the conversion and second cousin to the next lawspeaker Þorgeirr (*ÍF* I 46–7, 358), who also played a key role in Iceland's conversion, as ch. 7 below relates. Þorgeirr's genealogy is given slightly differently in *Landnámabók* and *Njáls saga* (*ÍF* I 274–5; XII 270–71). He is mentioned widely in the sagas, including *Reykdœla saga* and *Ljósvetninga saga* (both in *ÍF* X), which deals with the feuds between his sons and Guðmundr the Powerful. There is a later folk-tale that the waterfall Goðafoss near Ljósavatn got its name when Þorgeirr threw his idols into it after the acceptance of Christianity (Kålund 1877–82: II 150).

[53] Greenland is mentioned for the first time in 1053 in a letter from Pope Leo IX to Archbishop Adalbert of Bremen (*DI* I 18), and later in Adam of Bremen iv.37 (2002: 218) and *Historia Norwegie* (*HN* 3–4). Ari is the earliest Icelandic source for its discovery and settlement, which are described at greater length in *Landnámabók*, *Eiríks saga rauða* and *Grœnlendinga saga* (*ÍF* I 131–2; IV 200–202, 242–3).

[54] Ari's words suggest that he believed Eiríkr to have been born and bred in Breiðafjǫrðr, but other sources say that he came to Iceland from Jæren in Norway (*ÍF* I 130; IV 197; see further Ólafur Halldórsson 1980: 86–7).

[55] Contrast Adam of Bremen iv.397 (2002: 218), according to whom Greenland takes its name from the colour of the sea that surrounds it. In fact, the south of Greenland would have presented the first settlers with grassy slopes and shrubs, so the name may not be as propagandist as Ari assumes (Jones 1964: 46–7).

[56] This is the earliest occurrence in Old Icelandic of the name Vínland, which also appears in Adam of Bremen iv.39 (2002: 219). Adam and the sagas take it to derive from the wild grapes (*vínber*) believed to grow there, but other etymologies have also been suggested, relating it to grassland (*vin*, gen. *vinjar*) or to a generic term for berry (see the divergent views expressed by Lönnroth 1996, Crozier 1998 and Jónas Kristjánsson 2001). The location is most likely to have been in south-east Labrador or northern Newfoundland, where grapes might perhaps have grown in the more favourable climate of the period. By Ari's time, however, it had long been

forgotten and in 1121 according to Icelandic annals, a bishop of Greenland went in search of the country, presumably on a missionary enterprise (Jones 1964: 82–8).

[57] The etymology of *Skræling(j)ar* is uncertain, but it may be related to dialect Norwegian *skræla* 'to cry loudly, scream' or Icelandic *skrælna* 'to shrivel, dry out'. It is clearly a derogatory term; compare Modern Norwegian *skræling* 'weak or wretched person', Modern Icelandic *skrælingi* 'barbarian'. It is used for the indigenous inhabitants of Vínland in *Eiríks saga rauða* and *Grænlendinga saga* (*ÍF* IV 228–30, 256, 261–4), and of Greenland in *Historia Norwegie* (*HN* 3), without making any distinction between Indians and palaeo-Eskimos. The objects Ari refers to would have belonged to palaeo-Eskimos of the Early Dorset culture, who settled the west and east coast of Greenland between 700 BC and AD 200 (Gad 1970: 715; Jones 1964: 60, 91–4). However, his account forms an interesting literary parallel with the abandoned objects found in Iceland by the first settlers in ch. 1 above.

[58] Þorkell Gellisson was born at the earliest in 1030 and is unlikely to have travelled to Greenland much before 1050–60, which would make Eiríkr's companion extremely old. For this and other reasons it is possible that Greenland was settled later than Ari states (see Ólafur Halldórsson 1981: 204–5).

[59] Óláfr Tryggvason was king in Norway from 995 to 999/1000. Tradition has it that he was baptised by a hermit in the Scilly Isles, and the *Anglo-Saxon Chronicle* (*ASC* 126, 128) reports his baptism or confirmation in England under the sponsorship of King Ethelred the Unready. Adam of Bremen ii.36 (2002: 80), who is otherwise hostile to Óláfr, describes him as the first Christian king of Norway, and the earliest sources credit him with the conversion of five countries (Shetland, Orkney, the Faeroes, Iceland and Norway); later and less reliable sources also associate him with the conversion of Russia, Denmark and Greenland (see *Kristni saga* ch. 12 and note 75 below). It seems likely, however, that the importance of his missionary work has been exaggerated and that some particulars may even have been displaced from his namesake St Óláfr Haraldsson (Lönnroth 1965; Sawyer 1987); it has been argued that Oddr Snorrason and others wanted to set up Óláfr Tryggvason as a saint in his own right (Sverrir Tómasson 1988: 273–6). His reign is described in *Historia Norwegie*, Theodoricus, *Historia de antiquitate regum norwagiensium*, *Ágrip* and *Fagrskinna*, and also forms the subject of Oddr Snorrason's *Óláfs saga Tryggvasonar*, *Óláfs saga Tryggvasonar* in *Heimskringla* and *Óláfs saga Tryggvasonar in mesta*.

[60] Þangbrandr is also mentioned in *Landnámabók* (*ÍF* I 348), Oddr Snorrason 1932: 126–7, *Heimskringla* (*ÍF* XXVI 319–20, 328, 332–3), *Ágrip* 1995: 30–31, *HN* 20 and Theodoricus 1998: 15–16. His mission is recounted at length in *Kristni saga* chs 7–9, *ÓTM* I 149–50, 168; II 64–6, 150–60, 163–6 and *Njáls saga* (*ÍF* XII 256–69). Oddr Snorrason and Snorri Sturluson call him 'Saxon' and his name suggests a German origin, from OHG **thanc, danc* (cf. *dankjan* 'to think') and MHG **brant* 'firebrand, sword'. Theodoricus, however, calls him Theobrand (Theudobrand, Dietbrant) from Flanders, and a marginal annotation in *Þórðarbók* (in *Skarðsárbók* 1958: 164) names him Þorbrandr, a more familiar Norse name and probably therefore secondary to Þangbrandr.

[61] These men are also listed as the first converts by Theodoricus (1998: 15–16). Hallr's conversion is described at length in *Kristni saga* ch. 7, *ÓTM* I 151–6 and

Njáls saga (*ÍF* XII 256–7); he traced his ancestry from Hrollaugr and numbered among his descendants Bishop Magnús, St Jón, Sæmundr the Learned, Ari and the Sturlungs (*ÍF* I 317–18). On Gizurr the White, father of Bishop Ísleifr, see the genealogy of bishops (p. 13) and *Kristni saga* chs 9–12 and 14. He is prominent in *Njáls saga* among the opponents of Gunnarr and singled out in *Hungrvaka* (*ÍF* XVI 6) as the one 'who brought Christianity to Iceland'. Hjalti Skeggjason, who plays a more prominent role in *Kristni saga* chs 10–12 and the corresponding chapters of *Óláfs saga Tryggvasonar in mesta*, was married to Gizurr's daughter Vilborg (*ÍF* I 77, 79) and later acted as emissary of St Óláfr in Sweden (*ÍF* XXVII 77, 86–112).

[62] Ari's uncertainty on these matters is echoed in other sources. *Heimskringla*, *Njáls saga*, *Laxdœla saga* and *Óláfs saga Tryggvasonar in mesta* all reckon his stay at two years, but they diverge on whether he killed two, three or four men (*ÍF* V 125; XII 258–68; XXVI 320; *ÓTM* II 157–60). According to Theodoricus (1998: 15), Þangbrandr stayed in Iceland for 'almost two years', and *Kristni saga* says that he stayed three years and was responsible for a number of deaths. For a more detailed account of the killings, see *Kristni saga* ch. 9 below and references there.

[63] Ari's Icelandic perspective (and, presumably, audience) is clearly marked in this key passage both by his use of 'east' to refer to Norway (which is east of Iceland) and by his reference to 'our' countrymen.

[64] The situation in Norway upon Þangbrandr's return is also described (with more explicit criticism of Þangbrandr) in Oddr Snorrason 1932: 126–8, *Heimskringla* (*ÍF* XXVI 332–3), *Laxdœla saga* (*ÍF* V 125), *Njáls saga* (*ÍF* XII 269), *Kristni saga* ch. 11 and *ÓTM* II 163–6.

[65] Theodoricus' Thermo (1998: 16), who came to Norway from England with Óláfr. Þormóðr is also mentioned in Oddr Snorrason 1932: 128, *Heimskringla* (*ÍF* XXVI 347), ch. 12 of *Kristni saga* and *ÓTM* II 188, but only Theodoricus gives him a significant role, attributing Iceland's conversion to his preaching rather than to Gizurr and Hjalti's diplomacy.

[66] According to Jón Jóhannesson (1974: 131), this change of date may have been designed to allow more heathens from remote areas to get to the assembly on time, but it was more probably due to the fault in the calendar which, despite the *sumarauki*, would have been about a week out by this stage (Líndal 1974: 243).

[67] Lesser outlawry involved payment of a ransom (known as a *fjǫrbaugr* 'life-ring'), confiscation of property, and exile from Iceland for three years. The person condemned enjoyed legal immunity when abroad, but could be killed with impunity in Iceland if found outside designated sanctuaries or designated routes between them or from them to ship. If he had not gone abroad within three years, he became a full outlaw (*Grágás* 1980–2000: I 92–5, 98, 117–18; Hastrup 1985: 137–9).

[68] It is not at all clear that the concept of blasphemy (Ari's *goðgá*) existed in pagan times, and it may be that Hjalti was in fact outlawed for libel or 'shaming slander' (*níð*), which was more harshly punished when proclaimed at the Law-Rock (*Grágás* 1980–2000: II 198; Jakob Benediktsson 1974: 194). The events surrounding Hjalti's outlawry are described at greater length in ch. 10 of *Kristni saga* and *ÓTM* II 161–3.

[69] The wit of this verse lies in its word play: the Icelandic verb *geyja* 'bark' can also mean 'mock, abuse', and the noun *grey* 'female dog, bitch' carries connota-

tions of promiscuity appropriate to the Norse goddess of fertility (von See 1968). According to most, therefore, Hjalti is protesting his innocence of blasphemy: he does not wish to abuse the gods, but cannot help thinking that Freyja is a bitch (Ljungberg 1938: 199; Ohlmarks 1958: 296; Almqvist 1974: 18). Less likely is Genzmer's view (1928) that the first line is an accusative and infinitive construction ('I do not wish gods to bark'), so that Hjalti is declaring his distaste for gods that bark, rather than any reluctance to insult them. Possibly, however, Hjalti is parodying the worship of heathens, whom he envisages barking at the gods like dogs (Kress 1996: 54). The author of *Njáls saga* (*ÍF* XII 264) also had difficulties making sense of the verse, for he changed the first line to 'I do not hold back in blaspheming the gods'. Why Hjalti chooses Freyja as a focus for his attack is not entirely clear, but the accusation of promiscuity accords well with the scornful treatment of female goddesses in early translated saints' lives (e.g. *HMS* I 2–3, 569, II 233; cf. particularly *Clemens saga* 2005: 44–5), as well as reflecting her reputation in Eddic verse (Dronke 1997: 339–40). In some versions, the verse has two extra lines extending the insult to Óðinn: 'It has to be one or the other | Óðinn's a bitch or else Freyja' (Oddr Snorrason 1932: 128; *ÍF* XII 264; *ÓTM* II 162).

[70] There have been many plausible suggestions as to why fighting did not break out: that the Christians were more numerous than the heathens had expected, that news of Icelandic hostages in Norway prevented it or that moderate men on both sides intervened (Jón Jóhannesson 1974: 133–4). Among the medieval sources, Theodoricus (1998: 16) and *ÓTM* II 189 describe it as a miracle, but *Kristni saga* (ch. 12 below) gives a political explanation.

[71] The Icelandic verb (*kaupa at*) is ambiguous, and could mean either that Hallr and Þorgeirr negotiated a settlement, or that Hallr gave Þorgeirr money (either a bribe or the appropriate fee) to speak the law (Ólsen 1900: 86; Jón Jóhannesson 1974: 134–5). Later sources assume that a payment was made: half a mark in Oddr Snorrason (1932: 129), three marks in *Njáls saga* (*ÍF* XII 271), sixty ounces of silver in *Kristni saga* (ch. 12) and *ÓTM* II 191. They also differ on what the negotiations might have involved: Oddr states (confusingly) that Þorgeirr proclaimed the Christian law at once, *Kristni saga* that he agreed to proclaim both, while perhaps most plausibly, *Óláfs saga Tryggvasonar in mesta* allows Hallr to specify the key points to be included. Ari leaves the nature of the agreement deliberately murky.

[72] There has been much discussion about what Þorgeirr was doing under the cloak. Bjǫrn M. Ólsen (1900: 103), for example, argued that he was preparing his speech at the Althing, Sigurður Nordal (1990: 178) that he 'kept awake to listen to his inner voice', while Jan de Vries (1958–9) and Jón Hnefill Aðalsteinsson (1999: 103–23) have suggested that he was communing with *landvættir* or other supernatural powers in a shamanistic ritual. For the sense of the numinous, one might want to compare Njáll's mysterious 'mumbling' upon hearing of the new faith (*ÍF* XII 255).

[73] The exposure of children is associated with heathen times in a number of sagas (e.g. *ÍF* III: 56), and the eating of horse-flesh is forbidden in Icelandic laws of the Christian period (*Grágás* 1980–2000, I 49). This may have been because of an association with heathen sacrificial feasts, but the ban was widespread and not specifically directed against Scandinavia (Egardt 1962). The concessions Ari mentions are usually interpreted as provisional economic measures (Jón Jóhannesson 1974:

136–7; Steffensen 1966–9: 196–7), though Sveinbjǫrn Rafnsson (1979) has attempted to relate them to clauses in medieval penitentials. According to *Njáls saga* (*ÍF* XII 272), the two practices became unlawful when Christianity was introduced, but the same concessions extended to them as to heathen worship in general.

[74] The Icelandic legal system distinguished between a panel of neighbours (*búakviðr*) and witnesses (*vættir*). Panels consisted of five or nine men who were qualified by dwelling-place and economic status to deliver a verdict on the matter at hand. Witnesses, on the other hand, had to have seen or heard whatever they were testifying to, and were in this case more difficult to obtain (*Grágás* 1980–2000: I 63–4, 69–77, 141, 144–6; Jón Jóhannesson 1974: 136).

[75] This took place in *c*.1016 during the reign of St Óláfr (*ÍF* XXVII 77). Other accounts of Iceland's legal conversion to Christianity, all to some extent dependent on Ari, can be found in Oddr Snorrason 1932: 128–30, ch. 12 of *Kristni saga*, *Njáls saga* (*ÍF* XII 269–72) and *ÓTM* II 188–98.

[76] In Ari's time, the beginning of the Christian era was under dispute. Ari follows Bede in using Dionysius' chronology (*secundum æram vulgarem* 'by the common method of reckoning'), which eventually prevailed, but Icelandic texts from the second half of the twelfth century use Gerlandus' chronology, according to which the Christian era began seven years later (Ólafia Einarsdóttir 1964: 127–42). The exact date of Iceland's conversion is a tricky issue. Ari places it in the same summer as Óláfr Tryggvason's fall, which he dates to 1000, but Ólafia Einarsdóttir (1964: 74–80, 107–26; cf. also *ÍF* I xxiii–xxxv) has argued that it should in fact be dated to 999: she suggests that if, as seems likely, Ari used a calendar which began the year on 1st September, he would have dated Óláfr Tryggvason's fall on 9/10th September to 1000, and the conversion to 999 (we would now date both to 999). This also fits with what Ari says in ch. 9 about how Hallr was baptised at the age of three (in 998) one year before the conversion (p. 11).

[77] Friðrekr is mentioned in chs 1–4 of *Kristni saga*, *ÓTM* I 284–98, *Grettis saga* (*ÍF* VII 35) and *Vatnsdæla saga* (*ÍF* VIII 124–6). It has been suggested that Archbishop Adaldag of Bremen sent him to Iceland, but this is not mentioned in any source (Líndal 1974: 236). *Hungrvaka* (*ÍF* XVI 11–13) describes Friðrekr briefly as 'the only one who came out before [the time of Bishop Ísleifr] about whom stories are told', but has more detailed information about the other bishops. Bjarnharðr was among the English bishops in St Óláfr's entourage; he later went to Knútr the Great, who made him bishop of Skåne (at that time part of Denmark; Adam of Bremen ii.55, 57; 2002: 93–4; *HN* 25). Kolr was probably also sent to Iceland by St Óláfr; he stayed with Hallr in Haukadalr and was the first bishop to be buried at Skálaholt (*Skarðsárbók* 1958: 195). He may be the same Kolr who is said to have confirmed Víga-Glúmr on his deathbed *c*.1003 (*ÍF* IX 97–8). Hróðólfr (Roðulf) was among Óláfr's English bishops (Adam of Bremen ii.57, 64; 2002: 94, 100; *HN* 25) and may be related to the Norman Archbishop Robert who baptised Óláfr in Rouen in 1015; he was a kinsman of Edward the Confessor, whose mother Emma was Robert's sister. He was probably sent to Iceland by Archbishop Libentius *c*.1030, and lived at Bœr and Lundr in Borgarfjǫrðr (*ÍF* I 65, *Skarðsárbók* 1958: 195); English sources say that he returned to England in 1050, was appointed abbot of Abingdon and died there in 1052 (*ASC* 171–2 and *Chronicon monasterii*

de Abingdon 1858: 463–4). Jóhan is probably Adam's Johannes scotus (Adam of Bremen iii.21, 51; 2002:131, 157), who was bishop of Magdeburg before he was martyred in either Wendland or Mecklenburg in 1066. Bjarnharðr may be the same bishop whom Archbishop Adalbert sent to Norway (Adam of Bremen iii.77; 2002: 183). He stayed in Iceland in 1047/8–1067, probably because of the quarrels between Haraldr the Hard-Ruler and Adalbert, lived at Giljá and Steinsstaðir in Vatnsdalr and returned to Norway to become bishop in Selje and then in Bergen under Óláfr the Peaceful. Heinrekr is perhaps the bishop of Lund mentioned in Adam of Bremen iv.8 (2002, 192), who died of a drinking binge in 1066. On these men, see further Melsteð 1907–15: 720, 823–8; Jón Stefánsson 1946–53; Jón Jóhannesson 1974: 138–44; and Líndal 1974: 250–54.

[78] These are probably the same bishops mentioned disapprovingly in *Grágás* (1980–2000: I 38) and *Hungrvaka* (*ÍF* XVI 8–9), according to which they were contemporary with Ísleifr and considerably more lenient. Jörgensen (1874–8: 694) and Jón Jóhannesson (1974: 143) thought they were Paulicians from Armenia, a heretical dualist sect that denied the reality of Christ's body and rejected the Church's sacraments, hierarchy and cult (especially image worship). Magnús Már Lárusson (1960), however, has argued that they were more likely to be Eastern Orthodox bishops from Ermland, a district on the Baltic coast (in modern-day Poland), where a see of the Slavonic rite existed from *c*.1000 into the twelfth century. There were close connections between Scandinavia and the East during the reign of Prince Jaroslav of Kiev (1019–54), and there appear to have been Eastern Orthodox bishops in Norway and Sweden during the same period.

[79] Skapti was lawspeaker 1004–30. His sister, Þordís, was Gizurr the White's third wife and mother of Bishop Ísleifr (*Skarðsárbók* 1958: 185; *ÍF* XVI 6). Skapti is mentioned in numerous sagas, including *Njáls saga* (*ÍF* XII 141–2, 370–71, 406–11), *Grettis saga* (*ÍF* VII 146, 163–4, 177–8), *Flóamanna saga* (*ÍF* XIII 315–16, 321–2) and *Heimskringla* (*ÍF* XXVII 74, 217), and it was to him that St Óláfr addressed his request for the heathen provisions to be removed from the law. The portrait given here of his term of office is unique.

[80] The Fifth Court was a court of first instance for cases of false witness and breaches of legal procedure, and of second instance for cases that had failed to reach a unanimous verdict in the quarter courts. One judge was nominated by each of the forty-eight chieftains, and thirty-six of these passed judgement. Decisions were by majority (*Grágás* 1980–2000: I 83–8; Jón Jóhannesson 1974: 70–74). A detailed account of the institution of the Fifth Court can be found in *Njáls saga* (*ÍF* XII 242–6), which places it before the Conversion but is not usually taken to be historically accurate.

[81] In Iceland, all killings had to be announced in public or they counted as murder (*Grágás* 1980–2000: I 146). It appears from Ari's comment that it had previously been the custom for the rich and powerful to pronounce other men responsible for their killings so as to avoid outlawry themselves.

[82] On Ísleifr, see also ch. 14 of *Kristni saga*, *Hungrvaka*, *Ísleifs þáttr* (*ÍF* XVI 6–11, 335–8) and *Jóns saga helga* (*ÍF* XV 176–7, 181–3, 191–2). Some of this chapter is reproduced with minor changes in *Haukdœla þáttr* in *Sturl* I 58–9. Ísleifr's consecration at the hands of Archbishop Adalbert is usually dated to 1056

in accordance with Icelandic annals and the emended text of *Hungrvaka* (Bekker-Nielsen 1960). Adam of Bremen iii.77, iv.36 (2002: 183, 218) mentions it as the occasion of Iceland's 'conversion', by which he must mean its subordination to the see of Hamburg–Bremen.

[83] Kolr (or Kollr) is mentioned in ch. 14 of *Kristni saga*, *Hungrvaka* (*ÍF* XVI 9), *Jóns saga helga* (*ÍF* XV 181), *Sturl* I 58 and *Landnámabók* (*ÍF* I 386). He was the grandson of Ísleifr's cousin and died *c*.1120. On Jón, see note 101 below.

[84] About Þorvaldr we know only that he was a chieftain at Hraungerðr (*ÍF* XVI 6). Teitr's son, Hallr (d. 1150) was brother-in-law to Hafliði Másson. According to *Hungrvaka* (for which his son, Gizurr, was a source), he was elected bishop in 1149, but died in Utrecht on his way from Rome to Lund for consecration. He was renowned for his command of languages, and *Hungrvaka* says that he spoke the language of whatever country he travelled to as if it were his mother tongue (*ÍF* I 318, *ÍF* XVI 34, *Sturl* I 60).

[85] Hallr in Haukadalr was the brother of Bishop Þorlákr's grandfather and a distant relation of Hjalti Skeggjason (see *ÍF* I 383 and ch. 10 below). He was born in 995/6, died in 1089, and was almost eighty when Ari came to him. According to Snorri (*ÍF* XXVI 6–7), he had travelled widely and formed a trading partnership with St Óláfr.

[86] According to *Laxdœla saga* (*ÍF* V 229), Gellir died in Denmark on his way back from a pilgrimage to Rome and was buried at Roskilde. Ari's father, Þorgils, had drowned at a young age in Breiðafjǫrðr.

[87] Haraldr the Hard-Ruler. Together with Earl Tostig of Wessex, he led a force to England against Harold Godwineson in 1066, where he was defeated at the battle of Stamford Bridge (*ÍF* XXVIII 182–91; *Ágrip* 1995: 56–9; *Msk* 267–72; *ASC* 196–9). This event is often taken to mark the end of the Viking Age in Scandinavia.

[88] It is not clear whether Ari's *Frakkland* refers to an area in France or modern-day Germany. Magnús Már Lárusson (1967: 358) has suggested Franconia in the Upper Rhine region, while Foote (1984b: 115–20) argues on the basis of various geographical references in medieval Icelandic texts that it was a poorly defined region comprising the French kingdom of the Capetians, Burgundy, Lotharingia and the centre of the old Carolingian realm around Aachen and Liège. *Oddverja-annáll* (2003: 124) gives Sæmundr's place of study as Paris. His return to Iceland, like his studies abroad, became the subject of many folk-tales (see, for example, *ÍF* XV 339–42 and Jón Árnason 1954–61: I 469–88) and is variously dated in Icelandic annals to 1076, 1077 or 1078.

[89] In fact, Leo IX was pope in 1054 (cf. the correction in *Kristni saga* ch. 14, p. 51 below and *Sturl* I 58), and Victor II succeeded him in 1055. Ari's mistake here probably derives from Adam of Bremen iii.34 (2002: 141), who says that Leo IX died in the same year as Emperor Henry III, which was 1056 (Köhne 1987: 27–8).

[90] 5th July 1080.

[91] On Ari's contemporary Gizurr, see chs 15–17 of *Kristni saga*, *Hungrvaka* (*ÍF* XVI 14–22) and *Jóns saga helga* (*ÍF* XV 192–5, 202, 232). Most of this chapter is also taken up in *Haukdœla þáttr* in *Sturl* I 58–9.

[92] The Icelandic here (*rétt*) is ambiguous, and could mean that Gizurr's right name was Gisrøðr, that it was corrected to Gisrøðr or (if the word is read *rætt*) that

it was pronounced as Gisrøðr. Although the etymology of the name Gizurr is unclear, the first element is more likely to be related to Modern Icelandic *giska* 'to guess' than to the personal name Gísl, from which the form Gisrøðr would be derived (Ásgeir Blöndal Magnússon 1989: 248). Gis(f)røðr corresponds to German Gisfrid or Gisfred ('Peace-Pledge'), and it is possible that the alteration was made by German speakers (cf. *ÍF* I 22, note 2).

[93] Markús's grandfather Bjarni was second cousin to Skapti Þóroddson, and Markús himself was related to Þuríðr Snorradóttir, Ari Þorgilsson and Bishop Ísleifr (*ÍF* I 381 and note 3). As well as serving the longest series of terms of any lawspeaker, Markús travelled abroad and composed poetry for three kings: Ingi Steinkelsson of Sweden (1080–1111) and St Knútr (1080–86) and Eiríkr Sveinsson (d. 1103) of Denmark (*Edda Snorra Sturlusonar* 1848–87: III 252, 258, 260, 267, 271, 283). Parts of his *Eiríksdrápa* are preserved in *Knýtlinga saga* (*ÍF* XXXV 212–39). He died in 1107.

[94] Tithes were established as Church law during the fifth and sixth centuries, but met with fierce resistance in most newly-converted countries. Iceland was the first of the Scandinavian countries to pass tithe laws; an attempt to introduce them in Denmark in the 1080s was a significant factor in the rebellion against St Knútr that led to his death. Before tithes were introduced, priests probably charged fees for individual services (Adam of Bremen iv.31; 2002: 212). Tithes became an important source of income for chieftains owning churches, who received one half of them, which may explain why the law was so easily accepted in Iceland. Usually tithes were a 10% tax on gross income, but in Iceland, they were a 1% property tax, which, although it did not accord with canon law, made them easier to calculate in an agrarian economy (Orri Vésteinsson 2000: 67–80). A separate tithe law can be found in manuscripts of *Grágás* (1980–2000: II 221–31; see also *DI* I 70–162), but probably does not represent accurately the law of 1097.

[95] All previous bishops in Iceland, including Ísleifr, had been missionary bishops or bishops *in partibus infidelium*, meaning that they had the title of bishop without any territorial jurisdiction. It was only under Gizurr that Iceland was integrated into the diocesan system of the medieval Church.

[96] Although sometimes connected with the tithe law, this was more probably undertaken to see whether it was financially viable to set up a second episcopal see (Jón Jóhannesson 1974: 151–2).

[97] All householders with financial means above a certain level were required to pay a tax when not attending the Althing. This was levied by the chieftain with whom they were affiliated and used to pay the expenses of those householders who did attend. Being subject to the assembly attendance dues gave men both rights and responsibilities as participants in the assembly (for example, sitting on panels of neighbours) and in local affairs (*Grágás* 1980–2000: I 57–8, 150–51; Jón Jóhannesson 1974: 61).

[98] This happened in 1117–18. The first written copy of the laws became known as *Hafliðaskrá* 'Hafliði's scroll' and is mentioned in *Grágás* (1980–2000: I 191) as the most authoritative manuscript. Hafliði, a powerful chieftain from the north of Iceland, was married to Teitr's daughter Rannveig who was second cousin to Ketill Þorsteinsson's wife, Gróa; their daughter Valgerðr was married to the son

of Ari's cousin Oddný, daughter of Þorkell Gellisson. Hafliði probably had an important role in the establishment of the see at Hólar (Orri Vésteinsson 2000: 34–5). See further ch. 18 of *Kristni saga* below and notes 119–20 there.

[99] The Treatment of Homicide law can be found in *Grágás* (1980–2000: I 139–74). It deals with the definitions of and penalties for assault, wounds, killings and murder, and the legal procedures to be followed in the preparation of cases. Gísli Sigurðsson (2004: 58) describes the writing down of the laws as 'the first step in a movement led by the allies of the Church to encroach upon the secular domain of the lawspeaker'.

[100] Þorlákr was consecrated in Lund in 1118. Although it is unclear exactly how bishops were elected in Iceland before *c*.1150, the existing bishop (contrary to canon law) often appears to have nominated his successor directly (Orri Vésteinsson 2000: 144).

[101] Jón was descended from Hallr on Síða, second cousin to Teitr Ísleifsson's wife Jórunn and a pupil of Bishop Ísleifr; he was the first bishop to be consecrated at the newly-established archiepiscopal see in Lund (in 1106). He was recognised as a saint at the Althing in 1200. See further *Hungrvaka* (*ÍF* XVI 18, 24) and *Jóns saga helga* (especially *ÍF* XV 181–3, 196–200).

[102] Although in theory only one bishop could be appointed to a diocese, in cases of extreme need it was possible for a coadjutor to be consecrated to help the existing one and succeed him upon his death. According to *Hungrvaka* (*ÍF* XVI 23–4), Þorlákr was therefore consecrated to Reykjaholt rather than Skálaholt, but given permission to reside at Skálaholt if Gizurr was still living upon his return to Iceland.

[103] Tuesday 28th May 1118.

[104] This list probably comes from a crusader history related to Fulcher of Chartres's *Historia Hierosolymitana*, which also has a death list mentioning Paschal, Baldwin, Arnulf and Alexius (Skårup 1979). Alexius is also known in Old Icelandic tradition as Kirjalax, the emperor who received both King Eiríkr the Good and King Sigurðr Crusader in Miklagarðr (Constantinople); see *ÍF* XXVIII 252–4, 370–72; *Msk* 323–5; *Fagrskinna* 2004: 256; *ÍF* XXXV 236–8. The Swedish king Philip is mentioned in Swedish genealogies from the mid-thirteenth century on and in an Icelandic source from *c*.1254; he may be included in this list because he died on pilgrimage abroad (Ólafia Einarsdóttir 1964: 33–5; Faulkes 2005: 119).

[105] A lunar (or Metonic) cycle is a period of nineteen years after which the Moon's phases occur on the same days of the solar year. It was used during the Middle Ages to calculate the date of Easter, which was celebrated on the Sunday following the first New Moon on or after the vernal equinox (March 21). The oldest surviving Icelandic Easter table, AM 732 a VII 4to, begins with the new lunar cycle of 1121, and it is probable that Ari used a similar table for dating purposes, possibly with marginal annotations (Ólafia Einarsdóttir 1964: 93–106).

[106] Compare the genealogies in ch. 2, and see note 22. Here Ari organises his material according to the bishops' order of appointment and uses female links where necessary to trace their ancestry to the main settler in each quarter of the land. In the manuscripts there is a cross over the name of the first Christian in each genealogy (Hallr on Síða, Þórðr Horsehead and Goðmundr Eyjólfsson), except that the cross over Gizurr the White has been accidentally omitted.

¹⁰⁷ I.e. Þorfinnr karlsefni (literally 'makings of a man'), who 'discovered Vínland the good'; see *Landnámabók* (*ÍF* I 141, 241), *Eyrbyggja saga* (*ÍF* IV 135), *Eiríks saga rauða* and *Grœnlendinga saga* (*ÍF* IV 209–23, 241–68).

¹⁰⁸ Eyjólfr Valgerðarson is listed in *Landnámabók* (*ÍF* 1 396), *Heimskringla* (*ÍF* XXVI 271) and ch. 1 of *Kristni saga* among the most important chieftains in Iceland. *Jómsvíkinga saga* (1969: 99–100) cites a libellous verse he composed about King Haraldr Gormsson of Denmark. He appears, together with his equally well-known son Guðmundr the Powerful, in *Reykdœla saga*, *Ljósvetninga saga*, *Valla-Ljóts saga*, *Víga-Glúms saga* and *Njáls saga*.

¹⁰⁹ Other accounts of the Yngling dynasty of kings can be found in *Ynglingatal* and *Ynglinga saga* (in *ÍF* XXVI 9–83), *HN* 12–13, *Langfeðga tal frá Nóa* (*AÍ* III 57–8), *Ættartala Haralds frá Óðni* (in *Flb* I 27–8), *Af Upplendingakonungum* (in *Hauksbók* 1892–6: 456–7), and in Resen's manuscript (Faulkes 2005: 117–19). The relationship between these is complex and Ari stands closest to *Historia Norwegie* (see Ellehøj 1965: 109–41). It seems likely that the deviations in Snorri are due to his use of an earlier version of the lists in Resen's manuscript, which are mostly derived from English sources presumably not available to Ari (Faulkes 1977 and 2005).

¹¹⁰ *HN* 12 follows Ari, but has Yngvi as 'the first to rule the kingdom of Sweden'; in Snorri, Óðinn precedes Njǫrðr, and Freyr is identified with Yngvi (*ÍF* XXVI 24, cf. *Hauksbók* 1892–6: 457, *AÍ* III 58, Faulkes 2005: 118). *Flb* I 27 has the order Óðinn–Freyr–Njǫrðr–Freyr.

¹¹¹ Ari seems to have imagined a migration to Scandinavia from the Black Sea area (Thrace), in accordance with classical writings about the origin of the Germanic nations; he may also have been influenced by continental traditions whereby the origins of nations were traced back to the fall of Troy (Turks and Trojans being closely identified; see Faulkes 1978–9, especially 110–24). Compare *Ynglinga saga* (*ÍF* XXVI 14–16) and Snorri Sturluson (2005: 4–6).

¹¹² On the presence of euhemerised gods like Njǫrðr and Freyr in Icelandic genealogies, see Faulkes 1978–9: 94–95, 106–110. One might wish to compare West-Saxon genealogies tracing English kings back to Woden (Óðinn); it is clear from lists in Resen's manuscript that royal genealogies of this kind were well known in Iceland (Faulkes 1977 and 2005: 117–18).

¹¹³ *Ynglingatal* (as we have it) begins with Fjǫlnir. Snorri tells how he accidentally fell into a vat of mead whilst drunk on a visit to Frið-Fróði in Denmark (*ÍF* XXVI 25–6; see also *HN* 12).

¹¹⁴ Cf. *Langfeðgatal* (*AÍ* III 58), *HN* 12, 89 and Faulkes 2005: 118; *Heimskringla* (*ÍF* XXVI 31) and *Ættartala* (*Flb* I 27) both have the form Dómaldi.

¹¹⁵ Cf. *HN* 12 and Faulkes 2005: 118. *Heimskringla* (*ÍF* XXVI 37–9), *Ættartala* (*Flb* I 27) and *Langfeðgatal* (*AÍ* III 58) all have the order Agni–Alrekr.

¹¹⁶ According to Snorri, Aun sacrificed nine of his ten sons to Óðinn for long life, and became so old that he had to be carried around on a chair and drink milk out of a drinking horn like an infant (*ÍF* XXVI 47–50; see also *HN* 13 and *Flb* I 27).

¹¹⁷ Snorri correctly gives this nickname to Egill's son, Óttarr, who was killed in battle in Vendel in Jutland: the Danes left his body out to rot and sent a wooden crow back to the Swedes to show how little they thought him worth (*ÍF* XXVI 54,

cf. *Flb* I 27, *ÁÍ* III 58 and Faulkes 2005: 118). However, it is likely that the Vendel in question is actually the one in Swedish Upplǫnd, where Óttarr is traditionally believed to be buried (Nerman 1925: 145–8).

[118] Aðils is one of three kings whom Snorri says were buried at Uppsala, the centre of the old Swedish kingdom (*ÍF* XXVI 57–9). Both he and his father Óttarr are named among the Swedes in the Old English poem *Beowulf* (as Ohthere and Eadgils; 1950: 90). Aðils (Athislus) is also mentioned in books II and III of Saxo Grammaticus, *The History of the Danes* (1979–80: I 52–5, 73).

[119] *Braut* means 'road (cut through rocks, forest, etc.)', related to the Icelandic verb *brjóta* 'to break up'. Snorri describes how Ǫnundr cleared the forest land and built roads throughout Sweden during his reign (*ÍF* XXVI 62–3).

[120] According to Snorri, Ingjaldr got this nickname because it was rumoured that 'he killed twelve kings and broke faith with them all' (*ÍF* XXVI 71).

[121] Hálfdan is the last name Ari has in common with *Ynglingatal*, though Goðrøðr is later mentioned by Snorri (*ÍF* XXVI 75). Óláfr and Helgi appear to have been borrowed from a different genealogy (that of the descendants of King Dagr) and inserted here in order to link Ari's ancestors with the Ynglings (Steffensen 1970–73: 67–9). In *Laxdæla saga* and *Fóstbræðra saga* (*ÍF* V 3; VI 124), Óleifr the White is described as 'son of Ingjaldr, son of Fróði'.

[122] In *Þáttr af Ragnars sonum* (*FN* I 161–2) and *Heimskringla* (*ÍF* XXVI 87–8), Helgi's son by Sigurðr's daughter (Áslaug) is Sigurðr Hart.

[123] Óleifr (early form of the name Óláfr; Irish Amlaibh) raided in the British Isles and became king of Dublin and the surrounding area; he appears in Irish annals in 853–71. The genealogy given by Ari, which would make him contemporary with Haraldr the Fine-Haired, is chronologically incorrect at this point: Óleifr in fact belongs earlier and it has been suggested that he should be identified with Óláfr Geirstaðaálfr, son of Goðrøðr the Hunter-king, on whom see note 7 above (Steffensen 1970–73: 63–7; Smyth 1977: 101–12). According to Icelandic tradition, Óleifr was married to Auðr the Deep-minded (*ÍF* I 136; IV 4, 195).

[124] Þorsteinn was a petty king who raided widely in Scotland, but was eventually betrayed and killed by the Scots; *Laxdæla saga* (*ÍF* V 7) names Ari as an authority on 'the death of Þorsteinn, that he fell at Caithness' (cf. *ÍF* I 136; XXVI 122; XXXIV 8).

[125] Eyjólfr the Grey figures in *Gísla saga* and *Eyrbyggja saga* as Gísli's killer (*ÍF* IV 23–4; VI 111–17) and his son Þorkell plays an important role in *Laxdæla saga* as Guðrún's fourth husband (*ÍF* V 171–5, 199–207, 215–24); his grandson Gellir Bǫlverksson was lawspeaker 1054–62 and 1072–4. Ari marks Eyjólfr out as the first Christian in his family line, just as he marks out Óleifr feilan as the first settler.

[126] Gellir Þorkelsson, a chieftain at Helgafell, plays a role in *Ljósvetninga saga* (*ÍF* X 83, 89–92, 102) and *Bandamanna saga* (*ÍF* VII 326, 338–45, 351–2, 359) and was emissary for St Óláfr in his demand for control over Iceland (*ÍF* XXVII 220, 240–41). His mother was Guðrún Ósvífrsdóttir, and his journeys abroad and descendants are mentioned towards the end of *Laxdæla saga* (*ÍF* V 204, 215–16, 227–9). Ari's cousin, Brandr Þorkelsson, appears in a list of priests dated to 1143 (*DI* I 186).

KRISTNI SAGA
THE STORY OF THE CONVERSION

CHAPTER ONE: HERE BEGINS THE STORY OF THE CONVERSION

NOW [the story of] how Christianity came to Iceland begins with a man called Þorvaldr Koðránsson, son of Atli the Strong's brother. They [Koðrán and Atli] were the sons of Eilífr Eagle, son of Bárðr from Áll, son of Ketill Fox, son of Skíði the Old.[1] Koðrán lived at Giljá in Vatsdalr and was an excellent man. His son Þorvaldr went abroad and was on raids at first, but he used the booty he got for the release of men taken captive in battle—whatever he did not need to have for his own provisions. Because of this, he became famous and well loved.[2] Þorvaldr travelled far and wide in the southern lands.[3] In Saxland, in the south, he met a bishop called Friðrekr and accepted from him baptism and the true faith, and stayed with him for a while.[4] Þorvaldr asked the bishop to go to Iceland with him to baptise his father and mother and others of his relatives who were willing to follow his advice. The bishop granted him this.

Bishop Friðrekr and Þorvaldr came to Iceland the summer that the land had been inhabited for one hundred and seven years.[5] Þorkell Moon then held the office of lawspeaker, and these were then the greatest chieftains in the country: Eyjólfr Valgerðarson in the north and Víga-Glúmr, Arnórr kerlingarnef, Þorvarðr Spak-Bǫðvarsson and Starri and his brothers in Guðdalir, Þorkell krafla in Vatsdalr. And in the west, there was then Ari Másson, Ásgeirr Knattarson, Eyjólfr Grey, Gestr the Wise, Óláfr Peacock, Víga-Styrr; Snorri goði was eighteen years old and had taken over the farm at Helgafell; Þorsteinn Egilsson. And in the south, Illugi the Red and Þorkell Moon and Þóroddr goði, Gizurr the White, Ásgrímr Elliða-Grímsson, Hjalti Skeggjason, Valgarðr at Hof, Runólfr Úlfsson and the sons of Ǫrnólfr in Skógar. And in the east, the sons of Þórðr Freysgoði, Síðu-Hallr, Helgi Ásbjarnarson, Víga-Bjarni and Geitir.[6]

It is said that the bishop and Þorvaldr travelled around the Northern Quarter, and Þorvaldr preached the faith to people because the bishop did not at the time understand Norse. And Þorvaldr preached God's message boldly, but most people made little response to their words. Ǫnundr the Christian, son of Þorgils Grenjaðarson from Reykjardalr, accepted the faith, as did Hlenni the Old, son of Ormr Bag-Back, and Þorvarðr Spak-Bǫðvarsson in Áss in Hjaltadalr;[7] and Eyjólfr Valgerðarson had himself prime-signed.[8]

CHAPTER TWO: ABOUT ÞORVALDR AND THE BISHOP

The bishop and Þorvaldr stayed at Giljá with Koðrán for the first winter together with thirteen men. Þorvaldr asked his father to be baptised, but he was slow to respond. At Giljá there stood a stone to which he and his kinsmen used to sacrifice, and they claimed that their guardian spirit lived in it.[9] Koðrán said that he would not have himself baptised until he knew who was more powerful, the bishop or the spirit in the stone. After that, the bishop went to the stone and chanted over it until the stone broke apart. Then Koðrán thought he understood that the spirit had been overcome. Koðrán then had himself and his whole household baptised, except that his son Ormr did not wish to accept the faith.[10] He then went south to Borgarfjǫrðr and buys land at Hvanneyrr. Ormr married Þórvǫr, daughter of Ǫzurr and Bera, Egill Skalla-Grímsson's daughter. Their daughter was Yngvildr, who was married to Hermundr Illugason. Ormr later married Geirlaug, daughter of Steinmóðr from Djúpadalr. Their daughter was Bera, who was married to Skúli Þorsteinsson.[11]

The bishop and Þorvaldr set up house at Lækjamót in Víðidalr and lived there for four years. They travelled far and wide throughout Iceland to preach the faith. The bishop and Þorvaldr were at an autumn feast in Vatsdalr at Giljá with Óláfr.[12] Þorkell krafla and many other people had come there.[13] Two berserks turned up there, who were both called Haukr. They threatened to use force against people, went around howling, and strode through fire.[14] Then people asked the bishop to destroy them. After that the bishop consecrated the fire before they strode through, and they were severely burned. After that people attacked them and killed them, and they were carried up onto the mountain by the gill. That is why it has since been called Haukagil.[15] After that, Þorkell krafla had himself prime-signed, but many who had been present at this event were baptised.[16]

Þorvaldr and the bishop went to the Western Quarter to preach the faith. They came to Hvammr during the Althing, to the home of Þórarinn fylsenni, and he was then at the assembly, but his wife Friðgerðr was at home with their son Skeggi.[17] Þorvaldr preached the faith to people there, but meanwhile Friðgerðr was in the temple and sacrificed and each of them heard the other's words, and the boy Skeggi laughed at them.[18] Then Þorvaldr uttered this verse:

> I preached the precious faith,
> no man paid heed to me;
> we got scorn from the sprinkler
> —priest's son—of blood-dipped branch.
> And without any sense,
> old troll-wife against poet
> —may God crush the priestess—
> shrilled at the heathen altar.[19]

No one had themselves baptised as a result of their words in the Western Quarter, as far as is known, but in the Northern Quarter many people left off sacrifices and broke up their idols, and some refused to pay the temple tax.[20]

Chapter three: About Þorvarðr

Þorvarðr Spak-Bǫðvarsson had a church built on his farm in Áss. That greatly displeased those people who were heathen.

There was a man called Klaufi, son of Þorvaldr Refsson from Barð. He was a chieftain.[21] He is greatly displeased with Þorvarðr over this, and he went to see Arngeirr, Þorvarðr's brother, and gave him a choice of whether he would rather burn down the church or kill the priest the bishop had provided for it.[22]

Then Arngeirr answers: 'I am against any of my friends harming the priest, because my brother has ruthlessly avenged lesser wrongs. But I think it a good plan to burn down the church, although I want nothing to do with it.'

A little later, Klaufi went there at night, and planned to burn down the church. There were ten of them altogether, and when they came into the churchyard, it seemed to them as if fire were flying out of all the church windows, and they went away because the whole church seemed to them full of fire.[23] But when he heard that the church had not burned down, he went there on another night with Arngeirr, with the intention of burning down the church. And when they had broken into the church, then he tried to light a fire with dry birch-wood. The fire was slow to kindle. Then he lay down and blew at it across the threshold. Then an arrow flew over his head into the floor beside him, and a second came between his shirt and his side. Then he leaped up and said that he would not wait for the third.[24] Arngeirr then went home.

And this church was built sixteen years before Christianity was made law in Iceland, and it was still standing when Bótólfr was bishop at Hólar, without any repairs having been made to the turf on the outside.[25]

Chapter four: About Þorvaldr

Bishop Friðrekr and Þorvaldr went to the assembly, and the bishop asked Þorvaldr to preach the faith to people at the Law-Rock while he was present but Þorvaldr spoke. Then Heðinn from Svalbarð in Eyjafjǫrðr, a well-born man, answered him with many evil words. Heðinn was the son of Þorbjǫrn Skagason. He was married to Ragnheiðr, stepdaughter and niece of Eyjólfr Valgerðarson.[26] Then they asked poets to libel Þorvaldr and the bishop. This verse was then uttered:

> The bishop has
> borne nine children;
> Þorvaldr's father
> of them all.[27]

Because of that libel, Þorvaldr killed two men. The bishop asked why he had killed them.

'Because they said that the two of us had children together.'

The bishop answered: 'They lied about us, but you have misinterpreted their insult, because I might well have borne your children on my back.'

And when Þorvaldr and the bishop wished to ride to the assembly at Hegranes, the heathens came to meet them and pelted them with stones so that they did not manage to get any further. After that they were made outlaws according to heathen laws.

And that summer, after the Althing, the chieftains assembled a company and rode off with two hundred men, and intended to burn the bishop and Þorvaldr in their home. They stopped to graze their horses before they rode up to the homestead at Lækjamót. But when they were about to remount, birds flew up past them. At that their horses shied, and men fell from horseback, some broke their arms and some their legs or injured themselves on their own weapons. The horses ran away from some of them, and with that they went back home.[28]

The bishop and Þorvaldr did not become aware of this armed gathering until afterwards. They had then lived at Lækjamót for three years. They lived there for one more year. After that they went abroad. And when they got to Norway, they lay at anchor in a certain harbour. Then Heðinn came from Iceland to the same harbour and went straight up into the forest to cut wood. And when Þorvaldr became aware of this, he went with his slave and had him killed there. And when the bishop discovered this, he said now it would end their partnership that Þorvaldr was eager to take revenge. The bishop then went south to Saxland and died there, and he is truly a saint. But Þorvaldr spent some time on trading expeditions at first.

Chapter five: About Þangbrandr

In the days of King Haraldr Gormsson, Bishop Albert went from Bremen to Áróss in Jutland and took up residence there;[29] his chaplain was called Þangbrandr, son of Count Vilbald of Bremen. And when Þangbrandr was fully-grown, Bishop Hubert of Canterbury invited his brother Albert to visit him; at that feast Hubert gave gifts to Albert and all his companions.[30]

Then the bishop said to Þangbrandr: 'You have the manners of a knight, so I am giving you a shield, and on it is depicted a cross with the image of our Lord; that represents your clerical learning.'

A little later, Þangbrandr met Óláfr Tryggvason in Wendland.[31] Óláfr asked:

'Who is the man tortured on the cross that you Christians worship?'

Þangbrandr answers: 'Our Lord Jesus Christ.'

The king asks: 'Why was he tortured, or what crime did he commit?'

Then Þangbrandr told King Óláfr in detail about the passion of our Lord and the miracles of the cross. The king then asked to buy the shield, but Þangbrandr gave the shield to him, and the king gave him the value of the shield in refined silver, and said:

'If you ever need help or support, then come to me, and I will then repay you for the shield.'

Shortly afterwards, King Óláfr had himself baptised in the Scillies in Ireland.[32]

Þangbrandr buys a beautiful Irish girl with the silver. But when he got back with her, a man whom Emperor Otto the Young had sent there as a hostage wanted to take the girl off him, but he [Þangbrandr] was not willing to let her go.[33] The hostage was a great fighter, and challenged Þangbrandr to a battle, but Þangbrandr had the victory and killed him. Because of that Þangbrandr was not able to stay in Denmark, and he then went to King Óláfr Tryggvason, and he [Óláfr] received him well and he was ordained priest there and served as the king's chaplain for a while.

CHAPTER SIX: ABOUT STEFNIR

King Óláfr left Ireland and [went] east to Hólmgarðr, and from Hólmgarðr to Norway, as it is written in his saga, and preached Christianity there to the whole population.[34] He had the first church built on an island called Mostr. There he appointed Þangbrandr to sing mass on the island, and gave him a homestead and lands. He [Þangbrandr] was a very extravagant man and open-handed, and his money soon ran out. He then got himself a long ship and raided the heathen and plundered far and wide, and used the money to pay for his company of men.

King Óláfr came to Norway at the beginning of Gói.[35] With him were many Icelanders. One of them was called Stefnir. He was the son of Þorgils, son of Eilífr, son of Helgi bjóla from Kjalarnes.[36] King Óláfr sent Stefnir to Iceland the first summer he came to Norway, to preach God's message there. But when he got to Iceland, then people received him badly, and his kinsmen worst of all, because all people were then heathen in this country.

And he travelled boldly both north and south, and taught people the true faith, but they were not much moved by his teaching. And when he saw that it was not making headway, then he began to destroy temples and places of worship and to break up idols.[37] Then the heathens assembled a company of men and he then escaped with difficulty to Kjalarnes and stayed there with his kinsmen.

His ship lay ashore at Gufáróss. It was carried out to sea during the winter in floods and violent gales. The heathens uttered this verse about it:

> Now Stefnir's prow-falcon (sea
> streams through the hollow ship)
> is by fierce mountain flurry—
> fell weather—entirely destroyed.
> But we believe that—bonds
> must be in our land—such roaring
> (the river rages with ice)
> is ruled by the Æsir's power.[38]

The ship came ashore not much damaged, and Stefnir had it repaired in the spring.

That summer at the Althing, it was made law that kinsmen of Christians who were closer than fourth and more distantly related than second cousins must prosecute them for blasphemy.[39] That summer Stefnir was prosecuted for being a Christian. His kinsmen conducted the suit, because Christianity was then called a disgrace to one's family. The sons of Ósvífr the Wise, Þórólfr and Áskell, Vandráðr and Torráðr, prosecuted him, but Óspakr wanted no part in it.[40]

But Stefnir said: 'No harm will come to me from my outlawry. But because of this lawsuit, great misfortune will befall you in the space of a few years.'[41]

Stefnir went abroad in the summer and King Óláfr received him well.

Chapter seven: About Þangbrandr

When King Óláfr heard of the unruly things Þangbrandr was doing, he summoned him to him and laid charges against him, and said that he should not be in his service, when he was a robber. Þangbrandr asked the king to assign to him some difficult mission.

The king said: 'We two shall be reconciled, if you go to Iceland and manage to convert the country.'

Þangbrandr said: 'I will take the risk.'[42]

That summer Þangbrandr went to Iceland. He landed at Selvágar in northern Álptafjǫrðr to the north of Melrakkanes. And when people realised that Þangbrandr and his men were Christian, then the inhabitants refused to speak to them or to direct them to harbour.

Síðu-Hallr was then living at Á. He had been to Fljótsdalr, and when he came home, Þangbrandr went to see him and told him that King Óláfr had directed him to Hallr, if he landed in the Eastern Fjords, and asked him to guide them to harbour and give them any other assistance they needed. Hallr had them moved to Leiruvágr in southern Álptafjǫrðr and drew their ship ashore at the place that is now called Þangbrandshróf. And Hallr moved the cargo to his infield and put up a tent there in which Þangbrandr and his men stayed. Þangbrandr sang mass there. The day before Michaelmas, Þangbrandr and his men began to observe the feast at nones.[43]

Hallr was there in the tent at the time. He asked:

'Why are you stopping work now?'

Þangbrandr says: 'Tomorrow is the feast of the Archangel Michael.'

Hallr asked: 'Of what nature is he?'

Þangbrandr answers: 'He is appointed to receive the souls of Christians.'

Then Þangbrandr said many things about the glory of God's angels.[44] Hallr said:

'The one whom these angels serve must be powerful indeed.'

Þangbrandr says: 'God has given you this understanding.'

In the evening, Hallr said to his household: 'Tomorrow Þangbrandr and his men are observing a feast-day for their God, and I now wish you to benefit from this, and you shall not work tomorrow, and we shall now go and see the rites of Christians.'

In the morning, Þangbrandr held the divine service in his tent, and Hallr and his household went to see their rites, and heard the sound of bells, and smelled the scent of incense, and saw men clothed in costly material and fine cloth.[45] Hallr asked his household how they liked the rites of Christians, and they spoke well of them. Hallr was baptised the Saturday before Easter together with his whole household in the river there.[46] It has since been called Þváttá.

CHAPTER EIGHT: ABOUT ÞANGBRANDR

In the summer, Þangbrandr rode to the Althing with Hallr. But when they came to Skógahverfi, the heathens paid a man called Galdra-Heðinn to make the ground fall away beneath Þangbrandr. On the day they [Þangbrandr and Hallr] rode away from Kirkjubœr from the home of Surtr, son of Ásbjǫrn, son of Ketill the Foolish—all his forebears on the father's side were baptised[47]—then Þangbrandr's horse fell down into the ground, but he jumped off its back and stood on the brink unharmed.[48]

Þangbrandr baptised many people on that journey, Gizurr the White and Hallr in Haukadalr (he was then three years old) and Hjalti Skeggjason. Þangbrandr preached God's message outstandingly at the assembly, and many people then accepted the faith in the Southern Quarter and the Northern Quarter. He travelled on after the assembly, and intended to go to Eyjafjǫrðr by the eastern route. He baptised many people in Þangbrandslœkr in Øxarfjǫrðr and in Þangbrandspollr by Mývatn. But he did not manage to get any further than Skjálfandafljót because of the power of the people of Eyjafjǫrðr. He then turned back to the Eastern Fjords and taught the faith there. Þangbrandr went west from there by the southern route.

Chapter nine: The killing of Skeggbjǫrn

And when Þangbrandr taught the faith to people in Iceland, many began to libel him. Þorvaldr veili, who lived at Vík in Grímsnes, did so.[49] He composed verse about Þangbrandr, and he spoke this verse to Úlfr the poet:[50]

> To the unshakable Úlfr,
> Uggi's son (I have no hate
> for the wielder of steel), I send,
> straight out of hand, a message,
> that the spear-storm's strengthener drive out
> the spineless wolf of God
> to appease the divine powers,
> and we repulse the other.[51]

Úlfr uttered this verse in reply:

> I'll not catch the cormorant
> to cave of teeth flown, although
> the sender's a well-tried swimmer
> in Hárbarðr's sanctuary's fjord.
> Of the heeder of sail-yard's horse—
> great harm I guard against,
> evil is underway—it's
> unlike me to snap at the fly.[52]

Vetrliði the poet also composed libellous verse about Þangbrandr, as did many others. And when they came to Fljótshlíð in the west—and Guðleifr Arason from Reykjahólar was with him—they learned that Vetrliði the poet was cutting turf together with his servants. Þangbrandr and Guðleifr went and killed him there.[53] This was composed about Guðleifr:

> The shields' tester went south
> in the land, battle tools
> to thrust into poetry's smithy
> of Baldr of rust-hater's bed.
> The manly sword-tester made,
> out for blood, the murderous hammer
> repay Vetrliði the poet
> on the anvil of battle-hat's place.[54]

From there they went west to Grímsnes and found Þorvaldr veili at Hestlœkr and killed him there. They turned back from there and stayed a second winter with Hallr. And in the spring Þangbrandr prepared his ship for departure.

That summer, Þangbrandr was sentenced to outlawry for these killings. He put out to sea, and was driven back to Hítará in Borgarfjǫrðr; that place is now called Þangbrandshróf, down from Skipahylr, and the boulder to which he fastened his ship's cable still stands there on a rock. But once they had arrived there, the inhabitants of the district held a meeting in order to bar them from all trade. Þangbrandr went to Krossaholt and sang mass there and put up crosses.

There was a man called Kolr who lived in Lœkjarbugr. He had so much food that he hardly knew what to do with it. Þangbrandr went there and asked to buy food from him, but he refused to sell any. They took the food and left behind payment for it. Kolr went down to Hítarnes, and made a complaint to Skeggbjǫrn, who lived there. He went with Kolr to meet Þangbrandr, and [they] asked him to have what he had stolen restored and to pay compensation for it, but Þangbrandr refused flatly. They fought on the meadow land down from Steinsholt. Skeggbjǫrn fell there with eight other men. Skeggbjǫrn's burial-mound is there on the meadow, but the others were buried in Landraugsholt beside the meadow there, and the cairns can still be clearly seen. Two of Þangbrandr's men fell.[55]

And when Gizurr the White heard of these events, he invited Þangbrandr to stay with him, and he spent the third winter there. That winter, Þangbrandr's ship was carried out to sea from Hítará and was badly damaged, and came ashore south of Kálfalœkr. Steinunn, mother of Skáld-Refr, composed this about it:[56]

> Þórr drew Þvinnill's animal,
> Þangbrandr's long ship, from land,
> shook the prow's horse and hit it,
> and hurled it against the sand.

> On sea the ski of Atall's land
> will not swim henceforth,
> for a harsh tempest sent by him
> has hewn it into splinters.
>
> Before the bell's keeper (bonds
> destroyed the beach's falcon)
> the slayer of giantess-son
> broke the ox of seagull's place.
> Christ was not watching, when
> the wave-raven drank at the prows.
> Small guard I think God held
> —if any—over Gylfi's reindeer.[57]

In the spring, Þangbrandr went west to Barðastrǫnd to meet Gestr the Wise. There a Norwegian berserk challenged him to a duel. Þangbrandr agreed to this.

The berserk said: 'You will not dare to fight with me once you see what I can do. I walk barefoot through burning fire and I let myself fall unprotected onto the point of my sword, and neither harms me.'

Þangbrandr answers: 'God will decide that.'

Þangbrandr consecrated the fire and made the sign of the cross over the sword. The berserk's feet were burned when he strode through the fire and when he fell onto the sword, it pierced him through, and that brought about his death. Many good men were delighted at this, even though they were heathen. Gestr then had himself prime-signed together with some of his friends.[58]

Þangbrandr left the west and had his ship repaired. He called it Járnmeis.[59] He sailed south across the fjord to Hǫfn and put into the bay and lay there waiting to put out to sea. The place between Hǫfn and Belgsholt has since been called Járnmeishǫfði. He went abroad in the summer to join King Óláfr in Þrándheimr.

CHAPTER TEN

At the assembly that summer there was much discussion about the faith Þangbrandr had preached and some people then blasphemed greatly, but those who were baptised spoke out against the heathen gods, and because of this great divisions arose. Then Hjalti Skeggjason uttered this little verse at the Law-Rock:

> I don't wish to bark at the gods:
> It seems to me Freyja's a bitch.

Runólfr goði, son of Úlfr, son of Jǫrundr goði, took up that verse and prosecuted Hjalti for blasphemy.[60] He showed in this his tyranny and intransigence more than justice, because he was not able to hold the court until he convened it on Øxará bridge and had both ends of the bridge defended with weapons. Then nobody came forward to sum up the case until Þorbjǫrn, son of Þorkell from Guðdalir, joined the court and summed it up.[61] In that court, Hjalti was convicted as a lesser outlaw for blasphemy. That summer he went abroad on a ship he had had made at his home in Þjórsárdalr and took the ship along western Rangá to the sea. And as they travelled down along the river, then a man ran along the bank and had in his hands a spear and shield. Hjalti said to him:

'There is a wisp of straw where your heart should be.'[62]

He threw the spear at Hjalti, but Hjalti grabbed his shield and the spear went into it. Hjalti's men leaped onto the bank and seized him, and asked who he was. He said that he was called Narfi and that Runólfr had sent him for Hjalti's head, and thus he was to free himself from outlawry.

Hjalti said: 'I have a better plan for you. Come abroad with me, and I will get you reprieved.'

Hjalti went abroad and came north to Þrándheimr in the autumn to meet King Óláfr. His father-in-law, Gizurr the White, also arrived from Iceland then.

CHAPTER ELEVEN: ABOUT KJARTAN

King Óláfr had made Hálogaland Christian and he came to Niðaróss in the autumn.[63] There were then many Icelanders there who were in command of ships. Kjartan, son of Óláfr Peacock, Kálfr Ásgeirsson and Bolli Þorleiksson owned one ship. Halldórr, son of Guðmundr the Powerful, also had his own ship there, as did Kolbeinn, son of Þórðr Freysgoði, and Svertingr, son of Runólfr goði, Hallfrøðr Óttarsson and Þórarinn Nefjólfsson.[64] These men were all heathen. They lay at anchor in front of the town and intended to go south along the coast, but they did not get a wind before the king arrived from the north.[65]

One fine day, people from the town went swimming, and those on board the ships noticed that one man was a much better swimmer than the others. Bolli Þorleiksson said to his kinsman Kjartan:

'Why don't you try your hand at swimming against that able man?'

Kjartan said: 'I don't want to contend with him.'

'Where's your competitive spirit, then?' says Bolli, and threw off his clothes.

Then Kjartan leaped up and took off his clothes, and told Bolli to stay where he was. Kjartan jumped into the water and went for the man and pulled him down and held him under for a while. After that they came to the surface, and Kjartan pulled him down a second time. And when Kjartan wanted to come up, the man took hold of Kjartan and held him under for a while. The third time he pulled Kjartan down and held him under for so long that he was on the point of suffocating. Then they headed for shore, and this man asked Kjartan whether he knew with whom he had competed at swimming. He said that he did not know. The man gave Kjartan a scarlet cloak, and said that he must know now with whom he had competed at swimming. Kjartan realised that this man was King Óláfr. He thanked him for the gift in a fitting manner. The heathens were displeased that Kjartan had accepted gifts from the king.[66]

On Michaelmas day, many Icelanders went to hear the divine service and to see the customs of Christians. And when they had returned, they discussed amongst themselves what they thought of their rites. Kjartan spoke well of them, but few others did. The king soon became aware of this and sent for Kjartan, and asked whether he wished to accept Christianity. Kjartan said that he could make the offer such that he would not refuse it. The king asked what he wanted.

'That you give me no less honour here than I can expect in Iceland, even if I do not return there.'

The king agreed to this. Kjartan was then baptised and was entertained at the king's table while he was in white robes.[67]

At the same time, the priest Þangbrandr came to the king from Iceland and told what animosity people had shown him there, and declared that there was no hope that Christianity would make progress there. Then the king became so angry that he had many Icelanders seized and put in chains, threatened some with death and some with maiming, and others were stripped of their possessions. The king said that he would repay them for how disrespectfully their fathers in Iceland had received his communications.

Hjalti and Gizurr then spoke up on behalf of everyone, said that the king had declared that no one could previously have done anything deserving of punishment that there would not be pardon for, if they were willing to have themselves baptised.[68]

Gizurr claimed kinship with the king: his mother Óløf was the daughter of the lord Bǫðvarr, son of Víkinga-Kári, and Ástríðr, mother of King Óláfr, was the daughter of Bǫðvarr's brother, Eiríkr.[69]

Gizurr said that he fully expected that Christianity would make progress in Iceland, if wise counsel were followed.

'But Þangbrandr behaved there as here, in a very unruly manner; he killed several men there, and people thought it hard to take that from a foreigner.'

The Story of the Conversion

King Óláfr said: 'Everyone shall have peace, if you and Hjalti pledge that Christianity will make progress in Iceland. But I will take hostage those men who seem to me most highly bred among the Icelanders until it is found out which way this matter will go.'

For this the king named Kjartan Óláfsson, Halldórr, son of Guðmundr the Powerful, Kolbeinn, son of Þórðr Freysgoði, brother of Brennu-Flosi, and Svertingr, son of Runólfr goði.[70]

When Svertingr was mentioned, one man said: 'Svertingr does not deserve that Hjalti should speak up on his behalf, when his father prosecuted Hjalti without cause.'[71]

Þangbrandr answers: 'It will often prove true that Hjalti will behave better than those given to passionate anger; and treat Hjalti and Gizurr well, sir, because they often repay evil with good.'[72]

Hjalti and Gizurr agreed to plead the king's cause in Iceland, and after that all the Icelanders who were there were released and baptised. King Óláfr stood sponsor to Hallfrøðr at his baptism, because he refused to have himself baptised otherwise. The king then named him 'Troublesome Poet' and gave him a sword to confirm the name.[73]

Gizurr and Hjalti stayed with the king during the winter, and Gizurr sat opposite the king as his drinking partner, further in than the landed men.[74] The Icelandic hostages also stayed with the king [and received] good treatment.

Chapter Twelve: About Gizurr and Hjalti

In the spring, Hjalti and Gizurr prepared their ship to go to Iceland. Many people tried to dissuade Hjalti from going, but he paid no attention to this. That summer King Óláfr left the country to go south to Wendland. It was also then that he sent Leifr Eiríksson to Greenland to preach the faith there. Then Leifr discovered Vínland the Good. He also came across some people on a wreck in the sea. Because of this he was called Leifr the Lucky.[75]

Gizurr and Hjalti arrived off Dyrhólmaóss the same day that Brennu-Flosi rode across Arnarstakksheiðr to the Althing. He then learned from the people who had rowed out to them that his brother Kolbeinn had been taken hostage and all about the mission of Hjalti and his companions, and he communicated this news to the Althing.

They reached Vestmannaeyjar on the same day and moored their ship by Hǫrgaeyrr.[76] There they carried their baggage ashore, along with the wood King Óláfr had had cut for a church, and [he had] stipulated that the church should be built at the place where they put up the gangplanks to land. Before the church was erected, lots were cast for which side of the bay it should stand on and the lots indicated the north. There had previously been sacrifices and heathen places of worship there.[77]

They stayed two nights on the islands before they crossed to the mainland. That was on the day people were riding to the assembly. They were unable to get hold of any transport or riding horses east of Rangá, because every house there belonged to Runólfr's assembly men. They walked until they came to Skeggi Ásgautsson's home at Háfr. He provided them with horses to ride to the assembly, but his son Þorvaldr, who was married to Hjalti's sister Koltorfa, had already ridden from home.[78] And when they got to Laugardalr, they managed to persuade Hjalti to stay behind with eleven other men, because he had been convicted as a lesser outlaw.

Gizurr and his men rode on until they came to Vellankatla near Ǫlfusvatn. Then they sent word to the Althing that their friends and relations should ride to meet them. They had then heard that their enemies intended to bar them from the assembly field. But before they rode off from Vellankatla, Hjalti and his men arrived there and their kinsmen and friends had then come to meet them. They then rode to the assembly with a large company of men and went to the booth belonging to Ásgrímr Elliða-Grímsson, son of Gizurr's sister.[79] Then the heathens thronged together fully armed and it came very close to them fighting, and yet there were some who wished to prevent trouble, even though they were not Christians.

The priest whom King Óláfr had provided for Hjalti and Gizurr was called Þormóðr. He sang mass the next day on the brink of the gorge up above the booth belonging to the people of the Western Fjords. From there they proceeded to the Law-Rock. There were seven men wearing vestments. They had two crosses that now stand in eastern Skarð. One of them marks the height of King Óláfr, the other the height of Hjalti Skeggjason.[80]

The whole assembly was at the Law-Rock. Hjalti and his men had burning incense, and the scent could be smelt as strongly upwind as downwind. Hjalti and Gizurr then announced their mission outstandingly well. And people were amazed by how eloquent they were and how well they spoke, and such great fear came with their words that none of their enemies dared speak against them.[81] But what happened there was that one man after another named witnesses and each side, the Christians and the heathens, declared itself under separate laws from the other.

Then a man came running up and said that there had been a volcanic eruption at Ǫlfus and it was about to engulf the homestead of Þóroddr goði.[82] Then the heathens spoke up:

'It is no wonder that the gods are enraged by such talk.'

Then Snorri goði said: 'What were the gods enraged by when the lava we are standing on here and now was burning?'

After that people left the Law-Rock. Then the Christians asked Síðu-Hallr to speak their law, the one that was to go with Christianity. Hallr agreed with Þorgeirr goði, who then held the office of lawspeaker, for sixty ounces of silver, that he [Þorgeirr] should speak both laws, the Christian and the heathen, and he was not yet baptised at the time. And when people had returned to their booths, Þorgeirr lay down and spread a cloak over his head, and lay like that all day and all night, until the same time the next day.

The heathens then held a well-attended meeting and made a decision to sacrifice two people from each Quarter, and called on the heathen gods not to let Christianity spread throughout the country.

Gizurr and Hjalti held another meeting with the Christians, and they said that they also wished to hold a sacrifice of as many people as the heathens. They said this:

'Heathens sacrifice the worst people, and push them over cliffs and crags, but we shall make our selection on the basis of people's virtues and call it a victory offering to our Lord Jesus Christ.[83] We must therefore live better lives and be more careful to avoid sin than before, and Gizurr and I will come forward as the victory offering for our Quarter.'

And for the Eastern Quarter, these men came forward: Hallr from Síða and Þorleifr from Krossavík, north of Reyðarfjǫrðr, brother of Þórarinn from Seyðarfjǫrðr. Ingileif was their mother. Digr-Ketill had summonsed him for being a Christian at the direction of Brodd-Helgi. Then the weather had become so bad that Ketill was delighted when he arrived at Þorleifr's home in the evening and received good hospitality there. Because of this the summons was dropped.[84]

And from the Northern Quarter, Hlenni the Old and Þorvarðr Spak-Bǫðvarr's son came forward as the victory offering, and from the Western Quarter, Gestr Oddleifsson. There was no other volunteer. This displeased Hjalti and Gizurr. Then Ormr Koðránsson spoke up. He was staying at Gilsbakki, because Hermundr Illugason had married his daughter Gunnhildr:[85]

'There would be someone to volunteer for this if Þorvaldr the Far-Traveller, my brother, were living in the same country as myself. But I will now come forward, if you are willing to accept me.'

They agreed to this, and he was baptised at once.

And the next day, Þorgeirr got up and sent word to the booths that people should go to the Law-Rock. And when people had come to the Law-Rock, he said that he thought matters had come to a bad pass in the land, 'if people are not to have the same law in this country', and asked that they should not do so, and said that battles and warfare would arise from it, and that would clear the way for the laying waste of the land. He also spoke about two kings, one called Dagr who was in Denmark, and the other called Tryggvi who was in Norway.[86] They had for a long time been at war with each other, until inhabitants from both kingdoms had deprived them of power and made peace between them without them wanting it. And that policy had worked out in such a way that in the space of a few years they were sending gifts to one another, and their friendship had lasted as long as they both lived.

'And it seems advisable to me not to let those who oppose each other here with most vehemence prevail, and let us arbitrate between them, so that each side has its own way in something, but we all have the same law and the same religion, because this will prove true: if we tear apart the law, then we tear apart the peace.'

Þorgeirr brought the speech to an end in such a way that both sides agreed to observe the law he chose to proclaim. It was then Þorgeirr's proclamation that all people in Iceland should be baptised and believe in one God, but the old laws should stand as regards the exposure of children and the eating of horse-flesh. People had the right to sacrifice in secret if they wished, but it would be punishable by the lesser outlawry if witnesses were produced. These heathen provisions were abolished some years later. All the people from the Northern and Southern Quarters were baptised in Reykjalaug in Laugardalr when they rode away from the assembly, because they did not want to be immersed in cold water. When Runólfr was baptised, Hjalti said:

'Now we are teaching the old chieftain to nibble on the salt.'[87]

That summer the whole assembly was baptised when people rode home. Most of the Westerners were baptised in Reykjalaug in southern Reykjardalr. Snorri goði had most success with people of the Western Fjords.[88]

Chapter thirteen

The summer Christianity was made law in Iceland, one thousand years had passed from the Incarnation of our Lord Jesus Christ. That summer, King Óláfr disappeared from the Long Serpent by Svǫlðr in the south on the fourth [day] before the ides of September.[89] He had then been king in Norway for five years. Earl Eiríkr Hákonarson took power after him.

Þorvaldr Koðránsson and Stefnir Þorgilsson met up after the disappearance of King Óláfr.[90] They travelled both together far and wide around the world and all the way out to Jerusalem, and from there to Miklagarðr and then to eastern Kœnugarðr along the Dnieper.[91]

Þorvaldr died in Russia a short way from Pallteskja.⁹² He is buried on a mountain there at the church of John the Baptist, and they call him a saint. Brandr the Far-Traveller says this:

> I have come
> where Christ grants
> rest to Þorvaldr
> Koðrán's son.
> He is buried there
> on a high mountain
> up in Drafn
> at John's Church.⁹³

Stefnir then went north to Denmark.⁹⁴ And when he got to Denmark, he uttered this verse:

> I will not name,
> I'll take close aim:
> hooked is the nose
> of the nithing
> who lured King Sveinn
> from the land
> and drew Tryggvi's son
> into a trap.⁹⁵

Earl Sigvaldi thought he recognised a reference to himself in this verse, and because of that he had Stefnir killed.⁹⁶

Ari the Old has said this.⁹⁷

CHAPTER FOURTEEN: ABOUT GIZURR

Gizurr the White lived in Hǫfði before he built a farm in Skálaholt and moved his household there.⁹⁸ He set his whole mind on strengthening Christianity. He sent his son Ísleifr south to Saxland, and [Ísleifr] went to school there in a town called Herfurða.⁹⁹ And when he returned to Iceland, he married Dalla Þorvaldsdóttir, and their sons were Gizurr and Teitr the Enterprising of Haukadalr and Þorvaldr.¹⁰⁰

At first there were foreign bishops here teaching Christian doctrine. But when the people of the country realised what an excellent cleric Ísleifr was, they asked him to go abroad and have himself consecrated bishop, and he granted them this. He was fifty years old when he was consecrated bishop. Leo IX was then pope. He spent the following winter in Norway, and then went to Iceland, and was bishop for twenty-four years. He taught many excellent men and had them ordained priests, and two of them later became bishops: St Jón Ǫgmundarson and Kolr, bishop of the people of Vík.

Bishop Ísleifr died in Skálaholt on the third [day] before the nones of July;[101] that was on a Sunday. He had then been bishop for twenty-four years, and eighty years had then passed from the disappearance of King Óláfr Tryggvason. Ari the Learned, who has said most about the events written down here, was present at his burial when he was twelve years old.

Chapter fifteen: Gizurr consecrated bishop

After the death of Bishop Ísleifr, the people of the country asked his son Gizurr to be consecrated bishop. He went abroad and was consecrated bishop two years after the death of Bishop Ísleifr, in the days of King Óláfr the Peaceful, king of Norway. Gregory VII was then pope in Rome. Gizurr spent the winter after his consecration in Denmark, and returned to Iceland the following summer.[102] And when he had been in Iceland for one year, Markús Skeggjason took up the office of lawspeaker. He has been the wisest of Iceland's lawspeakers apart from Skapti.[103]

Bishop Gizurr was so popular with the people of the country that everyone was willing to obey his commands and prohibitions,[104] and through the popularity of Bishop Gizurr and the persuasions of the priest Sæmundr the Learned, who has been the best cleric in Iceland, and with the guidance of the lawspeaker Markús and other chieftains, it was made law that everyone should reckon up and value their property, whether it was in land or in movable possessions, and swear an oath that the valuation was correct and pay a tithe on it. It is a great mark of how obedient the people of the country were to the man who brought this about, that all the land was valued and all the property that was on it, and it was made law that it should be so as long as the land was inhabited.

Chapter sixteen: On tithing

Bishop Gizurr also laid down a law that the episcopal see in Iceland should be in Skálaholt, and he endowed the see with the estate there and many other assets both in land and movable property.

And when he thought that the see had become as rich as he wished, then he gave more than a quarter of his diocese to the end that there should be two episcopal sees in Iceland rather than one, just as the Northerners had asked him. And he had first had all the householders in Iceland counted, and there were then a full 840 in the Eastern Quarter and 1200 in the Southern Quarter and 1080 in the Western Quarter and 1440 in the Northern

Quarter, and only those who had to pay the assembly attendance dues were counted.

When Bishop Gizurr had been bishop for twenty-five years, Úlfheðinn Gunnarson took up the office of lawspeaker, for Markús was then dead. Then Bergþórr Hrafnsson took up the office of lawspeaker. And the first summer he spoke the law, a new pronouncement was made that the laws should be written down the following winter at the home of Hafliði Másson with the guidance of Bergþórr and other wise men. And they were to make new provisions in all cases where these seemed better to them than the old laws, and they were to be proclaimed the following summer and all those were to be kept which a majority of people did not oppose. Then the Treatment of Homicide law and many other things in the laws were written down and read aloud the following summer in the Law Council, and everyone was very pleased with this.

The bishop was forty when he was consecrated bishop, and when he had been bishop for twenty-four years, Jón, son of Qgmundr and Þorgerðr, daughter of Egill, son of Hallr from Síða, was consecrated bishop. Jón was then fifty-four. He was the first bishop at Hólar in Hjaltadalr.

Chapter Seventeen: The Death of Bishop Gizurr

Bishop Gizurr made the land so peaceful, that no great conflicts arose between chieftains, and the carrying of weapons almost ceased.[105] At that time, most men of high rank were educated and ordained priests, even though they were chieftains, as was Hallr Teitsson in Haukadalr and Sæmundr the Learned, Magnús Þórðarson in Reykjaholt, Símon Jǫrundarson in Bœr, Guðmundr Brandsson in Hjarðarholt, Ari the Learned, Ingimundr Einarsson at Hólar, Ketill Þorsteinsson at Mǫðruvellir in the north and Ketill Guðmundarson, the priest Jón Þorvarðsson and many others, though their names are not written down [here].[106]

Bishop Gizurr had Þorlákr, son of Runólfr Þorleiksson, consecrated bishop during his lifetime. Þorlákr was then thirty-two years old. Bishop Gizurr died in Skálaholt when he had been bishop for thirty-six years. That was thirty nights after Bishop Þorlákr had been consecrated. It was the third day of the week on the fifth [day] before the calends of June.[107] That year Pope Paschal died, as did Kirjalax king of the Greeks[108] and Baldwin king of Jerusalem and Arnulf patriarch in Jerusalem and Philip king of the Swedes. Iceland had then been inhabited for two hundred and forty years, the first half in heathendom and the second in Christianity. 1118 years had then passed from the Incarnation of our Lord Jesus Christ.

Chapter eighteen

The year that Bishop Gizurr died, there was a severe famine in Iceland.[109] There was such a violent storm during the 'quiet-bell' days that people were not able to hold the divine service in churches in some districts in the north of the country.[110] And on Good Friday, a merchant ship was hurled ashore beneath Eyjafjǫll and turned over in the air and came down upside down. It had twenty-seven rowing benches. On the first day of Easter, few people were able to go to the divine service to receive communion, and some died of exposure.

There was another storm the summer after Gizurr's death on the day people were riding to the assembly. The church at Þingvǫllr, for which King Haraldr Sigurðarson had had wood cut, was then destroyed.[111] That summer, thirty-five ships came out here and many were wrecked against the coast, and some broke apart in the sea beneath people, but only eight got away, including those that were already here, and none of them reached land before Michaelmas. Because of the large number of people [on the ships], there was a severe famine here.[112]

When Bishop Gizurr died, these were the greatest chieftains in Iceland: Hafliði Másson in the north and the sons of Ásbjǫrn Arnórsson in Skagafjǫrðr, Þorgeirr Hallason and the priest Ketill Þorsteinsson. And in the east, Gizurr Einarsson, Sigmundr Þorgilsson—he died that year on pilgrimage to Rome. And in the south, Hallr Teitsson, Skúli Egilsson. And in the west, Styrmir Hreinsson, Halldórr Egilsson, Þorgils Oddason, Þórðr Gilsson, Þórðr Þorvaldsson in Vatsfjǫrðr.[113]

One year after the death of Bishop Gizurr, Þorsteinn Hallvarðsson, a fine man, was killed.[114] And the following year there were many people at the assembly. There had been such great loss of life that year that the priest Sæmundr the Learned said at the assembly that no fewer people must have died of illness than had then come to the assembly.

That summer there was a great throng at the courts. Then Þorgils Oddason wounded Hafliði Másson. The case did not reach legal judgement. Þorgils was outlawed for the injury, and remained in Iceland as an outlaw over the winter.[115] There was then so little carrying of weapons that there was only one steel cap at the Althing, and almost every householder who was then in Iceland rode to the assembly.

And in the spring three years after the death of Bishop Gizurr, Bishop Jón at Hólar died on the ninth [day] before the calends of May.[116] That summer, Hafliði Másson rode to the assembly with 1440 men, and Þorgils Oddason with 840 men. They reached a settlement at the assembly with

Þorgils giving Hafliði sole arbitration. And he awarded sixty hundreds of six-ell ounce-units of marketable wares to be paid in gold or refined silver or suitable goods.[117] Hafliði himself was to value them, or those he appointed.

That summer Ketill Þorsteinsson of Mǫðruvellir was elected bishop in place of Bishop Jón, and he went abroad that summer.[118]

Hafliði Másson was first married to Þuríðr, daughter of Þórðr Sturluson. Their son was called Þórðr. He married Solvǫr, daughter of Ásgrímr Þórhallsson. Their son was called Ívarr.[119] Hafliði later married Rannveig, daughter of Teitr from Haukadalr. Their daughter was called Sigríðr, whom Þórðr in Vatsfjǫrði married. Their sons were Þórðr and Páll. Hafliði and Rannveig's second daughter was called Valgerðr; the priest Ingimundr, son of Illugi and Oddný, daughter of Þorkell Gellisson, married her.[120] Their son was Illugi, who drowned when he was moving lime for the stone church he had intended to build at Breiðabólstaðr in Vestrhóp.[121]

Earl Rǫgnvaldr kali was killed five nights after the first feast-day of Mary, and King Óláfr Tryggvason fought on the Long Serpent the day after the second feast-day of Mary.[122]

NOTES TO THE STORY OF THE CONVERSION

[1] The same genealogy is given in *Njáls saga* (*ÍF* XII 285), but Eilífr's descent is slightly different in *Landnámabók* (*ÍF* I 227–8) and *Þorvalds þáttr víðfǫrla* (*ÓTM* I 280), where he is the son of Atli, son of Skíði the Old, son of Bárðr in Áll (*jarl* in *Óláfs saga Tryggvasonar in mesta*). Only the *Hauksbók* version of *Landnámabók* mentions that Koðrán is *faðir Þorvalds víðfǫrla* (see *ÍF* I 227, note 9).

[2] According to a long and eulogistic account of Þorvaldr's youth in *Þorvalds þáttr*, Þorvaldr travelled to Denmark, became one of Sveinn Forkbeard's men and raided with him in the British Isles (*ÓTM* I 282–4). He won fame and popularity through giving his money to the poor and releasing captives, and eventually made good use of this by saving the king from captivity in Bretland (probably Wales). *ASC* 126–9, 134–6, 143–4 also mentions that Sveinn raided in England, but this was much later than the raids mentioned here.

[3] I.e. Saxony (which is south of Norway). On spatial orientation outside of Norway in the sagas, see Jackson 1998–2001: 76–81.

[4] For other sources on Friðrekr, see note 77 to *Íslendingabók* ch. 8 above.

[5] This looks back to the dating of the settlement to 874 in the *Sturlubók* and *Hauksbók* redactions of *Landnámabók* (*ÍF* I 42; see p. 16, note 14 above). Following *Kristni saga*, most Icelandic annals date Friðrekr's arrival in Iceland to 981; *Flateyjarbók* dates it to 982. At the end of *Þorvalds þáttr*, the missionaries' arrival in Iceland is dated to the year 981, one hundred and six years after the settlement (*ÓTM* I 300).

[6] The saga's lists of the greatest chieftains in the land should be compared with those in the *Sturlubók* and *Hauksbók* redactions of *Landnámabók* (*ÍF* I 209–10, 286, 334–6, 394–7). If, as seems likely, they are original to the saga, they suggest a close link with *Landnámabók* and confirm the strong historical interests of the author. Over half the chieftains here are sons or descendants of the settlers and chieftains in the lists in *Landnámabók*, and others are mentioned elsewhere in that work; some are also well known from sagas of Icelanders. On Víga-Glúmr, see *Víga-Glúms saga* and *Reykdœla saga* (*ÍF* IX and X). On Arnórr kerlingarnef, grandson of Hǫfða-Þórðr and great-grandfather of the lawspeaker Úlfheðinn Gunnarsson's wife, see *ÓTM* II 180–84 and *Flb* I 484–8. Starri and his brothers (Þorkell, Hróaldr and Þorgeirr) are mentioned in *Njáls saga* (*ÍF* XII 300, 352) and Starri in *Grettis saga* (*ÍF* VII 227); their sister Gunnhildr was the great-grandmother of Hafliði Másson. Ari Másson was father of Þangbrandr's companion Guðleifr and ancestor of Bishop Guðmundr Arason; *Landnámabók* (*ÍF* I 162) tells on the authority of Þorkell Gellisson that he was baptised in 'the land of white men', probably Scotland (*Alba*). On Ásgeirr Knattarson and his father-in-law Óláfr Peacock, see *Egils saga* (*ÍF* II 242) and *Laxdœla saga* (*ÍF* V). On Víga-Styrr, see *Heiðarvíga saga* (*ÍF* III). Snorri's takeover of the farm at Helgafell is mentioned in *Eyrbyggja saga* and *Ævi Snorra goða* (*ÍF* IV 24–6, 186) and *Gísla saga* (*ÍF* VI 117). On Þorsteinn, son of Egill Skalla-Grímsson, see *Egils saga* (*ÍF* II 274–300) and *Laxdœla saga* (*ÍF* V 114, 156–8). On Illugi the Red, whose brother Sǫlvi was the grandfather of the priest Magnús Þórðarson (ch. 17), see *Harðar saga* (*ÍF* XIII). On Valgarðr at Hof and his nephew Runólfr, whose son Svertingr was a hostage in 998, see *Njáls saga* (*ÍF* XII) and *Kristni saga* chs 10–12. On the sons of

Qrnólfr (Arnórr and Halldórr), see *Njáls saga* (*ÍF* XII 142, 291) and *Droplaugarsona saga* (*ÍF* XI 156). On the sons of Þórðr Freysgoði, two of whom appear later in this saga (Brennu-Flosi and Kolbeinn), see *Njáls saga* (*ÍF* XII 238). On Helgi Ásbjarnarson, his brother-in-law Víga-Bjarni, son of Brodd-Helgi, and Brodd-Helgi's brother-in-law Geitir, see *Vápnfirðinga saga*, *Droplaugarsona saga* and *Fljótsdæla saga* (all in *ÍF* XI); Geitir's grandson was Þorsteinn uxafótr 'ox's foot' (*Flb* I 275–8). On Þorkell Moon, Gizurr the White, Hjalti Skeggjason, Síðu-Hallr (Hallr on Síða), Eyjólfr Valgerðarson and Eyjólfr the Grey, see notes 52, 61, 108, 125 to *Íslendingabók*. On Þorvarðr Spak-Bǫðvarsson, Þorkell krafla, Gestr the Wise, Þóroddr goði, and Ásgrímr Elliða-Grímsson, see notes 7, 13, 58, 79, 82 below.

[7] Qnundr and Hlenni are both mentioned in *Landnámabók* (*ÍF* I 270–71, 278–9). Hlenni also appears in *Ljósvetninga saga* (*ÍF* X 54), *Njáls saga* (*ÍF* XII 271) and *Víga-Glúms saga* (*ÍF* IX 36), where he is said to be the son of Qrnólfr. On Þorvarðr Spak-Bǫðvarsson, see *ÓTM* II 178–80 and *Flb* I 487, where his ancestry is traced back to King Eiríkr at Uppsala and King Burizleifr of Russia (cf. *ÍF* I 236–7). The compiler of *ÓTM* nicknames him *hinn kristni* 'the Christian' and comments: 'Most people say that Þorvarðr Spak-Bǫðvarsson was baptised by Bishop Friðrekr, but the monk Gunnlaugr mentions that some people think he was baptised in England and brought from there wood for the church he had made on his farm'. This alternative tradition is not mentioned in *Þorvalds þáttr* or elsewhere.

[8] Prime-signing (Latin *primum signum* or *prima signatio*, cf. OF *primseignier*, ME *primseinen*) was originally a rite accompanying entry into the catechumenate and later one of the rituals accompanying baptism; it consisted in making the sign of the cross (*signare*) on the forehead (Molland 1968). Norse sources suggest that it was adopted prior to or even instead of baptism during the conversion period, because it gave the recipient the right to have dealings with Christians. Egill and Gísli, for example, were both prime-signed abroad (*ÍF* II 128–9, *ÍF* VI xlvi) and, in some accounts, Óláfr Tryggvason was prime-signed in Greece (*Flb* I 127). According to *Valla-Ljóts saga* (*ÍF* IX 237), Eyjólfr was prime-signed in Iceland just before his death.

[9] The Norse term is *ármaðr*, which in prose usually means 'steward', and perhaps we are meant to understand that the spirit is a steward to Koðrán's goods. However, the evidence of place-names (e.g. Ármannsfell) and folk-tales suggests that *ármaðr* could also refer to a *landvættr* or nature spirit living in mountains, hills and rocks (see Einar Ól. Sveinsson 2003: 161–3, and Jón Árnason 1954–61: I 201–2 on Jǫrundr, Ásmundr and Ármann). These beings later developed into elves and trolls, who typically oppose the coming of Christianity in kings' sagas, bishops' sagas and later folk-tales (see, for example, Oddr Snorrason 1932: 174–9, and *Guðmundar saga byskups* in *BS* I 560–61, 598–9). Similar beings are mentioned in *Landnámabók* (*ÍF* I 330–31), *Heimskringla* (*ÍF* XXVI 270–72) and *Þiðranda þáttr ok Þorhalls* (*ÓTM* II 150); and in a sermon in *Hauksbók* (1892–6: 167), women are forbidden to offer sacrifices to nature spirits living in stones. Sacrifice to stones is also mentioned in *Landnámabók* and *Harðar saga* (*ÍF* I 273; XIII 90–91). In *Þorvalds þáttr*, the spirit is called *spámaðr* 'prophet', a term not usually applied to non-humans, but which aids comparison with the Christian bishop, and so underlines the opposition between paganism and Christianity (*ÓTM* I 285–6).

[10] Compare the much longer and more didactic version of these events in *Þorvalds þáttr* (*ÓTM* I 284–8). Koðrán's conversion is also mentioned briefly in *Vatnsdæla saga* (*ÍF* VIII 124).

[11] This information about Ormr only occurs in *Kristni saga*, one of many indications that the author was well acquainted with traditions from the west of Iceland. Ormr is not known from elsewhere, but married into well-known families: his first father-in-law Ǫzurr was the brother of Þóroddr goði (*ÍF* I 392–3, II 241–2 and note 85) and his son-in-law, Hermundr Illugason, was the brother of Gunnlaugr ormstunga 'Serpent-Tongue' (*ÍF* III 58–9). Ormr's grandson, also called Ormr, married Herdís Bollason, the granddaughter of Guðrún from *Laxdæla saga* (*ÍF* V 226–7). Ormr's second father-in-law, Steinmóðr, was the grandson of Úlfljótr (*ÍF* I 266; *Íslendingabók* ch. 2, note 24) and his son-in-law Skúli was son of Þorsteinn Egilsson and a well-known poet; he was bowman to Earl Eiríkr at the Battle of Svǫlðr (*ÍF* II 276, 300; Oddr Snorrason 1932: 209–10). The genealogy conflicts with that given later in the saga (ch. 12), where Ormr's daughter is called Gunnhildr instead of Yngvildr. In *ÓTM* II 194, Hermundr Illugason is said to be married to Ormr's sister Gunnhildr, but naming patterns in the family line suggest that *Kristni saga* is more correct (see *ÍF* XV clxxvii).

[12] Óláfr's farm is elsewhere called Haukagil (*ÍF* VIII 98) and has probably been confused here with the name of Koðrán's farm Giljá. Óláfr, grandfather and fosterfather of Hallfreðr vandræðaskáld 'the troublesome poet' appears in *Vatnsdæla saga* and *Hallfreðar saga*. In *Þorvalds þáttr*, the feast is given in honour of Þorvaldr's marriage to his daughter Vigdís, but other sources state more reliably that she was married to Þorkell krafla (*ÓTM* I 288; II 306; *Skarðsárbók* 1958: 96).

[13] Þorkell krafla ('pawing') was the illegitimate son of Þorgrímr Kárnsárgoði and got his nickname from his exposure at birth, when he *kraflaði* 'pawed, scratched' at the cloth laid over his face (*ÍF* VIII 98). He plays a central role in *Vatnsdæla saga*, and also appears in *Landnámabók* (*ÍF* I 223), *Hallfreðar saga* (*ÍF* VIII 188–90, 193) and *Grettis saga* (*ÍF* VII 35).

[14] These are all typical characteristics of berserks in sagas of Icelanders, where they are primarily seen as a social menace, rather than the formidable warriors of the kings' sagas (Blaney 1982). Here, as in other conversion narratives, the berserks are representatives of paganism, and Friðrekr must use consecrated objects to overcome them. Indeed, in *Þorvalds þáttr*, the berserks are guests among the heathens rather than intruders. It is likely that this scene is modelled on Þangbrandr's defeat of a berserk in similar fashion at Gestr the Wise's (*Kristni saga* ch. 9 and *ÍF* XV 140, note 3).

[15] Both berserks are called 'Hawk' and the place is therefore called 'Hawks' Gill' after them. It seems likely that this is an example of back-formation, whereby an event is created out of a place-name.

[16] The scene with the berserks also occurs in *Þorvalds þáttr* (*ÓTM* I 288–90) and in *Vatnsdæla saga* (*ÍF* VIII 124–6), but *Kristni saga* is closest to (and probably borrows from) the version in *Vatnsdæla saga*, where Þorkell krafla is the main character (see Ólsen 1893: 311; Duke [Grønlie] 1998–2001: 350–53; *ÍF* XV clxxv). In the saga, Þorkell refuses to be baptised until the legal conversion of Iceland in the year 1000, but does admit an affinity with the new religion (*en kvazk þó hyggja,*

at sjá mundi góð 'but said, however, he thought that it must be good'). *Þorvalds þáttr* includes an additional scene in which Bishop Friðrekr, in full vestments, strides through the fire himself unharmed. This combines elements of the ordeal and the trial of strength, and recalls the fiery furnace scene in Daniel 3 and its many retellings in saints' lives.

[17] Þórarinn fylsenni was the son of Þórðr gellir, and his wife Friðgerðr was the daughter of Hǫfða-Þórðr. Her sister Herdís was married to Þorvaldr's uncle, Atli the Strong (*ÍF* I 241–2; V 13; VII 90–91). There are some later folk-tales about Skeggi, according to which he remained obdurately pagan throughout his life (Jón Árnason 1954–61: I 143–4).

[18] The version of this scene in *Þorvalds þáttr* locates Friðgerðr *inni* 'inside', probably at home (*ÓTM* I 290). The confrontation between Christian missionary and pagan female is a motif found elsewhere (compare Þangbrandr's encounter with Steinunn in ch. 9) and seems likely to reflect the historical role women played in home-based cults during the pagan period (Steinsland 1985–8; Grønlie 2006).

[19] This verse appears slightly differently in two manuscripts of *Þorvalds þáttr*, where the third and fourth lines run: 'We got moderate praise from the distributor of rings (generous man)' (*ÍF* XV clxxi–clxxiv). Although the reading in *Kristni saga* is probably more original, the other is thought-provoking in the contrast it draws between men and women's response to the new faith. 'Sprinkler of blood-dipped branch' (*hlauttein*) is a kenning for a pagan priest, a branch (*tein*) being used like an aspergillum, to sprinkle blood from the sacrificed animal (*hlaut*) around the temple (cf. *ÍF* IV 8–9). Old Norse *gyðja* is the feminine form of *goði* 'priest-chieftain' and can mean either 'priestess' or 'goddess'.

[20] The legal obligation under paganism for householders to pay tax for the support of the temple is mentioned in a number of sagas of Icelanders (*ÍF* II 293; IV 9; XI 33; XIII 193) and in the account of Úlfljótr's law in *Hauksbók* and related texts (*ÍF* I 315). It seems likely, however, that this is modelled on the Christian tithes or on Church taxes raised before tithes were introduced (Olsen 1966: 43–8).

[21] Klaufi is mentioned in *Víga-Glúms saga* (*ÍF* IX 35–6). His father was married to Þuríðr, daughter of Hǫfða-Þórðr and sister to the above Friðgerðr.

[22] Þorvarðr's brother Arngeirr is mentioned in *Sturl* I 56, 117 as ancestor to the powerful family of Ásbirnings. In *Þorvalds þáttr*, where the story is told slightly differently, a third brother, Þórðr, is also mentioned (*ÓTM* I 292–3).

[23] Ólafur Halldórsson notes that this may be the first literary example of the folk-tale motif whereby a hidden power protects itself by making a church or other building appear to be on fire (*ÍF* XV clxxix and references there). These may be related to the well-known story in Gregory's *Dialogues* of how an idol, thrown into a monastery kitchen, caused the illusion that it was on fire (*HMS* I 165–6). What is unusual here is that God, rather than heathen spirits, causes the illusion: *Þorvalds þáttr* explicitly makes it an example of how 'God protected his house' (*ÓTM* I 292).

[24] The folk-tale motif of the arrows is told almost unchanged of Earl Eiríkr in Oddr Snorrason 1932: 227 (cf. *ÍF* XXVI 362 and *ÓTM* II 274–5) and, using apples rather than arrows, in *Yngvars saga víðfǫrla* (*FN* III 386).

[25] The date at which this church was built is also mentioned in *Þorvalds þáttr* (*ÓTM* I 292–3) and the Icelandic annals (*anno* 984). Recent excavations have

shown that three churches stood on this site between the early eleventh and the late thirteenth centuries, but there is no evidence of anything earlier (*ÍF* XV 10, note 1). Bótólfr was a Norwegian and came to Hólar, where he was bishop 1238–46, from the Augustinian monastery of Helgisetr in Niðaróss (*Sturl* I 445).

[26] In *Landnámabók* (*ÍF* I 269–70), Heðinn is given the nickname *inn mildi* 'the generous' and said to have built Svalbarð 'sixteen years before the conversion', which suggests some confused memory of the date of Þorvarðr's church. It is likely that his role here has been influenced by that of his namesake Galdra-Heðinn in the accounts of Þangbrandr's mission (see ch. 8 and *ÍF* XV clxxviii–clxxix).

[27] Old Norse *bera*, like English 'to bear' can mean both 'to carry' and 'to give birth to' and this play on words is central to the meaning of the verse. On the one hand, it states quite innocently that the bishop has carried nine children (to baptism?) and perhaps that Þorvaldr was their godfather. On the other, Þorvaldr is accused of fathering children on the bishop in a homosexual relationship. This appears to be a conventional and symbolic insult, implying cowardice and effeminacy, and parallels to the wording of the verse can be found in both Eddic verse and saga literature (Kuhn 1962: 103, 136; *ÍF* XII 314). The ambiguity is probably intended as some form of protection against legal retribution, since the law allowed the victims of such libel (*níð*) to kill the perpetrator(s) with impunity (see *Grágás* 1980–2000: II 197–9).

[28] The helpfulness of birds is a common motif in Irish saints' lives (*VSH* I cxlvi), although no exact parallel to this miracle is found there. It is perhaps more reminiscent of the sudden mists that are conjured up to prevent attacks in the sagas, and of which *Njáls saga* (*ÍF* XII 38) provides a good example.

[29] Haraldr Gormsson, nicknamed 'Bluetooth' (died 985/8), proclaimed on his monument at Jelling that he had 'made the Danes Christian'. He was probably baptised some time before 965, when Otto I recognised him as Christian ruler of Denmark (Lund 1997: 164–5). According to Adam of Bremen ii.3–4 (2002: 55–7, 71), Archbishop Adaldag of Bremen (937–88) had set up three episcopal sees in Jutland in 948 at Schleswig, Ribe and Aarhus, and consecrated a number of bishops without sees, including a certain Adalbrecht. There is no evidence that these bishops ever made it to Denmark and no historical account of a Bishop Albert (Adalbert) of Bremen at this time; possibly Archbishop Adaldag is meant, and what lies behind this account is a tradition that he visited Jutland when he established the sees there. In *Óláfs saga Tryggvasonar in mesta*, the scene is set in Bremen, not in Jutland, perhaps because it has an alternative account of the establishment of these sees under Archbishop Unni (*ÓTM* I 121; *ÍF* XV clxxxv–clxxxvi).

[30] There was no Archbishop Hubert of Canterbury before Hubert Walter (1193–1205).

[31] According to *Heimskringla* (*ÍF* XXVI 262–3), Óláfr spent three years in Wendland immediately after his participation in the conquest of Denmark. What Þangbrandr is doing there is not clear. *ÓTM* I 148–9 places the meeting in Saxony in the context of Óláfr's raids in Frisia, Saxony and Flanders.

[32] In fact, the Scilly Isles are off the coast of Cornwall; the author was perhaps misled by Oddr Snorrason, who says that they are 'a short way from Ireland'. The saga follows here the account of Óláfr's baptism given in Theodoricus 1998: 10,

HN 19–20, Oddr Snorrason 1932: 43–5, *Fagrskinna* 2004: 114 and *Heimskringla* (*ÍF* XXVI 266–7). *Ágrip* 1995: 28–31 sets the scene in England.

[33] In *ÓTM* I 132–44, Otto the Young (reigned 983–1002) is credited with conquering Denmark and converting Haraldr Gormsson; *Kristni saga* perhaps shares this error when it refers to Otto having sent a hostage to Denmark. Other Icelandic sources refer either to an unspecified Otto (*ÍF* XXVI 255–62) or to Otto the Red, probably Otto II, who did in fact carry out a punitive raid against Haraldr in 974 (*Jómsvíkinga saga* 1969: 85–97; Oddr Snorrason 1932: 47–53; *ÍF* XXXV 93–4; see further Ólafur Halldórsson 2000: 72). *Veraldar saga* (1944: 71) follows Adam of Bremen (ii.3; 2002: 55–6) in attributing the conquest to Otto I, but this is not right. Óláfr is involved in this military conquest in most of the Icelandic sources, despite the fact that he was not, according to *Heimskringla*, as yet baptised.

[34] Hólmgarðr is the Norse name for Novgorod, where Snorri tells us that Óláfr spent his youth (*ÍF* XXVI 231); it became a major trading centre for Scandinavians in Russia during the ninth century. The only saga of Óláfr in which he travels to Norway from Russia is Oddr Snorrason's, but Oddr does not mention the church on Mostr until later, after Óláfr has made a trip to England to acquire missionaries (1932: 65–6, 187). According to *Heimskringla* (*ÍF* XXVI 291–3; cf. *ÓTM* I 208–10, 220–21), on the other hand, Óláfr goes straight from Ireland to Norway, and first takes land on Mostr, where he later has a church built. Either the compiler is using another saga of Óláfr (i.e. Gunnlaugr's) or he is conflating the information provided by Oddr Snorrason and Snorri Sturluson. On stories about the island Mostr, see further Ólafur Halldórsson 1990: 409–14.

[35] Gói, the second month in the Icelandic winter half-year, began on the Sunday between 8th and 14th February every year—that is, 10th February in 995 (Sveinbjǫrn Rafnsson 2001: 103–04).

[36] Helgi bjóla (or bjólan; from the Irish proper name *Béol(l)án* 'alive and safe', perhaps confused with Icelandic *bjóla* 'bucket?'), son of Ketill Flatnose, came to Iceland from the Hebrides and was a Christian (*ÍF* I 50–51, 396). His sons are named differently in *Landnámabók* and *Kjalnesinga saga*, but Eilífr is not mentioned in either, unless he can be identified with the Eilífr on Helgi's ship who lived at Eilífsdalr (*ÍF* XIV 3). Although one might expect a link between Stefnir's Christianity and that of his great-grandfather, none is made, and *ÓTM* I 301 says that he was baptised in Denmark during travels abroad. Stefnir is mentioned only in Oddr Snorrason's *Óláfs saga Tryggvasonar*, *Kristni saga* and *Óláfs saga Tryggvasonar in mesta*, and the name Stefnir does not appear to have been used in Iceland before the fourteenth century, except as a rendition of the English name Stephen (*ÍF* XV 103, note 3). If there is a deliberate parallel with the biblical proto-martyr Stephen, it resides in little more than the name (Sveinbjǫrn Rafnsson 2001: 101, note).

[37] This is not unusual behaviour for a medieval missionary. The destruction of temples and idols served as proof of the power of the Christian God over heathen gods, and is a common feature in saints' lives (cf. *HMS* I 559–60, 571).

[38] The verse uses the following two kennings: 'ship's hollow' (hold) and 'prow-falcon' (ship). The Norse for this last is *stafnvalr* and there is probably a deliberate pun on Stefnir's name, which may mean either 'steersman' from the verb *stefna*

'to steer' or 'man in the bows' from *stafn* 'prow'. *Æsir* (sg. *Áss*) is a name for one race of Norse gods, and the word *bǫnd* (literally 'bonds') relates to the gods in their power to hold all things together, which contrasts neatly with the dissolution of Stefnir's ship. The authenticity of this verse has been questioned because of its similarity to the verses composed about Þangbrandr's shipwreck (see ch. 9 and *ÍF* XV cxxxii), but it has also been suggested that there may have been a tradition of invective against missionaries using the motif of the failed sea-voyage (Jesch 1987: 12–13). Interestingly, the content of the verse is undermined by the prose frame, which states that Stefnir's ship was not so badly damaged after all (Grønlie 2004: 464–6).

[39] The specificity of this law has to do with the structure of the kinship system in Iceland, which stretched to collaterals at the fifth remove (Hastrup 1985: 76; cf. *Grágás* 1980–2000: I 175). Brothers and first cousins were too close to prosecute family members, but prosecution by those more distantly related than fourth cousins would lead to wealth and property passing outside the family.

[40] The sons of Ósvífr are named in *Landnámabók* as Óspakr, Þórólfr, Torráðr, Einarr, Þorkell and Þorbjǫrn (*ÍF* I 123), and in *Laxdœla saga* as Óspakr, Helgi, Vandráðr, Torráðr and Þórólfr (*ÍF* V 85–6). Sveinbjǫrn Rafnsson (2001: 105–06) has pointed out that Torráðr and Vandráðr are made-up names generally used as substitutes for unknown names or for people in disguise. The report that Óspakr refused to join the prosecution is often attributed to the status of Archbishop Eysteinn of Niðaróss (1160–88), who was his great-great-grandson (*ÍF* V 157; XXVIII 120). Ósvífr was the great-grandson of Helgi bjóla's brother Bjǫrn the Easterner, and was therefore Stefnir's third cousin.

[41] This must be a reference to the part played by the sons of Ósvífr in the death of Kjartan Óláfsson. They were all, with the possible exception of Óspakr, outlawed for his killing (*ÍF* V 156, 158).

[42] This account of how Þangbrandr came to be sent to Iceland is also found in *Heimskringla* (*ÍF* XXVI 319) and *ÓTM* II 65–6. It draws upon a common motif in short stories about Óláfr Tryggvason and Óláfr Haraldsson, wherein those who fall into the king's disfavour are assigned evangelising missions in order to regain it (cf. *Flb* I 421–2, II 231).

[43] 28th September at 3 pm.

[44] This replaces a long speech in *ÓTM* II 152–3. Runic inscriptions suggest that St Michael was a popular saint in Scandinavia during the conversion period, and there is an early reference to him in an eleventh-century skaldic verse by the Icelandic poet Arnórr jarlaskáld (Edwards 1982–5: 40–41; Whaley 1998: 312). St Michael was believed to aid the individual Christian against the devil and to escort souls to God after death. *Njáls saga* (*ÍF* XII 257) describes him as weighing up good and evil deeds and he is often depicted with scales in church art. There are twelfth-century sermons on St Michael in the Icelandic and Norwegian Homily Books and a fourteenth-century life by Bergr Sokkason (*Homiliu-bók* 1872: 88–92; *Gamal Norsk Homiliebok* 1931: 136–43; *HMS* I 676–713).

[45] The impression made by the rituals of Christian worship is emphasised in a number of related narratives, including Koðrán's conversion in *Þorvalds þáttr* (*ÓTM* I 284) and Kjartan's conversion in *Heimskringla* (*ÍF* XXVI 329–30).

[46] Easter and Pentecost were the canonical seasons for baptism until the twelfth

century and beyond, but it was performed out of season from an early date in emergencies and during missions to the pagans (Cramer 1993: 137–8).

[47] Ketill the Foolish was the grandson of Ketill Flatnose and came to Iceland from the Hebrides, where his family had been baptised. This genealogy is missing a link: according to *Landnámabók* and *Laxdœla saga*, Surtr was the son of Þorsteinn, son of Ásbjǫrn (*ÍF* I 234–5; V 3), while in *Njáls saga* (*ÍF* XII 259) and *ÓTM* II 156, Surtr is the son of Ásbjǫrn, son of Þorsteinn. *Landnámabók* states that *papar* had previously dwelt at Kirkjubœr and that 'heathens could not live there' (*ÍF* I 324–5).

[48] *Njáls saga* (*ÍF* XII 259–60) gives a longer and more dramatic account of this event, ending with the killing of Galdra-Heðinn at the hands of Guðleifr. It bears a striking resemblance to the many Irish tales in which criminals are swallowed alive by the earth (*VSH* I clxviii). Sigurður Nordal (1928), however, has shown that it is possible for a horse to sink into the ground in precisely this area (and only this area), since volcanic eruptions from Katla cause the formation of glacial cavities covered over by sand (*jǫkulhvörf*), which can give way when ridden over.

[49] Þorvaldr is also mentioned in *Heimskringla* (*ÍF* XXVI 320), *Njáls saga* (*ÍF* XII 261–4) and *ÓTM* II 157–8. According to *Háttatal* in Snorri Sturluson 1999: 18, he invented the poetic metre *skjálfhenda* 'shivering' when he was shipwrecked on a skerry. This may explain his nickname (*veill* 'ailing, wretched') and perhaps there is a link between the name of the verse-form and the occurrence of the adjective *úskelfr* 'unshakable' in his only surviving verse.

[50] Úlfr Uggason is a well-known poet, also mentioned in *Landnámabók* (*ÍF* I 111), *Njáls saga* (*ÍF* XII 152, 263) and *ÓTM* II 158. *Laxdœla saga* (*ÍF* V 80) says that he composed a poem (*Húsdrápa*) about the depictions on the wall of Óláfr Hǫskuldsson's hall. The 12 stanzas or parts of stanzas that survive of this are found only in *Skáldskaparmál* (see Snorri Sturluson 1998: 157, note to verse 8).

[51] This verse also appears in *Njáls saga* (*ÍF* XII 262) and *ÓTM* II 158, where there are some variant readings that affect its interpretation. The kennings in this version are the following: 'wielder of steel' (warrior), 'spear-storm's strengthener' (warrior: the spear-storm is battle), 'wolf of God' (God's messenger). For this last kenning, *Njáls saga* has the better reading *goðvargr* 'god-wolf', which can be interpreted as 'enemy' or 'outcast' of the gods; the word *vargr* has connotations of savagery, criminality and outlawry. The word *argr*, translated here as 'spineless', implies sexual deviancy and effeminacy; like the insult to Friðrekr, it was an extremely offensive term and its use carried heavy legal penalties (*Grágás* 1980–2000: II 198, 354, where it is translated 'womanish'). The meaning of the verse as a whole is far from clear: some have argued from the variant readings that Þorvaldr is urging Úlfr to push Þangbrandr off a cliff, perhaps as a sacrifice to the gods; others that he is to drive him from the land, either by outright violence or through verbal abuse (see Grønlie 2004: 467–8).

[52] This verse, unlike the first, is found in a very similar form in *Njáls saga* (*ÍF* XII 263) and *ÓTM* II 158. The kennings are as follows: 'the cormorant to cave of teeth flown' (fly, bait: the teeth's cave is the mouth), 'a well-tried swimmer in Hárbarðr's sanctuary's fjord' (poet: Hárbarðr is a name for Óðinn and his sanctuary's fjord is the mead of poetry), 'heeder of sail-yard's horse' (sailor: the sail-yard's

horse is a ship). The consistency of maritime imagery throughout this verse (fishing, swimming, sailing) is striking.

[53] The killing of Vetrliði is also mentioned in *Landnámabók* (*ÍF* I 348), *Heimskringla* (*ÍF* XXVI 320), *Njáls saga* (*ÍF* XII 260–61) and *ÓTM* II 157. *Þórðarbók* (in *Skarðsárbók* 1958: 164) adds the following information: 'Vetrliði libelled Þorbrandr; because of that Þorbrandr killed him at the turf-cutting; he defended himself with a turf-cutter from Guðleifr Arason of Reykjanes. Þorbrandr stabbed him with a spear. Ljóðarkeptr composed a praise-poem about Guðleifr.' Ljóðarkeptr appears to be the same person as Óðar- or Óttarr keptr, mentioned in *Skáldatal* among the poets of Knútr the Great (*Edda Snorra Sturlusonar* 1848–87, III 258, 267, 283). It seems likely that the stanza about Vetrliði's death, and perhaps other information about the missionaries' killings, comes from his poem (Sveinbjǫrn Rafnsson 1977: 26–8). The only surviving fragment of Vetrliði's work, probably from a poem addressing Þórr, is preserved in Snorri Sturluson 1998: 17.

[54] This verse is also found in *Njáls saga* (*ÍF* XII 260–61) and *ÓTM* II 157. The kennings in the *Kristni saga* text are as follows: 'shields' tester' (warrior), 'battle tools' (weapons), 'poetry's smithy' (breast), 'Baldr of rust-hater's bed' (warrior: the rust-hater or enemy is armour, and armour's bed is the sword), 'sword-tester (of blood)' (warrior, killer), 'murderous hammer' (probably axe), 'anvil of battle-hat's place' (nape of the neck: battle-hat's place is the head). It seems likely that the aggressors in this verse (tester of shields and sword-tester) are Þangbrandr and Guðleifr, both of whom took part in the killing, while the 'smithy (of the vessel) of poetry' refers to Vetrliði's breast, source of his libellous poetry. The parallel between poetry, violence and ironwork runs throughout the verse (see Grønlie 2004: 469–70).

[55] This story is told only in *Kristni saga* and is probably derived from oral tradition, as the link with place-names and landscape suggests (Ólsen 1893: 322–4; Sveinbjǫrn Rafnsson 1977: 26; *ÍF* XV cc). It once again shows the author's familiarity with Borgarfjǫrðr and the west of Iceland. Neither Kolr nor Skeggbjǫrn are known from elsewhere, but similar conflicts arising from refusal to sell food occur in both *Hænsa-Þóris saga* and *Njáls saga* (*ÍF* III 13–16; XII 121–2).

[56] Steinunn is mentioned in *Landnámabók* (*ÍF* I 100–01) and her son Skáld- (Poet-) or Hofgarða-Refr is also mentioned in *Eyrbyggja saga* (*ÍF* IV 30, 114) and *Heimskringla* (*ÍF* XXVII 358, 382). His poetry is frequently quoted in *Skáldskaparmál* (see Snorri Sturluson 1998: 155, note to verse 4). Steinunn was both descended from and married into a powerful family of priest-chieftains (*goðar*); her son's by-name Hofgarða- means 'of temple-courts'. Her two surviving verses are also preserved in *ÓTM* II 159 and *Njáls saga* (*ÍF* XII 265–7), where her encounter with Þangbrandr is expanded into an antagonistic exchange ending with the same two verses (in reverse order).

[57] The kennings are as follows: 'Þvinnill's animal' (ship: Þvinnill is the name of a sea-king), 'prow's horse' (ship), 'ski of Atall's land' (ship: Atall is a sea-king and his land is the sea), 'bell's keeper' (priest, Þangbrandr), 'beach's falcon' (ship), 'slayer of giantess-son' (Þórr), 'ox of seagull's place (ship: the sea-gull's place is the sea), 'wave-raven' (ship), 'Gylfi's reindeer' (ship: Gylfi is a sea-king). These verses have been generally admired for their metrical perfection, elegant kennings and mocking inversion of the motif of the successful sea-voyage in skaldic praise-

poetry. They are discussed in Ohlmarks 1958: 306–08, Guðrún Helgadóttir 1961: 119–22, Jesch 1987: 10–12, Straubhaar 2002: 267–9 and Grønlie 2006.

[58] This event is also described in *ÓTM* II 160 and *Njáls saga* (*ÍF* XII 267–9). It differs slightly in *Njáls saga*, where three fires are built, one consecrated by heathens, one by Þangbrandr and the third left unconsecrated. In a typical 'trial of strength', Gestr and his men agree to be converted if the berserk is afraid of the fire consecrated by Þangbrandr, which proves to be the case. Þangbrandr then strikes the berserk's arm with a crucifix—using the sign of the cross literally— before he and Guðleifr kill him. Gestr is well known in the sagas for his wisdom and prophetic skills: according to *Laxdœla saga* (*ÍF* V 196), he asks to be buried at Helgafell 'because that place will be the greatest in this district': a monastery was later built there.

[59] 'Iron basket'. In *Njáls saga* (*ÍF* XII 265, 269), Þangbrandr's ship is called *Vísundr* (Ox), presumably because of the kenning in Steinunn's verses (ox of the gull's place), but the heathens name it 'Iron basket' after it has been repaired.

[60] Runólfr's role in Hjalti's outlawry is also mentioned in *Landnámabók* (*ÍF* I 368), *Laxdœla saga* (*ÍF* V 125–6), and *ÓTM* II 162–3. It is not mentioned in *Njáls saga*, where Runólfr has a more extensive, and more sympathetic, role (*ÍF* XII 133, 135, 288–9, 308).

[61] Þorkell was one of the brothers of the chieftain Starri, mentioned in ch. 1. His son Þorbjǫrn is named only here and in *ÓTM* II 162.

[62] This comment alliterates in Icelandic (*Þér liggr **h**álmsvisk þar er **h**jartat skyldi*) and Vigfússon and Powell (1905: I 375) have suggested it belongs alongside Hjalti's other poetic utterances; see pp. 8, 24 (note 69), 44, 50 and 69 (note 87).

[63] The conversion of Hálogaland is described in Oddr Snorrason 1932: 140–43, *Heimskringla* (*ÍF* XXVI 324–8) and *ÓTM* II 127–34.

[64] There are conflicting accounts of these Icelanders in Norway. The A-text of Oddr Snorrason 1932: 122 says that there were three ships, one owned by Þórarinn Nefjólfsson and Kjartan Óláfsson, one by Hallfreðr and one by Brandr Vermundarson and Þorleifr Brandsson. The S-text, however, gives the owners of the ships as Kjartan and Bolli, Hallfreðr and Þórarinn and the brothers Brandr and Þorkell Styrsson. In *Laxdœla saga* (*ÍF* V 116), Kjartan arrives on a ship together with Bolli and Kálfr Ásgeirsson, and they join three other ships owned by Brandr Vermundarson, Hallfreðr and the brothers Bjarni and Þórhallr Skeggjason. In *Heimskringla* (*ÍF* XXVI 328–9), the men Óláfr later takes hostage are mentioned first (Kjartan, Halldórr Guðmundarson, Kolbeinn Þórðarson and Svertingr Runólfsson), and Þórarinn, Hallfreðr, Brandr and Þorleikr Brandsson are also said to be ship-owners. *ÓTM* II 161 mentions only the hostages and Þórarinn Nefjólfsson (Kjartan and Hallfreðr are treated separately). *Kristni saga* probably follows *Heimskringla* in including the hostages in its list of Icelanders, but has in common with *Laxdœla saga* the ship owned by Kjartan, Bolli and Kálfr (cf. Duke [Grønlie] 1998–2001: 353–8).

[65] Oddr Snorrason 1932: 122–3 says that the men tried three times to leave but 'they never got a good wind'; Snorri (*ÍF* XXVI 329) mentions one attempt 'but the wind was against them'. In *Laxdœla saga*, the king has forbidden all unconverted Icelanders to leave Norway (*ÍF* V 116). Typically, *ÓTM* II 161 incorporates both the weather motif and the king's ban.

Notes to the Story of the Conversion

[66] The swimming contest and accompanying dialogue occur in many different sources, including Oddr Snorrason 1932: 122–4, *Laxdæla saga* (*ÍF* V 116–18), the text of *Heimskringla* in *Fríssbók* (1871: 148–9), where it appears to have been interpolated from a manuscript of Oddr Snorrason's saga, and *ÓTM* I 359–61. In the earliest version of the scene (the A-text of Oddr Snorrason's saga), the dialogue is between Hallfreðr and Kjartan, and it is Hallfreðr who, with a premonition of his later troublesome relationship with Óláfr, refuses to compete. In *Laxdæla saga*, Bolli replaces Hallfreðr, but he and Kjartan have opposite roles to the ones here (perhaps the author was relying on his memory of the scene in the saga). In *Óláfs saga Tryggvasonar in mesta*, the different versions are conflated: a dialogue between Kjartan and Hallfreðr (from Oddr Snorrason) is followed by an exchange between Kjartan and Bolli (from *Laxdæla saga*). It seems likely that the swimming competition carries a symbolic value: Kjartan's immersion at the hands of Óláfr and the gift of a cloak foreshadow his later baptism and clothing in white robes (Weber 1987: 125–6; *ÍF* XV cl–cliv).

[67] This is closest to the account of Kjartan's baptism in *Heimskringla* (*ÍF* XXVI 329–30), which also takes place at Michaelmas and is preceded by bargaining: Kjartan asks for the king's friendship. In Oddr Snorrason 1932: 124–5 and *Laxdæla saga* (*ÍF* V 121–3), the conversion takes place at Christmas and in *Laxdæla saga*, Kjartan seeks out King Óláfr himself. A white robe (Latin *alb*) was traditionally worn for a week after baptism to symbolise 'the joy of regeneration and purity of life and the beauty of angelic splendour' (Fisher 1965: 60; quoted from Alcuin, epistle 134).

[68] Again, this is close to Hjalti and Gizurr's speech in *Heimskringla* (*ÍF* XXVI 332): 'You will not, king, go against your words, because you declared that no one shall have done so much to anger you that you will not forgive those who wish to have themselves baptised and to abandon heathenism.'

[69] This would make Óláfr and Gizurr second cousins. In *Heimskringla* (*ÍF* XXVI 328), Bǫðvarr's brother is named Sigurðr and his son is Eiríkr, but this Sigurðr is not mentioned elsewhere.

[70] Each of these hostages comes from a different quarter of Iceland: Kjartan from the west, Halldórr from the north, Kolbeinn from the east and Svertingr from the south. They appear for the first time in Oddr Snorrason 1932: 127, where Óláfr's involvement in the conversion is emphasised; the A-text says that there are four, but names only two, while the S-text gives all four names. They are also mentioned in *Laxdæla saga* (*ÍF* V 126), *Heimskringla* (*ÍF* XXVI 347) and *ÓTM* II 165. The attempt to involve all four quarters of Iceland in the conversion begins with the genealogies in Ari's *Íslendingabók* and is notable in this incident and in the sacrifice planned by Gizurr and Hjalti in ch. 12 below.

[71] In *ÓTM* II 165–6, Hjalti speaks up on behalf of the hostages, asking Óláfr to treat them well. It seems likely that such a speech has been dropped from *Kristni saga*, leaving only this one reference to it.

[72] Cf. Romans 12: 17, 21; 1 Peter 3: 9.

[73] Hallfreðr's baptism is also mentioned in Oddr Snorrason 1932: 125–6, *Laxdæla saga* (*ÍF* V 123) and *Heimskringla* (*ÍF* XXVI 330–32). There is an extended account in *Hallfreðar saga* (*ÍF* VIII 151–5), which shares some features

with that of Kjartan's baptism (Lindow 1997a). There are many references in the sagas to the giving of 'naming gifts' along with a nickname (ÍF VI 171–2; IX 157; Flb I 234, 289, 464), and this presumably derives from the custom of giving children gifts at their naming or, in Christian times, baptism.

[74] This was a great honour, as descriptions of Norse drinking customs in other sagas suggest (cf. ÍF II 122; Msk 280).

[75] Leifr's mission to Greenland, his rescue of people from a shipwreck and discovery of Vínland are also described in Heimskringla (ÍF XXVI 347–8), Eiríks saga rauða (ÍF IV 211–12) and AÍ I 12. Greenland, however, is not mentioned among the countries converted by Óláfr Tryggvason in the oldest sources, and it has been suggested that it is more likely to have been converted by St Óláfr c.1015 (Ólafur Halldórsson 1978: 381–9; 1981). Leifr's role is probably a fiction, perhaps to be attributed to Gunnlaugr Leifsson.

[76] Hǫrgr is a heathen place of worship, probably 'a pile of stones set up in the open as an altar' (Turville-Petre 1964: 239); eyrr is a spit of sand or gravel jutting out into the sea.

[77] This is reminiscent of the church Óláfr has built on Mostr, and the building of churches on the ruins of pagan temples is not uncommon in hagiography (e.g. HMS I 560). A document from 1269 mentions a church named Klemenskirkja 'Clement's church' on Heimaey in the Vestmannaeyjar (DI II 66), and the (now obsolete) place-name Klemenseyri probably once indicated its location (Þorkell Jóhannesson 1938: 57). Hofmann (1994) has argued that this church was the one erected by Gizurr and Hjalti and that it was modelled on Óláfr Tryggvason's 'Clement's church' in Niðaróss.

[78] Skeggi and his son Þorvaldr are mentioned in Landnámabók (ÍF 1: 367–8), as is their aid to Hjalti and his companions. Þorvaldr's daughter, Þorlaug, was married to Egill Síðu-Hallsson, and their daughter was Þorgerðr, mother of Bishop Jón Ǫgmundarson.

[79] Ásgrímr Elliða-Grímsson's genealogy is given in Landnámabók (ÍF I 264, 267) and he is mentioned in a number of sagas, most notably Njáls saga (ÍF XII 72–3).

[80] These crosses are also mentioned in Oddr Snorrason 1932: 128. Whether they mark the physical height of the two men or their spiritual stature is not clear; see the different opinions expressed by Groth 1895: xxxv and Finnur Jónsson (Oddr Snorrason 1932: xxxi). The term hæð 'height' is used symbolically for Latin maiestas in various homilies and saints' lives (Leifar 1878: 62; Homiliubók 1872: 14, 90; Thomas saga 1869: 458), but there are other examples where it is clearly literal (AÍ I 25; ÍF XXVIII 230).

[81] This contradicts what is said in ÓTM II 190 about the 'great noise and uproar' following Gizurr and Hjalti's announcement; but there is a similar scene in Heimskringla (ÍF XXVI 305–06), where three opponents of Óláfr Tryggvason rise to oppose him at an assembly, but find themselves unable to speak a word.

[82] Þóroddr was father of Skapti the Lawspeaker and father-in-law of Gizurr the White (ÍF I 392–3), and this anecdote implies that he had been converted to Christianity. Theodoricus (1998: 16) lists 'Þorgils of Ǫlfus' as one of the first converts. This may mean Þóroddr's son-in-law, Þorgils Ørrabeinsstjúpr (Jón Hnefill Aðalsteinsson 1999: 64–5; Lange 1989: 137–8), or it may be a mistake for Þóroddr

himself or represent a conflation of Þorgils and Þóroddr (Jón Jóhannesson 1974: 129; Perkins 1985: 793–5). *Flóamanna saga* mentions that Þorgils 'was among the first to accept the faith', but it is probable that the saga is using Theodoricus as a source (*ÍF* XIII 274, cxlix–cl). Cf. Theodoricus 1998, 70 (note 93).

[83] Cf. Romans 12: 1; Hebrews 13: 15–16. This passage has been used to support the theory that the death penalty was originally sacral in character; it can be connected with the reading of Þorvaldr veili's verse whereby Úlfr is urged to push Þangbrandr off a cliff (see note 51 above and Ólafur Lárusson 1928). There are other references to Norse literature to throwing people off cliffs (*Skarðsárbók* 1958: 189; *Gautreks saga* in *FN* III 6–7), as well as to human sacrifice at legal assemblies (*ÍF* I 126; IV 18), and there is some evidence that the elderly and dependents could be sacrificed during famines (*ÍF* X 169–70; *ÓTM* II 178, 180). The practice, however, does not seem to have been widespread and no archaeological evidence has as yet been found in Iceland (Briem 1945: 167–72; Turville-Petre 1964: 252–5; Jón Hnefill Aðalsteinsson 1999: 184–98).

[84] The full story is told in *Vápnfirðinga saga* (*ÍF* XI 33–5), where Þorleifr is more specifically said to be prosecuted *um hoftoll* (for not paying the temple-tax) rather than for being a Christian. Þórarinn from Seyðarfjǫrðr is also mentioned in *Landnámabók* (*ÍF* I 298) and *Droplaugarsonar saga* (*ÍF* XI 158).

[85] On Gunnhildr, see note 11 to ch. 2 above.

[86] These two kings are not named in other versions of Þorgeirr's speech, and attempts to identify them have not been successful; they are most likely invented types.

[87] In Icelandic, this forms two lines of alliterative verse: *Gǫmlum kennu vér nú goðanum | at geifla á saltinu* (Vigfússon and Powell 1905: I 375). It refers to the salt traditionally placed on the tongue of the catechumen during initiation rites as a symbol of divine wisdom (Fisher 1965: 7, 83, 160).

[88] *Eyrbyggja saga* says that 'Snorri goði pleaded most with the people of the Western Fjords that Christianity should be accepted' (*ÍF* IV 136).

[89] 10th September. Ari says that Óláfr 'fell the same summer' (see *Íslendingabók* ch. 7 and note 76 above). Rumours that he survived the battle of Svǫlðr seem to have circulated early (they are recorded by Hallfreðr in his *Erfidrápa* and *Rekstefja*) and are mentioned in *HN* 23, Theodoricus (1998: 18), *Ágrip* (1995: 32–5) and, with citation of Hallfreðr's stanzas, in Snorri's *Heimskringla* (*ÍF* XXVI 367–70). For later traditions that Óláfr ended his life as a monk in Syria or Greece, see Oddr Snorrason 1932: 240–47 and *ÓTM* II 318–21, 340–49.

[90] *ÓTM* I 301 places Þorvaldr and Stefnir's travels together between their missions, and mentions separately (I 300) that Þorvaldr travelled to Jerusalem, Greece, Constantinople and the East, where he founded a monastery on a mountain called Drǫfn. *Flb* I 300–302 dramatically abridges his journeys, but includes a meeting between Þorvaldr and Óláfr Tryggvason that supposedly took place when Óláfr accompanied Otto III on a mission to the East. If there is any historical reality behind all this, then Þorvaldr was perhaps among the clerics who arrived in Russia after the marriage of Princess Anna, sister of Basil II and Constantine VIII, to Vladimir of Kiev in 989. Vladimir's conversion was one of the conditions for this marriage (Ellis Davidson 1976: 254–5; Blöndal 1978: 197–9).

[91] The first element of Kœnugarðr, the Norse name for Kiev, is probably a corruption of the Old Russian name for the inhabitants of the area, Kijane (Blöndal 1978: 3; Ásgeir Blöndal Magnússon 1989:536; in Kjan-gorod, the Old Russian name of the town, *gorod* = ON *garðr*). Together with Jerusalem and Constantinople, it became an important site of pilgrimage for Scandinavians during the Middle Ages (Franklin and Shepherd 1996: 303–13).

[92] Polotsk, in modern-day Belorus. It lay on an important trading route along the Western Dvina, and was the seat of a Scandinavian magnate by the 970s; by the mid-eleventh century it was the seat of a bishop and possessed a cathedral of St Sophia (Franklin and Shepherd 1996: 152, 250–51).

[93] Neither Brandr nor his verse is known from elsewhere, though 'far-traveller' is a common by-name of travellers in the East (cf. Þorvaldr, Yngvarr, Ǫrvar-Oddr). Vigfússon and Powell (1905: I 372) connect him with the prior Brandr in *Landnámabók* (*ÍF* I 137) who compiled a genealogy of the people of Borgarfjǫrðr, but this is based on the mistaken description of Þorvaldr as 'a sainted Borgfrith man'. The place-name Drafn has not been identified.

[94] According to *ÓTM* II 305, Stefnir made his way to Denmark after a pilgrimage to Rome.

[95] This verse also occurs in Oddr Snorrason 1932: 194–5, with a parallel translation into Latin, and in *ÓTM* II 305. The A-text of Oddr Snorrason's saga does not attribute it to Stefnir, and Bætke (1970) has suggested that the Latin version may in fact be Oddr Snorrason's own composition, only later 'translated' into Icelandic. This is contested by Andersson in his translation (2003: 20–21). A nithing (from ON *níðingr*) is a coward or villain; in ON it could also be used of an apostate, which is how Oddr Snorrason translates it into Latin. Andersson (2003: 22–4) suggests that the 'hooked' nose is a veiled reference to the archetypal traitor, Judas Iscariot.

[96] Sigvaldi was Earl of Jómsborg in Wendland and his treacherous acts towards Sveinn Forkbeard and Óláfr Tryggvason are told in *Jómsvíkinga saga* (1969: 154–9)—which also mentions his ugly nose (132), Oddr Snorrason 1932: 109–12, 193–4, *Heimskringla* (*ÍF* XXVI 272–3, 350–53) and *ÓTM* I 175–7, II 248–58. The same account of Stefnir's death occurs in *ÓTM* II 305, but according to Oddr Snorrason 1932: 195 (S-text), he was killed after composing an insulting verse about Sigvaldi's daughter. *Óláfs saga Tryggvasonar in mesta* seems to register an awareness of this when it insists upon the exclusivity of its own version: 'This alone was the cause of Stefnir's death.'

[97] Ari Þorgilsson 'the Learned'. It is not clear whether this refers to what comes before it (the death of Stefnir) or to what comes after (the lives of Ísleifr and Gizurr), the main source for which is chs 9 and 10 of Ari's *Íslendingabók*. Stefnir's death is not otherwise mentioned in Ari's writings, but might conceivably have been part of his *konunga ævi* (see Ellehøj 1965: 50–51).

[98] *Landnámabók* and *Flóamanna saga* (*ÍF* I 378; XIII 267, 318) confirm that Gizurr and his father Teitr lived at Hǫfði. According to *Hungrvaka* (*ÍF* XVI 5 and note 3), however, Teitr was the first to build a farm at Skálaholt, though Gizurr later had the first church built there. In fact, archaeological research has shown that Skálaholt was settled before the time of either man.

[99] Ísleifr's schooling at Herfurða (Herford in Westphalia) is mentioned in *Hungrvaka* and *Jóns saga helga* (*ÍF* XV 176–7, XVI 6), which also says that his son Gizurr was sent to school there. The convent at Herford was probably founded *c*.789 and later ceded to Ludwig the Pious. It had close links to Corvey (founded in 822), from where Ansgar was sent to Denmark and Sweden, and was an important centre for mission and education. The abbess during Ísleifr's time was Godesti (1002–40), daughter of Bernhard I of Saxony (973–1011) and sister of Bernhard II (1011–59), whose son Ordulf (1059–72) was married to the daughter of St Óláfr (Adam of Bremen ii.79; 2002: 108; *ÍF* XXVII 447). The link between Ísleifr and Herford can also be documented from other sources: the appendix to *Skarðsárbók* (1958: 189) mentions that Ísleifr instituted a fast observed in Herford, and two Icelandic calendars, one from Skálaholt, record the feast day of St Pusinna, Herford's patron saint (Gjerløw 1980).

[100] The Icelandic *marglátr* usually means 'changeable, inconstant, loose', but may also carry the meaning 'enterprising' (i.e. one who takes up many tasks), and this seems likely here in view of Teitr's studies and status as Ari's foster-father (Kahle 1905: 45).

[101] 5th July 1080.

[102] According to *Hungrvaka* and *Jóns saga helga* (*ÍF* XV 192; XVI 15–16), Gizurr went to see Gregory VII in Rome before his consecration, because the Archbishop of Hamburg–Bremen, Liemar, had been excommunicated by the pope. He was eventually consecrated by Archbishop Hartwig of Magdeburg. *Jóns saga* adds that Gizurr spent the following year in Denmark and Gautland, but this is probably a misunderstanding of ch. 10 of *Íslendingabók*, according to which Gizurr spent the year before his consecration in Gautland and the year after in Denmark.

[103] On Markús Skeggjason, see note 93 to ch. 10 of *Íslendingabók* above, and compare *Hungrvaka* (*ÍF* XVI 17): 'He was a very wise man and a very great poet.'

[104] Compare *Hungrvaka* (*ÍF* XVI 16): 'Everyone wished to sit or stand as he commanded, young and old, rich and poor, women and men, and it was right to say that he was both king and bishop over the land while he lived.' This echoes Haraldr Sigurðarson's famous comment on Gizurr: 'He could be a viking chieftain, and has the makings for it. Given his temperament, he could be a king, and that would be fitting. The third possibility is a bishop, and that is probably what he will become, and he will be a most outstanding man' (*Msk* 255).

[105] On the idea of a 'Golden Age' during the reign of Gizurr, see Orri Vésteinsson 2000: 63–7.

[106] A large number of chieftains were ordained priests in the early and mid-twelfth century, but the practice was condemned by Archbishop Eiríkr Ívarsson of Niðaróss in 1190 (*DI* I: 290–91). This list moves clockwise from south to north. Magnús Þórðarson was the great-grandfather of Guðný, mother of the Sturlungs, and his daughter Oddný was the step-mother of Bishop Magnús Einarsson at Skálaholt (*ÍF* I 78–9, XVI 28). Guðmundr Brandsson (d. 1151) was descended from Þórðr Víkingsson, who was rumoured to be a son of Haraldr the Fine-Haired. He was a close relative and friend of Þorgils Oddason, as well as second cousin to Ari the Learned (*ÍF* I 180, 183; *Sturl* I 13, 36; *ÍF* XVI 33). Ingimundr Einarsson (d. 1169/70), a descendant of Ari Másson from ch. 1, was a cousin of

Þorgils Oddason and a well-known poet and story-teller; some of his verses are preserved in *Þorgils saga ok Hafliða* (*BS* I 418; *Sturl* I 13–4, 23–7). On Hallr Teitsson, Sæmundr the Learned and Ketill Þorsteinsson, see notes 1, 2 and 84 to *Íslendingabók*. Hallr, Ingimundr, Ketill Guðmundsson (d. 1158) and Jón Þorvarðsson (d. 1150) all appear in a list of priests from 1143 sometimes attributed to Ari and compiled for bishops Ketill Þorsteinsson and Magnús Einarsson; this also includes the sons of Sæmundr (Eyjólfr and Loptr), Ari's son Þorgils and Ketill's son Rúnólfr (*DI* I 185–6).

[107] 28th May 1118.

[108] Kirjalax is the Norse name for Alexius, on whom see ch. 10 of *Íslendingabók* and note 104.

[109] The whole of this chapter can also be found in the appendix to *Skarðsárbók* (1958: 193–5), where it is somewhat fuller and seems to be copied from a source other than *Hauksbók* (Jón Jóhannesson 1941: 16–19; *Skarðsárbók* 1958: xxxix–xl, *ÍF* XV cxxxvi–vii).

[110] *Dymbildagar* is the Icelandic name for the three days before Easter (Maundy Thursday, Good Friday and Holy Saturday). *Dymbil* may be derived from the adjective *dumbr* 'dumb, silent', although it is perhaps more likely related to *demba* and *dumpa* from Gmc **demb-* 'to strike, fall with a thump'; it refers to having a wooden tongue in a bell, because bells were rung in Holy Week with a wooden tongue rather than a metal one (cf. Danish *dimmeluge*, Swedish *dymmelvecka*). This custom of damping or silencing the sound of church bells from Maundy Thursday until the Mass of the Easter Vigil dates from at least the eighth century, cf. Old English *swigdagas*, French *semaine muette*, German *die stille Woche* (Hardison 1965: 126, 161).

[111] According to *Heimskringla* (*ÍF* XXVII 214), St Óláfr sent the wood for the church at Þingvellir, but *Msk* 204 and *Flb* IV 120 both say that Haraldr sent a bell.

[112] The catastrophes of 1118 are also related in *Hungrvaka* (*ÍF* XVI 20–21) and mentioned briefly in some Icelandic annals. *Hungrvaka* adds: 'It seemed to the wisest men that Iceland drooped after the fall of Bishop Gizurr in the same way as the Roman Empire after the fall of Pope Gregory.' The pope referred to is Gregory I and the state of Rome after his death is described in John the Deacon's *Gregorii vita*, translated into Icelandic c.1200 (*HMS* I 395–6; see also the reference in *ÍF* XVII 134). *Páls saga biskups* (*ÍF* XVI 328) gives Ari as the source of the remarks in *Hungrvaka* and, if this is right, it might explain the reference to Gregory in ch. 10 of *Íslendingabók* (Louis-Jensen 1976).

[113] The sons of Ásbjǫrn, grandson of Arngeirr Spak-Bǫðvarsson in ch. 3, were Arnórr, Þorsteinn and Bǫðvarr (*Sturl* I 53). Þorgeirr Hallason (d. 1169), a chieftain in Eyjafjǫrðr, was married to Ingimundr Einarsson's sister and their son Ari was father of Bishop Guðmundr at Hólar (*ÍF* I 266; *Sturl* I 35, 66, 116–17, 124). Gizurr Einarsson is not known from elsewhere, though he may be the Gizurr mentioned in *ÍF* I 182, 295. Sigmundr Þorgilsson was ancestor of the Svínfelling dynasty and married to Markús Skeggjason's sister (*Sturl* I 53). Skúli Egilsson and Halldórr Egilsson were second cousins and descendants of Egill Skalla-Grímsson (*ÍF* I 95–7; XIV 247; *Sturl* I 74). Styrmir Hreinsson was grandson of Hermundr Illugason in ch. 2 and his cousin's daughter was married to Þorgils

Notes to the Story of the Conversion 73

Oddason (*Sturl* I 40, 49). On Þorgils himself, see *Melabók* (*ÍF* I 153, 162), *Msk* 369–70, *Sturl* I 12–56 and later in this chapter. He was a grandson of Ari Másson (whose sister Valgerðr was Ari's grandmother) and a friend of Sæmundr the Learned, who fostered his son Oddi. Þorgils's social standing is highlighted by the story that the reputed son of the Norwegian king Magnús Bareleg, Sigurðr slembidjákn, spent a year with him in Iceland. He died at the monastery of Þingeyrar in 1151. Þórðr Gilsson was a descendant of Víga-Sturla and Snorri goði, and grandfather of Snorri Sturluson (*ÍF* I 166; *Sturl* I 52, 64). On Þórðr Þorvaldsson, descendant of Snorri goði and great-grandson of Ásgeirr Knattarson in ch. 1, see *Sturl* I 54–5, the genealogies later in this chapter and note 120.

[114] The killing of Þorsteinn Hallvarðsson is included among the important events of Þorlákr's episcopate in *Hungrvaka* (*ÍF* XVI 27), and *Landnámabók* (*ÍF* I 388) mentions 'Hallvarðr, father of Þorsteinn, whom Einarr the Shetlander killed'.

[115] The dispute between Þorgils and Hafliði is also mentioned in *Hungrvaka* (*ÍF* XVI 27) during Þorlákr's episcopate and related at length in *Þorgils saga ok Hafliða* in *Sturl* I 12–50.

[116] 23rd April 1121. There is a fuller description in *Jóns saga helga* (*ÍF* XV 238–9).

[117] A 'six-ell ounce-unit' was the value of an ounce-unit of homespun, that is, six ells of cloth two ells wide and of stipulated quality (one ell was 49.2 cm). At the standard rate, 8 such ounce-units of homespun were equivalent to one weighed ounce of silver. A hundred in this context has the duodecimal value of 120, so Hafliði awarded himself 7200 ounce-units in all, that is 900 ounces of silver or the price of 360 cows. *Þorgils saga ok Hafliða* (*Sturl* I 49, 50) puts the price at 600 ounces of silver (or 240 cows) and specifies the means of payment as 'land in the Northern Quarter, gold and silver, goods from the East, ironwork, valuable objects costing no less than the price of a cow, gelded horses—an ungelded horse only if it were accompanied by a mare, and a mare only if accompanied by a stallion, and no horse older than twelve or younger than three years old'. Both awards are unusually high.

[118] In *Skarðsárbók* 1958: 194, the relevance of Ketill's appointment as bishop is made clearer by the fuller account of the disagreement between Þorgils and Hafliði and the comment that 'Ketill managed to bring an end to the difference with his persuasion'. In *Þorgils saga ok Hafliða* (*Sturl* I 47–8), Ketill's abilities as peacemaker are explicitly said to qualify him for the role of bishop.

[119] Hafliði's marriage to Þuríðr is mentioned in *Landnámabók* (*ÍF* I 182) and *Sturl* I 12; Þuríðr's father Þórðr, the son of Víga-Sturla was married to the daughter of Snorri goði. Little is known about Hafliði's son Þórðr, Þórðr's wife Solvǫr or their son Ívarr, but the Þorsteinn Ívarsson mentioned in *Íslendinga saga* (*Sturl* I 243) appears to be this Ívarr's son.

[120] Hafliði's marriage to Rannveig is mentioned in *Sturl* I 12, 54–5, as are the children of Þórðr and Sigríðr, there called Páll, Snorri, Teitr and Ívarr. Þórðr is probably an error for Snorri, since he and Páll are the most frequently mentioned of the four sons. The death of Ingimundr Illugason is given in Icelandic annals under 1150 and that of Valgerðr at Breiðabólstaðr is mentioned under 1154. It has been suggested that Ingimundr's father Illugi was the same Illugi that gave up his land at Hólar when the new bishopric was created there (*ÍF* XV 195–6; XVII 218–19).

[121] Most Icelandic churches would have been constructed of turf with wooden gable walls, if not built entirely of timber; stone churches were extremely rare in Iceland in the Middle Ages. Excavations have shown that a stone church was begun at Breiðabólstaðr, perhaps by Illugi, but it was never completed. Other stone churches were begun at Hólar in the fourteenth century and perhaps in Hítardalr (Lilja Árnadóttir and Kiran 1997: 36–8).

[122] On Earl Rǫgnvaldr kali, see *Orkneyinga saga*, according to which (*ÍF* XXXIV 140) he was originally called Kali. But it is likely that *kali* was at first a nickname (probably meaning 'cold') that only later came to be used as a proper name (Ásgeir Blöndal Magnússon 1989: 442). He was joint ruler of Orkney from c.1127–9, martyred in 1158/9, and recognised as a saint shortly after his death (*ÍF* XXXIV xc, 282). The first feast-day of Mary is the Assumption (15th August) and the second is the Nativity (8th September), so Óláfr's death is dated a day later than in ch. 13. This statement has little to do with *Kristni saga*, and was most likely copied into the saga by accident from a miscellany following it in *Hauksbók* (see Ólafur Halldórsson 1990: 462).

BIBLIOGRAPHY

Abrams, Lesley. 1996. 'Kings and Bishops and the Conversion of the Anglo-Saxon and Scandinavian Kingdoms', in *Church and People in Britain and Scandinavia*, ed. Ingmar Brohed, 15–28. Lund.

Adam of Bremen. 2002. *History of the Archbishops of Hamburg–Bremen*, trans. Francis J. Tschan. New York.

Adomnán's Life of Columba. 1991. Ed. and trans. Alan O. Anderson and Marjorie O. Anderson. Oxford.

Ágrip af Nóregskonungasǫgum: A Twelfth-Century Synoptic History of the Kings of Norway. 1995. Ed. and trans. Matthew J. Driscoll. Viking Society for Northern Research, Text Series 10. London.

A Í = *Alfræði íslenzk: Islandsk encyklopædisk litteratur*. 1908–18. Ed. N. Beckman and Kr. Kålund. 3 vols. Copenhagen.

Almqvist, Bo. 1974. *Norrön Niddiktning. Nid mot missionärer*. Nordiska Texter och undersökningar 23. Uppsala.

Andersson, Theodore M., trans. 2003. Oddr Snorrason. *The Saga of Olaf Tryggvason*. Islandica 52. Ithaca, NY

Árni Magnússons Levned og skrifter. 1930. Ed. Finnur Jónsson. 2 vols.

ASC = *The Anglo-Saxon Chronicles*. 2000. Trans. and ed. Michael Swanton. London.

Ásgeir Blöndal Magnússon. 1989. *Íslensk orðsifjabók*. Reykjavík.

Baetke, Walter. 1970. 'Die Óláfs saga Tryggvasonar des Oddr Snorrason und die Jómsvíkinga saga. Zur Historiographie des nordischen Frühmittelalters', in *Formen Mittelalterlicher Literatur: Siegfried Beyschlag zu seinem 65. Geburtstag*, ed. Bernd Naumann and Otmar Werner, 1–18. Göppingen.

Barði Guðmundsson. 1967. *The Origin of the Icelanders*, trans. Lee M. Hollander. Lincoln, Nebr.

Barnard, L. W. 1976. 'Bede and Eusebius as Church Historians', in *Famulus Christi*, 106–24.

Bede's Ecclesiastical History of the English People. 1969. Ed. and trans. Bertram Colgrave and R. A. B. Mynors. Oxford.

Bekker-Nielsen, Hans. 1960. 'Hvornaar blev Ísleifr Gizurarson bispeviet?' *Opuscula* 1: 335–8. Bibliotheca Arnamagnæana 20.

Bekker-Nielsen, Hans. 1972. 'The use of *rex* in *Íslendingabók*', in *Studies for Einar Haugen presented by friends and colleagues*, ed. Evelyn Scherabon Firchow et al., 53–8. The Hague.

Benedikz, Benedikt. 1976. 'Bede in the Uttermost North', in *Famulus Christi*, 334–43.

Beowulf and the Fight at Finnsburg. 1950. Ed. Fr. Klaeber. Boston, Mass.

Björn Sigfússon. 1944. *Um Íslendingabók*. Reykjavík.

Blaney, Benjamin. 1982. 'The Berserk Suitor: The Literary Application of a Stereotyped Theme', *Scandinavian Studies* 54: 279–94.

Bloch, Marc. 1992. *The Historian's Craft*, trans. Peter Putnam. Manchester.

Blöndal, Sigfús. 1978. *The Varangians of Byzantium*, trans. and rev. Benedikt S. Benedikz. Cambridge.

Brenner, Oskar. 1878. *Über die Kristni-Saga: Kritische Beiträge zur altnordischen Literaturgeschichte*. Munich.

Briem, Ólafur. 1945. *Heiðinn siður á Íslandi*. Reykjavík.

Brooks, Nicholas. 1999. *Bede and the English*. Jarrow.

BS = *Biskupa sögur*. 1858–78. Ed. Jón Sigurðsson, Guðbrandur Vigfússon, Þorvaldur Björnsson and Eiríkur Jónsson. 2 vols. Kaupmannahöfn.

BVO = *Bedae venerabilis opera, Pars* II. *Opera exegetica* 2. 1962. Ed. D. Hurst. Corpus Christianorum, Series Latina 119. Turnhout.

Charles Edwards, Thomas M. 1976. 'The Social Background to Irish *Peregrinatio*', *Celtica* 11: 43–59.

Christiansen, Aksel E. 1975. 'Om kronologien i Aris Íslendingabók og dens laan fra Adam af Bremen', in *Nordiske Studier: Festskrift til Chr. Westergård-Nielsen på 65-årsdagen den 24. november 1975*, ed. Johs. Brøndum-Nielsen, Peter Skautrup and Allan Karker, 23–34. Copenhagen.

Chronicon monasterii de Abingdon 1. 1858. Ed. Joseph Stephenson. Rerum Britannicarum medii ævi Scriptores 2. London.

Clemens saga. 2005. Ed. Helen Carron. Viking Society for Northern Research, Text Series 17. London.

Clunies Ross, Margaret. 1997. 'Textual Territory: the Regional and Genealogical Dynamic of Medieval Icelandic Literary Production', *New Medieval Literatures* 1: 9–30.

Colgrave, Bertram, ed. 1940. *Two Lives of Saint Cuthbert: A Life by an Anonymous Monk of Lindisfarne and Bede's Prose Life*. Cambridge.

Cramer, Peter. 1993. *Baptism and Change in the Early Middle Ages c.200–1150*. Cambridge.

Crozier, Alan. 1998. 'The *Vinland hypothesis: A reply to the historians', *Gardar* 29: 37–66.

Davis, R. H. C. 1976. *The Normans and their Myth*. London.

Dicuil. 1967. *Liber de mensura orbis terrae*. Ed. J. J. Tierney. Scriptores Latini Hiberniae 6. Dublin.

DI = *Diplomatarium Islandicum: Íslenskt fornbréfasafn*. 1857–1972. 11 vols. Ed. Jón Sigurðsson and Jón Þorkelsson. Copenhagen.

Dronke, Ursula. 1997. *The Poetic Edda* II. *Mythological Poems*. Oxford.

Duke [Grønlie], Siân. 1998–2001. '*Kristni saga* and its Sources: Some Revaluations', *Saga-Book* 25: 345–66.

Edda Snorra Sturlusonar. 1848–87. Ed. Jón Sigurðsson and Finnur Jónsson. 3 vols. Hafniæ.

Edwards, Diana. 1982–5. 'Christian and Pagan References in Eleventh-Century Norse Poetry: the case of Arnórr Jarlaskáld', *Saga-Book* 21: 34–53.

Egardt, Brita. 1962. 'Hästkött', *KLNM* 7: 280–81.

Einar Arnórsson. 1942. *Ari fróði*. Reykjavík.

Einar Ól. Sveinsson. 1948a. 'Á ártíð Ara fróða', *Skírnir* 122: 30–49.

Einar Ól. Sveinsson. 1948b. *Landnám í Skaftafellsþingi*. Skaftfellinga rit 2. Reykjavík.

Einar Ól. Sveinsson. 2003. *The Folk-Stories of Iceland*, rev. Einar G. Pétursson, trans. Benedikt Benedikz, ed. Anthony Faulkes. Viking Society for Northern Research, Text Series 16. London.

Eldjárn, Kristján. 1956. *Kuml og haugfé úr heiðnum sið á Íslandi.* Reykjavík.
Ellehøj, Svend. 1965. *Studier over den ældste norrøne historieskrivning.* Copenhagen.
Ellis Davidson, Hilda R. 1976. *The Viking Road to Byzantium.* London.
Fagrskinna. A Catalogue of the Kings of Norway. 2004. Trans. Alison Finlay. Leiden.
Famulus Christi: Essays in Commemoration of the Thirteenth Centenary of the Birth of the Venerable Bede. 1976. Ed. Gerald Bonner. London.
Faulkes, Anthony. 1977. 'The Genealogies and Regnal Lists in a Manuscript in Resen's Library', in *Sjötíu ritgerðir helgaðir Jakobi Benediktssyni 20. júlí 1977*, ed. Einar G. Pétursson and Jónas Kristjánsson, 177–90. Reykjavík.
Faulkes, Anthony. 1978–9. 'Descent from the gods', *Mediaeval Scandinavia* 11: 92–125.
Faulkes, Anthony. 2005. 'The Earliest Icelandic Genealogies and Regnal Lists', *Saga-Book* 29: 115–19.
Fellows-Jensen, Gillian. 1996. 'Language contact in Iceland: the evidence of names', in *Language contact across the North Atlantic*, ed. P. Sture Ureland and Iain Clarkson, 115–24. Tübingen.
Finnur Jónsson. 1920–24. *Den oldnorske og oldislandske litteraturs historie.* 3 vols. Copenhagen.
Finnur Jónsson, ed. 1930. Ari hinn fróðe Þorgilsson, *Íslendingabók.* Copenhagen.
Fisher, J. D. C. 1965. *Christian Initiation: Baptism in the Medieval West.* London.
Flb = Flateyjarbók. 1944–5. Ed. Sigurður Nordal. 4 vols. Reykjavík.
FN = Fornaldarsögur Norðurlanda. 1943–4. Ed. Guðni Jónsson and Bjarni Vilhjálmsson. 3 vols. Reykjavík.
Foot, Sarah. 1996. 'The Making of *Angelcynn*: English Identity before the Norman Conquest', *Transactions of the Royal Historical Society*, 6th series, 6: 25–49.
Foote, Peter. 1974. 'Secular attitudes in early Iceland', *Mediaeval Scandinavia* 7: 31–44.
Foote, Peter. 1984a. 'On the Conversion of the Icelanders', in *Aurvandilstá: Norse Studies*, ed. Michael Barnes, Hans Bekker-Nielsen and Gerd Wolfgang Weber. Viking Collection: Studies in Northern Civilization 2, 56–64. Odense.
Foote, Peter. 1984b. 'Aachen, Lund, Hólar', in *Aurvandilstá: Norse Studies*, ed. Michael Barnes, Hans Bekker-Nielsen and Gerd Wolfgang Weber. Viking Collection: Studies in Northern Civilization 2, 101–20. Odense.
Foote, Peter. 1993a. 'Historical Studies: Conversion Moment and Conversion Period', in *Viking Revaluations: Viking Society Centenary Symposium 14–15 May 1992*, ed. Anthony Faulkes and Richard Perkins, 137–44. London.
Foote, Peter. 1993b. 'Conversion', in *Medieval Scandinavia: an Encyclopedia*, ed. Philip Pulsiano, 106–08. New York.
Franklin, Simon and Jonathan Shepard. 1996. *The Emergence of Rus 750–1200.* London.
Fríssbók. Codex Frisianus: en samling af norske kongesagaer. 1871. Ed. C. R. Unger. Christiania.
Gad, Finn. 1970. 'Skrællinger', *KLNM* 15: 715–18.
Gamal Norsk Homiliebok Cod. AM 619 4º. 1931. Ed. Gustav Indrebø. Oslo.

Genzmer, Felix. 1928. 'Der Spottvers des Hjalti Skeggjason', *Arkiv för nordisk filologi* 44: 311–14.

Gísli Sigurðsson. 2004. *The Medieval Icelandic Saga and Oral Tradition: A Discourse on Method*, trans. Nicholas Jones. Publications of the Milman Parry Collection of Oral Literature 2. Cambridge, Mass.

Gjerløw, Lilli. 1980. 'Skálholt and Herford', *Liturgica Islandica* I, 189–212. Bibliotheca Arnamagnæana 35. Copenhagen.

Gougaud, Dom Louis. 1932. *Christianity in Celtic Lands: A History of the Churches of the Celts, their Origin, their Development, Influence and Mutual Relations*, trans. Maud Joynt. London.

Grágás. 1980–2000. *Laws of Early Iceland. Grágás*, trans. Andrew Dennis, Peter Foote and Richard Perkins. 2 vols. University of Manitoba Icelandic Studies 1 and 5. Winnipeg, Canada.

Groth, P., ed. 1895. Oddr Snorrason. *Saga Ólafs konungs Tryggvasonar*. Christiania.

Grønlie, Siân. 2004. 'Preaching, Insult and Wordplay in the Old Icelandic Kristniboðsþættir', *Journal of English and Germanic Philology* 103: 458–74.

Grønlie, Siân. 2005. '*Kristni saga* and Medieval Conversion History', *Gripla* 16: 137–60.

Grønlie, Siân. 2006. '"Neither Male Nor Female"? Redeeming Women in the Icelandic Conversion Narratives', forthcoming in *Medium Ævum* 75.

Guðrún P. Helgadóttir. 1961. *Skáldkonur fyrri alda* 1. Akureyri.

Hagnell, Eva. 1938. *Are Frode och hans författarskap*. Lund.

Halldór Hermannsson. 1930. *The Book of the Icelanders*. Islandica 30. Ithaca, NY.

Halldór Hermannsson. 1932. *Sæmund Sigfússon and the Oddaverjar*. Islandica 22. Ithaca, NY.

Halldór Hermannsson. 1948. 'Ari Þorgilsson fróði', *Skírnir* 122: 5–29.

Hardison, O. B. 1965. *Christian Rite and Christian Drama in the Middle Ages*. Baltimore, ML.

Hastrup, Kirsten. 1985. *Culture and History in Medieval Iceland: An Anthropological Analysis of Structure and Change*. Oxford.

Hastrup, Karen. 1990. *Island of Anthropology: Studies in Past and Present Iceland*. Viking Collection: Studies in Northern Civilization 5. Odense.

Haugen, Einar, ed. 1972. *First Grammatical Treatise: The Earliest Germanic Phonology*, 2nd ed. London.

Hauksbók, udgiven efter de arnamagnæanske håndskrifter no. 371, 544 og 675, 4to samt forskellige papirshåndskrifter. 1892–6. Ed. Eiríkur Jónsson and Finnur Jónsson. Copenhagen.

Hauksbók: The Arnamagnæan Manuscripts 371, 4to, 544, 4to and 675, 4to. 1960. Ed. Jón Helgason, Manuscripta Islandica 5. Copenhagen.

Heather, Peter. 1996. *The Goths*. Oxford.

Hermann Pálsson. 1957. 'Játmundar saga', *Skírnir* 131: 139–51.

Hermann Pálsson. 1965. 'Fyrsta Málfræðiritgerðin og upphaf íslenzkrar sagnaritunar', *Skírnir* 139: 159–77.

Hermann Pálsson. 1997. *Keltar á Íslandi*. Reykjavík.

HMS = Heilagra manna sögur: Fortællinger og legender om hellige mænd og kvinder. 1877. Ed. C. R. Unger. 2 vols. Christiania.

HN = *A History of Norway and the Passion and Miracles of the Blessed Óláfr*, trans. Devra Kunin and ed. Carl Phelpstead. 2001. Viking Society for Northern Research, Text Series 13. London.

Hofmann, Dietrich. 1994 'Zur Geschichte der Clemenskirche auf den Vestmannaeyjar', in *Sagnaþing helgað Jónasi Kristjánssyni sjötugum 10. apríl 1994*, ed. Gísli Sigurðsson, Guðrún Kvaran and Jónas Kristjánsson, 433–43. 1994.

Holtsmark, Anne, ed. [1967]. Ari Þorgilsson hinn fróði. *Íslendingabók*. Oslo.

Homiliu-bók: Isländska Homilier efter en handskrift från tolfte århundradet. 1872. Ed. Theodor Wisén. Lund.

Howe, John M. 1997. 'The Conversion of the Physical World: The Creation of a Christian Landscape', in Muldoon 1997, 63–78.

Howe, Nicholas. 1989. *Migration and Mythmaking in Anglo-Saxon England*. New Haven, Conn.

Hughes, Kathleen. 1960. 'The Changing Theory and Practice of Irish Pilgrimage', *Journal of Ecclesiastical History* 11: 143–51.

ÍF = *Íslenzk fornrit*. 1933–. Vols 1– . Reykjavík.

Jackson, Tatjana N. 1998–2001. 'On the Old Norse System of Spatial Orientation', *Saga-Book* 25: 72–82.

Jakob Benediktsson. 1974. 'Landnám og upphaf allsherjarríkis', in *Saga Íslands* I: 153–96.

Jesch, Judith. 1987. 'Women Poets in the Viking Age: an Exploration', *New Comparison* 4: 2–15.

Jochens, Jenny. 1999. 'Late and Peaceful: Iceland's Conversion through Arbitration in 1000', *Speculum* 74: 621–55.

Jómsvíkinga saga. 1969. Ed. Ólafur Halldórsson. Reykjavík.

Jón Árnason. 1954–61. *Íslenzkar þjóðsögur og ævintýri. Ný útgafa*, ed. Árni Böðvarsson and Bjarni Vilhjálmsson. 6 vols. Reykjavík.

Jón Hnefill Aðalsteinsson. 1997. *Blót í norrænum sið: Rýnt í forn trúarbrögð með þjóðfræðilegri aðferð*. Reykjavík.

Jón Hnefill Aðalsteinsson. 1999. *Under the Cloak: A Pagan Ritual Turning Point in the Conversion of Iceland*. Reykjavík.

Jón Jóhannesson. 1941. *Gerðir Landnámabókar*. Reykjavík.

Jón Jóhannesson. 1974. *A History of the Old Icelandic Commonwealth*. Trans. Haraldur Bessason. Manitoba, Canada.

Jón Stefánsson. 1946–53. 'Rúðólf of Bœ and Rudolf of Rouen', *Saga-Book* 13: 174–82.

Jónas Kristjánsson. 1980. 'Annálar og Íslendingasögur', *Gripla* 4: 295–319.

Jónas Kristjánsson. 2001. 'Bréf til Haralds Bessasonar frá Jónasi Kristjánssyni', in *Bréf til Haralds til heiðurs Haraldi Bessasyni sjötugum 14. apríl 2001*, ed. Baldur Hafstað and Gísli Sigurðsson, 256–72. Reykjavík.

Jones, Gwyn. 1964. *The Norse Atlantic Saga, Being the Norse Voyages of Discovery and Settlement to Iceland, Greenland, America*. London.

Jörgensen, Adolf D. 1874–8. *Den nordiske kirkes grundlæggelse og første udvikling*. Copenhagen.

Kahle, Bernhard, ed. 1905. *Kristnisaga, þáttr Þorvalds ens víðförla, þáttr Ísleifs biskups Gizurarsonar, Hungrvaka*. Altnordische Saga-Bibliothek 11. Halle.

KLNM = *Kulturhistorisk leksikon for nordisk middelalder fra vikingetid til reformationstid*. 1956–78. 22 vols. Copenhagen.

Knirk, James E. 1981. *Oratory in the Kings' Sagas*. Oslo.

Krag, Claus. 1991. *Ynglingatal og Ynglingesaga. En studie i historiske kilder*. Studia Humaniora 2. Oslo.

Kress, Helga. 1996. '"Grey þykir mér Freyja". Um konur, kristni og karlveldi í íslenskum fornbókmenntum', in *Konur og kristsmenn: þættir úr kristnisögu Íslands*, ed. Inga Huld Hákonardóttir, 13–63. Reykjavík.

Kristni-saga, sive Historia religionis Christianæ in Islandiam introductæ. 1773. Ed. Hannes Finsson. Hafniæ.

Kuhn, Hans, ed. 1962. *Edda: Die Lieder des Codex Regius nebst verwandten Denkmälern* I. Heidelberg.

Köhne, Roland. 1987. 'Wirklichkeit und Fiktion in den mittelalterlichen Nachrichten über Isleif Gizurarson', *Skandinavistik* 17: 24–30.

Kålund, Kristian. 1877–82. *Bidrag til en historisk-topografisk Beskrivelse af Island*. 2 vols. Copenhagen.

Lamb, Raymond. 1992. 'Church and Kingship in Pictish Orkney: A Mirror for Carolingian Continental Europe', in *Medieval Europe 1992. Preprinted Papers* 6: *Religion and Belief*, 101–06. York.

Lamb, Raymond. 1993. 'Carolingian Orkney and its Transformation', in *The Viking Age in Caithness, Orkney and the North Atlantic*, ed. Colleen E. Batey, Judith Jesch and Christopher D. Morris, 260–71. Edinburgh.

Lange, Gudrun. 1989. *Die Anfänge der isländisch-norwegischen Geschichtsschreibung*. Studia Islandica 47. Reykjavík.

Leifar fornra kristinna fræða íslenzkra. 1878. Ed. Þorvaldur Bjarnarson. Christiania.

Lilja Árnadóttir and Ketil Kiran, eds. 1997. *Church and Art: The Medieval Church in Norway and Iceland*. Reykjavík.

Líndal, Sigurður. 1969. 'Sendiför Úlfljóts. Ásamt nokkrum athugasemdum um landnám Ingólfs Arnarsonar', *Skírnir* 143: 5–26.

Líndal, Sigurður. 1974. 'Upphaf kristni og kirkju', in *Saga Íslands* I: 227–88.

Lindow, John. 1997a. '*Akkerisfrakki*. Traditions concerning Óláfr Tryggvason and Hallfreðr Óttarsson vandræðaskáld and the Problem of the Conversion', in *Sagas and the Norwegian Experience / Sagaene og Noreg. Preprints*, 409–18. Trondheim.

Lindow, John. 1997b. '*Íslendingabók* and Myth', *Scandinavian Studies* 69: 454–64.

Ljungberg, Helge. 1938. *Den nordiska religionen och kristendomen: Studier över det nordiska religionsskiftet under vikingatiden*. Nordiska texter och undersökninger 11. Stockholm.

Louis-Jensen, Jonna. 1976. 'Ari og Gregor', in *Nordiska Studier i filologi och lingvistik. Festskrift tillägnad Gösta Holm på 60-årsdagen den 8. juli 1976*, ed. Lars Svensson, Anne Marie Wieselgren and Åke Hansson, 273–9. Lund.

Lund, Niels. 1997. 'The Danish Empire and the End of the Viking Age', in *The Oxford Illustrated History of the Vikings*, ed. P. Sawyer, 156–81. Oxford.

Lönnroth, Erik. 1996. 'The Vinland Problem', *Scandinavian Journal of History* 21: 39–47.

Lönnroth, Lars. 1965. 'Studier i Olaf Tryggvasons saga', *Samlaren* 84: 54–94.

Lönnroth, Lars, Vésteinn Ólason and Anders Piltz. 2003. 'Literature', in *The Cambridge History of Scandinavia* I. *Prehistory to 1520*, ed. Knut Helle, 487–520. Cambridge.

Magnús Már Lárusson. 1960. 'On the so-called "Armenian" bishops', *Studia Islandica* 18: 23–38.

Magnús Már Lárusson. 1962. 'Interkalation', *KLNM* 7: 441–4.

Magnús Már Lárusson. 1967. 'Gizurr', *Kirkjuritið* 33: 350–69.

Magnús Stefánsson. 1975. 'Kirkjuvald eflist', in *Saga Íslands* II, ed. Sigurður Líndal, 57–144. Reykjavík.

Markus, R. A. 1975. *Bede and the Tradition of Ecclesiastical Historiography*. Jarrow.

Maurer, Konrad. 1867. *Ueber die Ausdrücke: altnordische, altnorwegische & isländische Sprache*. München.

Maurer, Konrad. 1870. 'Über Ari Thorgilssohn und sein Isländerbuch', *Germania* 15: 291–321.

Maurer, Konrad. 1891. 'Über Ari Fróði und seine Schriften', *Germania* 36: 61–96.

McTurk, Rory. 1991. *Studies in Ragnars saga loðbrókar*. Medium Ævum Monographs 15. Oxford.

Melsteð, Bogi Th. 1907–15. 'Ferðir, siglingar og samgöngur milli Íslands og annara landa á dögum þjóðveldisins', *Safn til sögu Íslands* IV, 585–910.

Molland, Einar. 1968. 'Primsigning', *KLNM* 13: 439–44.

Moreland, John. 2000. 'Ethnicity, Power and the English', in *Social Identity in Early Medieval Britain*, ed. William O. Frazer and Andrew Tyrrell, 23–51. London.

Morris, Christopher D. 2004. 'From Birsay to Brattahlíð: Recent Perspectives on Norse Christianity in Orkney, Shetland and the North Atlantic Region', in *Scandinavia and Europe 800–1350: Contact, Conflict and Coexistence*, ed. Jonathan Adams and Katherine Holman, 177–95. Turnhout.

Msk = Morkinskinna. The Earliest Icelandic Chronicle of the Norwegian Kings (1030–1157). 2000. Trans. Theodore M. Andersson and Kari Ellen Gade. Islandica 51. Ithaca, NY.

Muldoon, James, ed. 1997. *Varieties of Religious Conversion in the Middle Ages*. Gainesville, Fla.

Mundal, Else. 1984. 'Íslendingabók, ættar tala og konunga ævi', in *Festskrift til Ludvig Holm-Olsen*, ed. Bjarne Fidjestøl et al., 255–71. Øvre Ervik.

Mundal, Else. 1994. 'Íslendingabók vurdert som bispestolskrønike', *Alvíssmál* 3: 63–72.

Nerman, Birger. 1925. *Det svenska rikets uppkomst*. Föreningen för svensk kulturhistoria böcker 6. Stockholm.

Nordal, Sigurður. 1928. 'Þangbrandur á Mýrdalssandi', in *Festskrift til Finnur Jónsson, 29. maj 1928*, ed. Johs. Brøndum-Nielsen et al., 113–20. Copenhagen.

Nordal, Sigurður. 1990. *Icelandic Culture*, trans. Vilhjálmur T. Bjarnar. Ithaca, NY.

Oddr Snorrason. 1932. *Saga Óláfs Tryggvasonar*. Ed. Finnur Jónsson. Copenhagen.

Oddverjaannáll. 2003. In *Oddaannálar og Oddverjaannáll*. Ed. Eiríkur Þormóðsson and Guðrún Ása Grímsdóttir. Stofnun Árna Magnússonar á Íslandi, Rit 59. Reykjavík.
Ohlmarks, Åke. 1958. *Tors skalder och Vite-Krists: Trosskiftestidens isländska furstelovsskalder 980–1013*. Uppsala.
Ólafia Einarsdóttir. 1964. *Studier i kronologiske metode i tidlig islandsk historieskrivning*. Bibliotheca Historica Lundensis 13. Copenhagen.
Ólafur Halldórsson. 1978. *Grænland í miðaldaritum*. Reykjavík.
Ólafur Halldórsson. 1980. 'Ætt Eiríks rauða', *Gripla* 4: 81–91.
Ólafur Halldórsson. 1981. 'The Conversion of Greenland in Written Sources', in *Proceedings of the Eighth Viking Congress*, ed. Hans Bekker-Nielsen, Peter Foote and Olaf Olsen, 203–16. Odense.
Ólafur Halldórsson. 1990. *Grettisfærsla. Safn ritgerða eftir Ólaf Halldórsson gefið út á sjötugsafmæli hans 18. apríl 1990*. Stofnun Árna Magnússonar á Íslandi, Rit 38. Reykjavík.
Ólafur Halldórsson. 2000. *Danish Kings and the Jomsvikings in the Greatest Saga of Óláfr Tryggvason*. London.
Ólafur Lárusson. 1928. 'Vísa Þorvalds veila', in *Festskrift til Finnur Jónsson, 29. maj 1928*, ed. Johs. Brøndum-Nielsen et al., 263–73. Copenhagen.
Ólafur Lárusson. 1958. *Lög og saga*. Reykjavík.
Ólsen, Björn M. 1893. 'Om Are Frode', *Aarbøger for nordisk oldkyndighed og historie* 8: 207–352.
Ólsen, Björn M. 1900. *Um kristnitökuna árið 1000 og tildrög hennar*. Reykjavík.
Olsen, Olaf. 1966. *Hørg, hov og kirke: historiske og arkaeologiske vikingetidsstudier*. Copenhagen.
Orri Vésteinsson. 2000. *The Christianization of Iceland: Priests, Power and Social Change 1000–1300*. Oxford.
Orrman, Eljas. 2003. 'Church and Society', in *The Cambridge History of Scandinavia* I. *Prehistory to 1520*, ed. Knut Helle, 421–62. Cambridge.
ÓTM = *Óláfs saga Tryggvasonar en mesta*. 1958–2000. Ed. Ólafur Halldórsson. 3 vols. Editiones Arnamagnæana, A 1–3. Copenhagen.
Perkins, Richard. 1985. 'Christian elements in *Flóamanna saga*', in *The Sixth International Saga Conference, 28.7.–2.8. 1985: Workshop Papers* II, 793–811. Copenhagen.
Pizarro, Joaquín Martínez. 1985. 'Conversion Narratives: Form and Utility', in *The Sixth International Saga Conference, 28.7.–2.8. 1985: Workshop Papers* II, 813–32. Copenhagen.
Pohl, Walter. 1997. 'Ethnic Names and Identities in the British Isles: A Comparative Perspective', in *The Anglo-Saxons from the Migration Period to the Eighth Century: An Ethnographic Perspective*, ed. John Hines, 7–32. Woodbridge.
Rollason, David. 2001. *Bede and Germany*. Jarrow.
Russell, James C. 1994. *The Germanization of Early Medieval Christianity: A Sociohistorical Approach to Religious Transformation*. New York.
Saga Íslands I. 1974. Ed. Sigurður Líndal. Reykjavík.

Bibliography

Sawyer, Peter. 1987. 'Ethelred II, Olaf Tryggvason and the Conversion of Norway', *Scandinavian Studies* 59: 299–307.
Sawyer, Peter, Birgit Sawyer and Ian Wood. 1987. *The Christianisation of Scandianavia: Report of a Symposium held at Kungälv, Sweden, 4–9 August 1985*. Alingsås.
Saxo Grammaticus. 1979–80. *The History of the Danes. Books I–IX*. Ed. Hilda Ellis Davidson, trans. Peter Fisher. 2 vols. Cambridge.
Schier, Kurt. 1975. 'Iceland and the Rise of Literature in 'terra nova': Some Comparative Reflections', *Gripla* 1: 168–81.
Schreiner, Johan. 1927. *Saga og oldfunn. Studier til Norges eldste historie*. Oslo.
von See, Klaus. 1968. 'Der Spottvers des Hjalti Skeggjason', *Zeitschrift für deutsches Altertum und deutsche Literatur* 97: 155–8.
Sigurður Þórarinsson. 1974. 'Sambúð lands og lýðs í ellefu aldir', in *Saga Íslands* I: 27–97. Reykjavík.
Skarðsárbók: Landnámabók Björns Jónssonar á Skarðsá. 1958. Ed. Jakob Benediktsson. Reykjavík.
Skårup, Poul. 1979. 'Ari frodes dødsliste for året 1118', *Opuscula* 6: 18–23. Bibliotheca Arnamagnæana 33.
Smalley, Beryl. 1974. *Historians in the Middle Ages*. London.
Smyth, Alfred P. 1977. *Scandinavian Kings in the British Isles 850–880*. Oxford.
Snorri Sturluson. 1998. *Edda. Skáldskaparmál*. Ed. Anthony Faulkes. London.
Snorri Sturluson. 1999. *Edda. Háttatal*. Ed. Anthony Faulkes. London.
Snorri Sturluson. 2005. *Edda. Prologue and Gylfaginning*. Ed. Anthony Faulkes. London.
Steffensen, Jón. 1966–9. 'Aspects of Life in Iceland in the Heathen Period', *Saga-Book* 17: 177–205.
Steffensen, Jón. 1970–73. 'A Fragment of Viking History', *Saga-Book* 18: 59–78.
Steinsland, Gro. 1985–8. 'Husfruer, gydjer og volver', in *Kvinnenes kulturhistorie: Fra antikken til år 1800* I. Ed. Kari Vogt, Sissel Lie, Karin Gundersen and Jorunn Bjørgum, 126–30. Oslo.
Straubhaar, Sandra Ballif. 2002. 'Ambiguously Gendered: The Skalds Jórunn, Auðr and Steinunn', in *Cold Counsel: Women in Old Norse Literature and Mythology. A Collection of Essays*, ed. Sarah M. Anderson and Karen Swenson, 261–71. New York.
Sturl = *Sturlunga saga*, 1946. Ed. Jón Jóhannesson, Magnús Finnbogason and Kristján Eldjárn. 2 vols. Reykjavík.
Sveinbjörn Rafnsson. 1977. 'Um kristniboðsþættina', *Gripla* 2: 19–31.
Sveinbjörn Rafnsson. 1979. 'Um kristnitökufrásögn Ara prests Þorgilssonar', *Skírnir* 153: 167–74.
Sveinbjörn Rafnsson. 1997. 'The Atlantic Islands', in *The Oxford Illustrated History of the Vikings*, ed. P. Sawyer, 110–33. Oxford.
Sveinbjörn Rafnsson. 1999. 'Olaf Tryggvason och Olaf Haraldsson i den äldste historieskrivning', in *Kongemøte på Stiklestad: Foredrag fra seminar om kongedømme i vikingetid og tidlig middelalder*, ed. Olav Skevik, 105–17. Verdal.

Sveinbjörn Rafnsson. 2001. *Sögugerð Landnámabókar: Um íslenska sagnaritun á 12. og 13. öld*. Ritsafn Sagnfræðistofnunar 35. Reykjavík.
Sverrir Tómasson. 1975. 'Tækileg vitni', in *Afmælisrit Björns Sigfússonar*, ed. Björn Þorsteinsson and Sverrir Tómasson, 251–87. Reykjavík.
Sverrir Tómasson. 1988. *Formálar íslenskra sagnaritara á miðöldum. Rannsókn bókmenntahefðar*. Stofnun Árna Magnússonar á Íslandi, Rit 33. Reykjavík.
Theodoricus Monachus. 1998. *Historia de antiquitate regum norwagiensium. An Account of the Ancient History of the Norwegian Kings*, trans. David and Ian McDougall with an introduction by Peter Foote. Viking Society for Northern Research, Text Series 11. London.
Thomas saga erkibiskups. 1869. Ed. C. R. Unger. Christiania.
Thorsteinn Vilhjálmsson. 1993. 'Time-reckoning in Iceland before literacy', in *Archaeoastronomy in the 1990s*, ed. Clive L. N. Ruggles, 69–76. Loughborough.
Trausti Einarsson. 1968. 'Hvernig fann Þorsteinn surtur lengd ársins?' *Saga* 6: 139–44.
Tugéne, Georges. 1982. 'L'histoire "ecclésiastique" du peuple anglais: Réflexions sur le particularisme et l'universalisme chez Béde', *Recherches Augustiniennes* 17: 129–72.
Turville-Petre, Gabriel. 1953. *Origins of Icelandic Literature*. Oxford.
Turville-Petre, Gabriel. 1964. *Myth and Religion of the North: The Religion of Ancient Scandinavia*. London.
Turville-Petre, Joan. 1978–81. 'The Genealogist and History: Ari to Snorri', *Saga-Book* 20: 7–23.
Veraldar saga. 1944. Ed. Jakob Benediktsson. Copenhagen.
Vigfússon, Guðbrand and F. York Powell, eds and trans. 1905. *Origines Islandicae: A Collection of the More Important Sagas and other Native Writings Relating to the Settlement and Early History of Iceland*. 2 vols. Oxford.
de Vries, Jan. 1942. *Altnordische Literaturgeschichte* II. Berlin.
de Vries, Jan. 1958–9. 'Ein Problem in der Bekehrungsgeschichte Islands', *Zeitschrift für deutsches Altertum* 89: 75–82.
VSH = *Vitae Sanctorum Hiberniae*. 1910. Ed. Charles Plummer. 2 vols. Oxford.
Ward, Benedicta. 1976. 'Miracles and History: A Reconsideration of the Miracle Stories used by Bede', in *Famulus Christi*, 70–76.
Weber, Gerd Wolfgang. 1987. 'Intellegere historiam. Typological Perspectives of Nordic Prehistory (in Snorri, Saxo, Widukind and others)', in *Tradition og historieskrivning: Kilderne til Nordens ældste historie*, ed. Kirsten Hastrup and Preben Meulengracht Sørensen, 95–141. Acta Jutlandica 63: 2, Humanistik Serie 61. Århus.
Whaley, Diana. 1998. *The Poetry of Arnórr Jarlaskáld: An Edition and Study*. Turnhout.
Wood, Ian. 1999. 'The Use and Abuse of Latin Hagiography in the Early Medieval West', in *East and West: Modes of Communication. Proceedings of the First Plenary Conference at Menda*, ed. Evangelos Chrysos and Ian Wood, 93–109. Leiden.
Wood, Ian. 2001. *The Missionary Life: Saints and the Evangelisation of Europe 400–1050*. Harlow.

Wormald, Patrick. 1983. 'Bede, the Bretwaldas and the Origins of the *Gens Anglorum*', in *Ideal and Reality in Frankish and Anglo-Saxon Society*, ed. Patrick Wormald, Donald Bullough and Roger Collins, 99–129. Oxford.

Würth, Stephanie. 2005. 'Historiography and Pseudo-History', in *A Companion to Old Norse-Icelandic Literature and Culture*, ed. Rory McTurk, 155–72. Oxford.

Þórir Óskarsson. 2005. 'Rhetoric and Style', in *A Companion to Old Norse–Icelandic Literature and Culture*, ed. Rory McTurk, 354–71. Oxford.

Þorkell Jóhannesson. 1938. *Örnefni í Vestmannaeyjum*. Reykjavík.

INDEX OF PERSONAL NAMES

Abraham, bishop from Ermland 10 (see note 78)
Aðils [Eadgils/Athisl] at Uppsala, son of Óttarr 14 (see note 118)
Agni, son of Alrekr 14 (see note 115)
Albert [Adalbert], bishop in Bremen/Århus 38 (see note 29)
Alexius I Comnenus, Byzantine emperor 1081–1118 13 (see note 104), 53
Álfr in the Dales [Eysteinsson], brother of Þórólfr 6
Alrekr, son of Dagr 14 (see note 115)
Ari Másson, father of Guðleifr, chieftain in 981 35 (see note 6)
Ari Þorgilsson the Learned or the Old (1067/8–1148) 3, 10, 11, 14, 51, 52, 53
Arngeirr Spak['Wise']-Bǫðvarsson, brother of Þorvarðr 37 (see note 22)
Arnórr kerlingarnef ['Old Woman's Nose'], [Bjarnarson], chieftain in 981 35 (see note 6)
Arnulf [Arnaldus (Malecorne) of Rohea], Latin patriarch of Jerusalem 1099, 1112–18 13, 53
Ásbjǫrn Arnórsson, father of Arnórr, Þorsteinn and Bǫðvarr, chieftains in 1118 54 (see note 113)
Ásbjǫrn, son of Ketill the Foolish 41 (see note 49)
Ásgeirr Knattarson, chieftain in 981 35 (see note 6)
Ásgrímr Elliða-Grímsson, chieftain in 981 35, 48 (see note 79)
Ásgrímr Þorhallsson, father of Solvǫr 55
Áskell, son of Ósvífr the Wise 40 (see note 40)
Ástríðr, daughter of Eiríkr Víkinga-Kárason, mother of Óláfr Tryggvason 46
Atall, sea-king (in kenning) 44
Atli the Strong, son of Eilífr Eagle, brother of Koðrán 35
Auðr [Unnr, the Deep-Minded], daughter of Ketill Flatnose, settler 4 (see note 22), 13

Aun the Old, son of Jǫrundr 14 (see note 116)
Baldr, a god 43
Baldwin I, king of crusader state of Jerusalem 1100–1118 13, 53
Bárðr from Áll, son of Ketill Fox 35 (see note 1)
Bera, daughter of Egill Skalla-Grímsson, wife of Ǫzurr 36
Bera, daughter of Ormr Koðránsson, wife of Skúli Þorsteinsson 36
Bergþórr Hrafnsson, lawspeaker 1117–22 12, 53
Bjarnharðr [Bernard, the Saxon], foreign bishop in Iceland 10 (see note 77)
Bjarnharðr [Bernard, Vilráðsson] the Book-Learned, foreign bishop in Iceland 10 (see note 77)
Bjarni the Wise [Þorsteinsson], father of Skeggi, born c.960 11
Bjǫrn, son of King Haraldr the Fine-Haired 10
Bolli Þorleiksson, Kjartan's foster-brother (died 1007) 45
Bótólfr, bishop in Hólar 1238–46 37 (see note 25)
Brandr the Far-Traveller 51 (see note 93)
Brandr, son of Þorkell Gellisson, Ari's cousin 14 (see note 126)
Braut-Ǫnundr, son of Yngvarr 14 (see note 119)
Brennu['Burning']-Flosi, son of Þórðr Freysgoði 47
Brodd['Spike']-Helgi [Þorgilsson] (died 974) 49
Bǫðvarr, son of Víkinga-Kári, father of Ólǫf, lord (hersir) in Norway 46
Christ 3, 9, 13, 39, 44, 49, 50, 51, 53
Dagr, Danish king 50 (see note 86)
Dagr, son of Dyggvi 14
Dalla Þorvaldsdóttir, wife of Bishop Ísleifr, mother of Bishop Gizurr 51
Digr['Stout']-Ketill 49

Index of Personal Names

Dómaldr [Dómaldi], son of Vísburr 14 (see note 114)
Dómarr, son of Dómaldr 14
Dyggvi, son of Dómarr 14
Edmund, St, king of East Anglia 885–69/70 3 (see note 11) 5, 9, 13
Egill Crow of Vendill, son of Aun the Old 14 (see note 117)
Egill, son of Hallr on Síða 13, 53
Egill Skalla-Grímsson, father of Bera and Þorsteinn 36
Einarr [Auðunarson], son of Helga Helgadóttir 13
Eilífr Eagle, son of Bárðr from Áll 35 (see note 1)
Eilífr, son of Helgi bjóla 39 (see note 36)
Eiríkr at Uppsala [Bjarnarson, the Victorious], Swedish king c.970(?)–95 9
Eiríkr Hákonarson [the Powerful], Norwegian earl 1000–14, died 1022 9, 50
Eiríkr Víkinga-Kárason, brother of Bǫðvarr 46
Eiríkr the Red [Þorvaldsson] 7 (see note 54)
Eyjólfr, son of Goðmundr the Powerful 13
Eyjólfr Valgerðarson [Einarson], chieftain in 981 13 (see note 108), 35, 37
Eyjólfr [the Grey], son of Þórðr Gellir, chieftain in 981 14 (see note 125), 35
Eysteinn, son of Aðils 14
Eysteinn Fart, son of Hálfdan Whiteleg, king in Upplǫnd 3
Eysteinn, son of Magnús, Norwegian king 1103–23 13
Eyvindr the Easterner [Bjarnarson], father of Helgi the Lean 4 (see note 23)
Fjǫlnir, son of Freyr 14 (see note 113)
Freyja, goddess 8 (see note 69), 44
Freyr, a god, son of Njǫrðr 14
Frið-Fróði, legendary Danish king 14
Friðgerðr, wife of Þórarinn fylsenni 36 (see note 17)
Friðrekr, foreign bishop in Iceland 10 (see note 77), 35, 36, 37, 38
Galdra['Spells']-Heðinn 41

Geirlaug, daughter of Steinmóðr, second wife of Ormr Koðránsson 36
Geitir [Lýtingsson], chieftain in 981 (died 987) 35 (see note 6)
Gellir Bǫlverksson [grandson of Eyjólfr the Grey], lawspeaker 1054–62, 1072–4 10, 11
Gellir Þorkelsson, Ari's grandfather and foster-father, son of Þorkell Eyjólfsson and Guðrún Ósvífrsdóttir (1017–73) 6, 10, 14 (see note 126)
Gestr [Oddleifsson] the Wise, chieftain in 981 (died 1019/20) 35, 44 (see note 58), 49
Gisrøðr, see Gizurr Ísleifsson
Gizurr Einarsson, chieftain in 1118 54 (see note 113)
Gizurr son of Ísleifr, bishop of Iceland 1082–1105 and in Skálaholt 1106–18 3, 10, 11 (see notes 91 and 92), 12, 13, 51, 52, 53, 54
Gizurr the White, son of Teitr Ketilbjarnarson, father of Bishop Ísleifr 7 (see note 61), 8, 10, 13, 35, 42, 43, 45, 46, 47, 48, 49, 51
God 35, 36, 39, 41, 42, 44, 50
gods 8, 44, 48, 49
Goðiskálkr, foreign bishop in Iceland 10
Goðmundr/Guðmundr the Powerful, son of Eyjólfr Valgerðarson (954–1025) 13 (see note 108), 45, 47
Goðmundr Þorgeirsson, lawspeaker 1123–34 12
Goðrøðr the Hunter-King, son of Hálfdan the Bounteous 3 (see note 7)
Goðrøðr, son of Hálfdan Whiteleg 14 (see note 121)
Goðrøðr, son of Bjǫrn, grandfather of St Ólafr 10
Gregory I, pope 590–604 13
Gregory VII, pope 1073–85 12, 52
Grímr geitskor, Úlfljótr's foster-brother 4 (see note 27), 5
Grímr Svertingsson, lawspeaker 1002–3 10
Guðleifr, son of Ari Másson 42, 43

Guðmundr Brandsson, priest and chieftain (died 1151) 53 (see note 106)
Guðmundr the Powerful, see Goðmundr the Powerful
Gunnarr [Hlífarson], husband of Helga Óleifsdóttir, father of Þórunn 6
Gunnarr, son of Úlfljótr 4 (see note 24)
Gunnarr the Wise [Þorgrímsson], father of Úlfheðinn, lawspeaker 1063–65, 1075 10, 11, 12
Gunnarr, brother of Þorvaldr kroppinskeggi 5
Gunnhildr, daughter of Ormr Koðránsson, see Yngvildr
Gylfi, sea-king (in kenning) 44
Hafliði Másson, Teitr Ísleifsson's son-in-law, chieftain in 1118 (died 1130) 12 (see note 98) 53, 54, 55
Hálfdan the Bounteous but Stingy-with-Food, son of Eysteinn Fart 3 (see note 6)
Hálfdan the Black, son of Goðrøðr 3
Hálfdan Whiteleg, son of Óláfr Treefeller 3, 14 (see note 121)
Hálfdan, son of Sigurðr Bastard, grandfather of King Haraldr Sigurðarson 10
Halldórr Egilsson, chieftain in 1118 54 (see note 113)
Halldórr, son of Guðmundr the Powerful, hostage in Norway (died 1014) 45, 47
Hallfreðr/Hallfrøðr Óttarson 'Troublesome Poet' 45, 47 (see note 76)
Hallfríðr, daughter of Snorri Karlsefnisson, mother of Bishop Þorlákr Runólfsson 13
Hallr Órœkjuson, one of Ari's informants 5 (see note 32)
Hallr, son of Teitr Ísleifsson (died 1150) 10 (see note 84), 53, 54
Hallr in Haukadalr [Þórarinsson], Ari's foster-father (995/6–1089) 10 (see note 85), 11, 12, 42
Hallr Þorsteinsson on/from Síða, chieftain in 981 7 (see note 61), 8, 13, 35, 41, 43, 49, 53

Hallsteinn, son of Þórólfr Mostrarskeggi and Ósk Þorsteinsdóttir 5
Haraldr [Bluetooth] Gormsson, Danish king (died 985/8) 38 (see note 29)
Haraldr [of Grenland], son of Goðrøðr, father of St Óláfr 10
Haraldr the Fine-Haired, son of Hálfdan the Black, Norwegian king 3 (see note 8), 4, 5, 7, 10
Haraldr [the Hard-Ruler], son of Sigurðr, Norwegian king 1046–66 10, 11 (see note 87), 54
Hárbarðr, name for Óðinn 42
Haukr, name of two berserks 36
Heðinn [the Generous], son of Þorbjǫrn Skagason 37 (see note 26), 38
Heinrekr, foreign bishop in Iceland (died 1066?) 10 (see note 77)
Helga, daughter of Helgi the Lean 13
Helga, daughter of Óleifr feilan, wife of Gunnarr [Hlífarson] 6
Helgi Ásbjarnarson, chieftain in 981 (died 1008) 35 (see note 6)
Helgi bjóla, son of Ketill Flatnose 39 (see note 36)
Helgi the Lean, son of Eyvindr the Easterner, settler 4 (see note 22), 13
Helgi, son of Óláfr Goðrøðarson 14 (see note 121)
Hermundr Illugason, son-in-law of Ormr Koðránsson 36 (see note 11), 49
Hersteinn, son of Þorkell Blund-Ketilsson 6 (see note 45)
Hjalti Skeggjason, son-in-law of Gizurr the White 7 (see note 61), 8, 35, 42, 44, 45, 46, 47, 48, 49, 50
Hlenni the Old, son of Ormr Bag-Back [or Ǫrnólfr] 35 (see note 7), 49
Hrafn, son of [Ketill] Hœngr, lawspeaker c.930–49 5
Hrollaugr, son of Rǫgnvaldr, settler 4 (see note 22), 13
Hróðólfr [Roðulf] foreign bishop in Iceland (died 1052) 10 (see note 77)

Index of Personal Names

Hubert, bishop of Canterbury 38 (see note 30), 39
Hœngr [Ketill Þorkelsson], settler 5
Hœsna-Þórir (died 962) 6 (see note 44)
Hǫrða-Kári [Ásláksson], father of Þorleifr the Wise 4
Illugi the Red [Hrólfsson], chieftain in 981 35 (see note 6)
Illugi, father of Ingimundr 55 (see note 120)
Illugi, son of Ingimundr Illugason (died 1171) 55
Ingileif, mother of Þorleifr and Þórarinn Ásbjarnarson 49
Ingimundr Einarsson, priest and chieftain (died 1169/70) 53 (see note 106)
Ingimundr, son of Illugi, husband of Valgerðr Hafliðadóttir, priest (died 1150) 55 (see note 120)
Ingjaldr the Evil, son of Braut-Ǫnundr 14 (see note 120)
Ingjaldr, son of Helgi and great-grandson of Ragnarr loðbrók 14 (see note 122)
Ingólfr [Arnarson], first settler in Iceland 4, 5
Ísleifr Gizurarson, born 1006, bishop of Iceland 1056–80 3, 10 (see note 82), 11, 13, 51, 52
Ívarr [the Boneless], son of Ragnarr loðbrók 3 (see note 10)
Ívarr, son of Þórðr Hafliðason 55 (see note 119)
Jesus Christ, see Christ
Jóan, see Jón Ǫgmundarson
Jófríðr, daughter of Gunnarr and Helga, wife of Þorsteinn Egilsson 6
Jóhan, foreign bishop in Iceland (died 1066) 10 (see note 77)
Jón Þorvarðsson, priest and chieftain (died 1150) 53 (see note 109)
Jón/Jóan Ǫgmundarson, bishop at Hólar 1106–21 10, 13 (see note 101), 52, 53, 54, 55
Jǫrundr goði, father of Úlfr 45
Jǫrundr, son of Yngvi Agnason 14
Kálfr Ásgeirsson 45
Karlsefni [Þorfinnr], son of Þórðr Horsehead 13 (see note 107)
Ketilbjǫrn Ketilsson, settler 4 (see note 22), 7, 13
Ketill Flatnose [son of Bjǫrn buna] 4 (see note 22)
Ketill Guðmundarson, priest and chieftain (died 1158) 53 (see note 106)
Ketill the Foolish [son of Jórunn], grandson of Ketill Flatnose 41 (see note 47)
Ketill Fox, son of Skíði the Old 35
Ketill, son of Þorsteinn, bishop in Hólar 1122–45 3 (see note 1), 13, 53, 54, 55
Kirjalax, see Alexius
Kjartan, son of Óláfr Peacock, hostage in Norway (died 1003/4) 45, 46, 47
Klaufi, son of Þorvaldr Refsson 37 (see note 21)
Koðrán, son of Eilífr Eagle, father of Þorvaldr the Far-Traveller 35, 36, 51
Kolbeinn Flosason, lawspeaker 1066–71 10, 11
Kolbeinn, son of Þórðr Freysgoði, hostage in Norway 45, 47
Kolr, slave or freedman 5
Kolr, foreign bishop in Iceland 10 (see note 77)
Kolr [Þorkelsson], bishop in Vík (died c.1120) 10 (see note 83), 52
Kolr in Lœkjarbugr 43 (see note 55)
Koltorfa Skeggjadóttir, sister of Hjalti, wife of Þorvaldr Skeggjason 48
Leifr the Lucky, son of Eiríkr the Red 47 (see note 75)
Leo VII, pope 936–9 11 (see note 89)
Leo IX, pope 1049–54 51
Magnús [the Good], son of King Óláfr Haraldsson, Norwegian king 1035–47 13
Magnús Þórðarson, priest and chieftain 53 (see note 106)
Markús Skeggjason, lawspeaker 1084–1107 11 (see note 93), 12, 52, 53

Michael, St, Archangel 41 (see note 44)
Narfi, outlaw 45
Njǫrðr, son of Yngvi 14
Oddný, daughter of Þorkell Gellisson, mother of Ingimundr Illugason 55
[Tungu-]Oddr [Ǫnundarson], father of Þorvaldr (died c.965) 9 (see note 43)
Óláfr at Haukagil, grandfather and foster-father of Hallfreðr Óttarsson 36 (see note 12)
Óláfr, son of Goðrøðr, son of Hálfdan Whiteleg 14 (see note 121)
Óláfr the Peaceful Haraldsson, Norwegian king 1066–93 11, 52
Óláfr the Stout Haraldsson, St, Norwegian king 1015/16–30 4 (see note 20), 10, 13
Óláfr, son of King Haraldr the Fine-Haired 7
Óláfr Peacock [Hǫskuldsson], chieftain in 981 (died 1006) 35 (see note 6), 45
Óláfr [the Swede], son of Eiríkr at Uppsala, Swedish king 995–1022 9
Óláfr Treefeller, son of Ingjaldr the Evil, father of Hálfdan Whiteleg 3 (see note 5), 14
Óláfr Tryggvason, Norwegian king 995–999/1000 7 (see note 59), 8, 9, 10, 11, 13, 39, 40, 41, 44, 45, 46, 47, 48, 50, 52, 55
Óleifr [Óláfr] feilan, son of Þorsteinn the Red (886–948) 6 (see notes 43 and 46) 13, 14
Óleifr [Óláfr] hjalti, father of Ragi and Þórarinn 5 (see note 35)
Óleifr [Óláfr] the White, son of Ingjaldr Helgason 14 (see note 123)
Ólǫf [Álǫf], daughter of Bǫðvarr, mother of Gizurr the White 46
Ormr Bag-Back, father of Hlenni the Old 35
Ormr, son of Koðrán, brother of Þorvaldr the Far-Traveller 36 (see note 11), 49
Ósk, daughter of Þorsteinn the Red 5

Óspakr, son of Ósvífr the Wise 40 (see note 40)
Ósvífr the Wise Helgason, grandfather of Gellir Þorkelsson (died 1019/20) 6 (see note 39), 40
Óttarr [Ohthere], son of Egill 14 (see notes 117 and 118)
Otto the Young, German king 983–1002, Holy Roman Emperor 996–1002 39 (see note 33)
Páll, son of Þórðr Þorvaldsson (died 1171) 55 (see note 120)
Paschal II, pope 1099–1118 13, 53
Peter, bishop from Ermland 10 (see note 78)
Philip, Swedish king (died 1118) 13 (see note 104), 53
Phocas, Byzantine emperor 602–10 13
Ragi, son of Óleifr hjalti, brother of Þórarinn 5 (see note 35), 7
Ragnarr loðbrók [Sigurðarson] 3 (see note 10), 14
Ragnheiðr, niece and step-daughter of Eyjólfr Valgerðarson 37
Rannveig, daughter of Teitr Ísleifsson, second wife of Hafliði Másson 55 (see note 120)
Runólfr, son of Úlfr Jǫrundarson, chieftain in 981 35 (see note 6) 45, 47, 48, 50
Runólfr Þorleiksson, brother of Hallr in Haukadalr 12, 53
Rǫgnvaldr [Eysteinsson], earl in Mœrr 4
Rǫgnvaldr kali [Kolsson], St, earl in Orkney c.1127/9–58/9 55 (see note 122)
Síðu-Hallr, see Hallr Þorsteinsson
Sighvatr Surtsson, lawspeaker 1076–83 11
Sigmundr Þorgilsson, chieftain in 1118 54 (see note 113)
Sigríðr, daughter of Hafliði Másson, wife of Þórðr Þorvaldsson 55
Sigurðr [Sow], son of Hálfdan Sigurðarson (died 1018) 10
Sigurðr Bastard, son of King Haraldr the Fine-Haired 10

Index of Personal Names

Sigurðr [Crusader], son of King Magnús, Norwegian king 1103–30 13

Sigurðr [Snake-in-Eye], son of Ragnarr loðbrók 14

Sigvaldi, earl of Jómsborg 51 (see note 96)

Símon Jǫrundarson, priest and chieftain 53

Skáld['Poet']-Refr [Gestsson], son of Steinunn 43 (see note 56)

Skapti, son of Þóroddr goði, lawspeaker 1004–30 10 (see note 79), 52

Skeggbjǫrn at Hítarnes 42, 43 (see note 55)

Skeggi Ásgautsson, father of Þorvaldr 48 (see note 78)

Skeggi, son of Bjarni, father of Markús and Þórarinn 11

Skeggi, son of Þórarinn fylsenni and Friðgerðr 36 (see note 17)

Skíði the Old, father of Ketill Fox 35

Skúli Egilsson, chieftain in 1118 54 (see note 113)

Skúli, son of Þorsteinn Egilsson, son-in-law of Ormr Koðránson 36 (see note 11)

Snorri, son of Karlsefni 13

Snorri goði [Þorgrímsson], father of Þuríðr, chieftain in 981 (963/4–1031) 3, 35 (see note 6), 49, 50

Solvǫr, daughter of Ásgrímr Þórhallsson, wife of Þórðr Hafliðason 55

Spak('Wise')-Bǫðvarr, father of Þorvarðr 49

Starri or Hólmgǫngu['Duel']-Starri, [son of Eiríkr in Guðdalir], chieftain in 981 35 (see note 6)

Stefnir, son of Þorgils Eilífsson 39 (see note 36), 40, 50, 51

Steinmóðr [Gunnarsson], father-in-law of Ormr Koðránsson 36 (see note 11)

Steinunn [Dálksdóttir or Refsdóttir], mother of Skáld-Refr, poet 43 (see note 56)

Steinn Þorgestsson, lawspeaker 1031–3 10

Stephen, bishop from Ermland 10 (see note 78)

Styrmir Hreinsson, chieftain in 1118 54 (see note 113)

Surtr, son of Ásbjǫrn 41 (see note 47)

Svegðir, son of Fjǫlnir 14

Sveinn [Forkbeard], son of Haraldr Gormsson, king of Denmark 986–1014 and England 1013–14 9, 51

Svertingr, son of Runólfr goði, hostage in Norway 45, 47

Sæmundr Sigfússon [the Learned], priest and chieftain (1056–1133) 3 (see note 2), 9, 11, 52, 53, 54

Teitr, son of Bishop Ísleifr and Ari's foster-father (c.1040–1110) 3 (see note 9), 4, 8, 9, 10, 11, 51, 55

Teitr, son of Ketilbjǫrn Ketilsson 7, 13

Torráðr, son of Ósvífr the Wise 40 (see note 40)

Tryggvi, Norwegian king 50 (see note 86)

Tryggvi, son of Óláfr, son of King Haraldr the Fine-Haired 7, 51

Tungu-Oddr, see Oddr

Uggi, father of Úlfr 42

Úlfheðinn, son of Gunnarr the Wise, lawspeaker 1108–16 5 (see note 33), 7, 12, 53

Úlfljótr, lawspeaker 4 (see note 24), 5

Úlfr, son of Jǫrundr goði 45

Úlfr, son of Uggi, poet 42 (see note 50)

Valgarðr at Hof [Jǫrundarson], chieftain in 981 35 (see note 6)

Valgerðr, daughter of Hafliði Másson, wife of Ingimundr Illugason (died 1154) 55 (see note 120)

Vandráðr, son of Ósvífr the Wise 40 (see note 40)

Vanlandi, son of Svegðir 14

Vetrliði [Sumarliðason], poet 42 (see note 53), 43

Víga('killer')-Bjarni [Brodd-Helgason], chieftain in 981 35 (see note 6)

Víga('killer')-Glúmr [Eyjólfsson], chieftain in 981 (died c.1003) 36 (see note 6)

Víga('killer')-Styrr [Þorgrímsson], chieftain in 981 (died 1008) 35 (see note 6)
Víkinga('Vikings')-Kári, father of Bǫðvarr 46
Vilbald, father of Þangbrandr, count of Bremen 38
Vísburr, son of Vanlandi 14
Yngvarr, son of Eysteinn 14
Yngvi, son of Agni 14
Yngvi, father of Njǫrðr and progenitor of Ynglings 14 (see note 110)
Yngvildr/Gunnhildr, daughter of Ormr Koðránsson, wife of Hermundr Illugason 36 (see note 11), 49
Þangbrandr [Þorbrandr, Theobrand], son of Vilbald, foreign priest 7 (see note 60), 8, 11, 38, 39, 40, 41, 42, 43, 44, 46, 47
Þórarinn Ásbjarnarson, son of Ingileif and brother of Þorleifr 49 (see note 84)
Þórarinn Nefjólfsson 45
Þórarinn Ragi's brother, son of Óleifr hjalti, lawspeaker c.950–69 5 (see note 35), 7, 11
Þórarinn [Skeggjason], brother of Markús 11
Þórarinn fylsenni ['Foal's Forehead'?], son of Þórðr gellir, husband of Friðgerðr 36 (see note 17)
Þorbjǫrn Skagason, father of Heðinn 37
Þorbjǫrn, son of Þorkell [Eiríksson] 45 (see note 61)
Þórdís, daughter of Ǫzurr Hrollaugsson 13
Þórðr Freysgoði [Ǫzurarson], father of Brennu-Flosi and Kolbeinn, chieftain in 981 35 (see note 6), 45, 47
Þórðr gellir, son of Óleifr Feilan (died c.965) 6 (see notes 43 and 46), 7, 13, 14
Þórðr Gilsson, grandfather of Snorri Sturluson, chieftain in 1118 54 (see note 113)
Þórðr, son of Hafliði Másson and Þuríðr Þórðardóttir 55 (see note 119)
Þórðr Horsehead, son of Þórhildr Ptarmigan 13

Þórðr, son of Víga-Sturla, father of Þuríðr (1165–1237) 55 (see note 119)
Þórðr, son of Þórðr Þorvaldsson (died 1194) 55 (see note 120)
Þórðr Þorvaldsson, son-in-law of Hafliði Másson, chieftain in 1118 54 (see note 113), 55
Þorgeirr Hallason, chieftain in 1118 (died 1169) 54 (see note 113)
Þorgeirr Þorkelsson [or Tjǫrvason, Ljósvetningagoði], lawspeaker 985–1001 7 (see note 52), 9, 10, 49, 50
Þorgerðr, daughter of Egill Hallsson, mother of Bishop Jón Ǫgmundarson 13, 53
Þorgils, son of Eilífr Helgason, father of Stefnir 39
Þorgils Grenjaðarson, father of Ǫnundr the Christian 35
Þorgils Oddason, chieftain in 1118 (died 1151) 54 (see note 113), 55
Þorgils, son of Þorkell Gellisson and father of Ari 14 (see note 126)
Þórhildr Ptarmigan, daughter of Þórðr gellir 13
Þóríðr (Þuríðr), daughter of Snorri goði (1025/6–1112/13) 3 (see note 9)
Þórir kroppinskeggi, uncle of Þorvaldr 5 (see note 31)
Þorkell [Eiríksson], father of Þorbjǫrn, brother of Starri 45 (see note 61)
Þorkell, son of Eyjólfr the Grey (978/9–1026) 14 (see note 125)
Þorkell Gellisson, Ari's uncle (b. c.1030) 3 (see note 9), 4, 7, 14, 55
Þorkell Blund-Ketilsson, father of Hersteinn (died c.962) 6 (see note 45)
Þorkell Tjǫrvason [grandson of Þorgeirr Þorkelsson?], lawspeaker 1034–53 10
Þorkell krafla [Þorgrímsson], chieftain in 981 35, 36 (see note 13)
Þorkell Moon, son of Þorsteinn Ingólfsson, lawspeaker 970–84 5, 6, 7 (see note 52), 35
Þorlákr [son of Runólfr], bishop in Skálaholt 1118–33 3 (see note 1), 12, 13, 53

Index of Personal Names

Þorleifr, son of Ingileif and half-brother of Þórarinn 49 (see note 87)
Þorleifr the Wise, son of Hǫrða-Kári 4 (see note 26)
Þorlcikr, Hallr in Haukadalr's brother 12
Þormóðr [Thermo], foreign priest 8 (see note 65), 48
Þóroddr goði [Eyvindarson], father of Skapti, chieftain in 981 35, 48 (see note 82)
Þórólfr Fox [Eysteinsson], brother of Álfr in the Dales 6 (see note 47)
Þórólfr Mostrarskeggi [Ǫrnólfsson], settler (died 918) 5 (see note 38)
Þórólfr, son of Ósvífr the Wise 40 (see note 40)
Þórr, a god 43
Þorsteinn Black, son of Hallsteinn 5 (see note 38), 6
Þorsteinn, son of Egill Skalla-Grímsson, chieftain in 981 (died 1015) 6, 35 (see note 6)
Þorsteinn, son of Eyjólfr Goðmundarson, father of Bishop Ketill 13
Þorsteinn Hallvarðsson (died 1119) 54 (see note 114)
Þorsteinn, son of Ingólfr, father of Þorkell Moon 5 (see note 30), 7
Þorsteinn the Red, son of Óleifr the White 5, 13, 14 (see note 124)
Þórunn, daughter of Gunnarr and Helga, wife of Hersteinn Þorkelsson 6
Þorvaldr, son of Bishop Ísleifr Gizurarson 10 (see note 84), 51
Þorvaldr the Far-Traveller, son of Koðrán Eilífsson 35, 36, 37, 38, 49, 50, 51
Þorvaldr kroppinskeggi, nephew of Þórir and brother of Gunnarr 5
Þorvaldr Refsson, father of Klaufi 37
Þorvaldr, son of Skeggi, brother-in-law of Hjalti 48 (see note 78)
Þorvaldr, son of Tungu-Oddr 6
Þorvaldr veili, poet 42 (see note 49), 43
Þorvarðr [the Christian] Spak-Bǫðvarsson, chieftain in 981 35 (see note 7), 37, 49
Þórvǫr, daughter of Ǫzurr and Bera Egilsdóttir, first wife of Ormr Koðránsson 36
Þuríðr, daughter of Snorri goði, see Þóríðr
Þuríðr, daughter of Þórðr Sturluson, first wife of Hafliði Másson 55 (see note 119)
Þvinnill, sea-king (in kenning) 43
Æsir 40 (see note 38)
Ǫgmundr, father of Bishop Jón 53
Ǫnundr the Christian, son of Þorgils Grenjaðarson 35 (see note 7)
Ǫrnólfr, foreign bishop in Iceland 10
Ǫrnólfr in Skógar, father of Halldórr and Arnórr (died 997), chieftains in 981 35 (see note 6)
Ǫzurr, son of Hrollaugr 13
Ǫzurr, brother of Þóroddr goði, father of Þórvǫr 36 (see note 11)

INDEX OF PLACES AND PEOPLES

Á (river), see Þváttá
Áll (Ål in Hallingdal, Buskerud?), in Norway 35
Álptafjǫrðr (Northern, now Hamarsfjörður), fjord in eastern Iceland 41
Álptafjǫrðr (Southern, now Álftafjörður), fjord in eastern Iceland 41
Angles, inhabitants of East Anglia in England 3, 13
Arnarstakksheiðr, coastal path between Mýrdalr and Mýrdalssandr in southern Iceland 47
Áróss (Århus), in Jutland 38
Áss (now Neðri-Áss), farm in Hjaltadalr in Skagafjǫrðr 35, 37
Barð, farm in Fljót in Skagafjǫrðr 37
Barðastrǫnd, coastal area along north coast of Breiðafjǫrðr 44
Belgsholt, farm in Borgarfjǫrðr 44
Bláskógar ('Black Woods'), wooded area near Þingvellir in southwest Iceland 5
Borgarfjǫrðr, fjord and district in western Iceland 5, 6, 36, 43
Breiðabólstaðr, farm on Síða in south-east Iceland 13
Breiðabólstaðr, farm in Vestrhóp 55
Breiðafjǫrðr, ('broad') fjord and district in western Iceland 4, 5, 6, 7, 13, 14
Breiðafjǫrðr Quarter, see Western Quarter
Bremen, in northern Germany 38
Bœr, farm in Borgarfjǫrðr 53
Canterbury, in England 38
Dales (now Breiðafjarðardalir), valleys in Breiðafjǫrðr in western Iceland 6
Danes 9
Denmark 9, 12, 39, 50, 51, 52
Djúpadalr (now Stóridalr), farm in Eyjafjǫrðr in northern Iceland 4, 36
Dnieper, river running through present-day Ukraine to the Black Sea 50
Drafn, near Polotsk (not identified) 51
Dyrhólmaóss (now Dyrhólaós), estuary in Mýrdalr in southern Iceland 47
Eastern Fjords 5, 41, 42

Eastern Fjords Quarter, see Eastern Quarter
Eastern Quarter 12, 49, 52
Easterner 4 (see note 23)
Eiríksfjǫrðr (Tunugdliarfik), in Greenland 7
England 11, 13
Ermland 10 (see note 78)
Eyjafjǫll, mountains east of Rangá district in southern Iceland 54
Eyjafjǫrðr, fjord and district in northern Iceland 4, 7, 13, 37, 42
Eyjafjǫrðr Quarter, see Northern Quarter
Fljótsdalr, area in eastern Iceland 41
Fljótshlíð, area south-east of Rangá district in southern Iceland 42
Frakkland 11 (see note 88)
Gautland (Götaland, probably Västergötland), area in southern Sweden 11
Giljá (Stóra Giljá), farm in Vatsdalr in northern Iceland 35
Giljá, see Haukagil
Gilsbakki, farm on Hvítá in Mýrar north of Borgarfjǫrðr 49
Greenland 3, 7, 47
Greeks 13, 53
Grímsnes, area east of Þingvallavatn in south-west Iceland 42, 43
Guðdalir (Goðdalir), valleys in Skagafjǫrðr (probably Svartárdalur, Vesturárdalur and Austurdalur, see *ÍF* I 231) 35, 45
Gufáróss, river mouth at head of Borgarfjǫrðr in western Iceland 40
Gulaþing ('Gula Assembly'), legal area in western Norway that had its central assembly on the island of Gulǿy in Hǫrðaland 4
Háfr, farm near Þjórsá in south-west Iceland 48
Hálogaland (Hålogaland), in northern Norway 45
Haukadalr, farm in Biskupstunga in south-west Iceland 10, 11, 12, 42, 51, 53, 55

Index of Place-Names

Haukagil ('Hawks' Gill'), farm in Vatsdalr in northern Iceland 36 (see note 12)

Hegranes, headland in Skagafjǫrðr in northern Iceland, site of regional assembly 38

Helgafell, mountain and farm on Snæfellsnes in western Iceland 35

Herfurða (Herford), in Westphalia in present-day Germany 51 (see note 99)

Hestlœkr (now Slauka), stream running into Hvítá in Grímsnes (see *ÍF* XV 137) 43

Hítará, river in Mýrar north of Borgarfjǫrðr 43

Hítarnes, farm in Hnappadalr north of Hítará 43

Hjaltadalr, area in Skagafjǫrðr 35, 53

Hjarðarholt, farm in Laxárdalr in western Iceland 53

Hof, farm on Rangárvellir in southern Iceland 35

Hólar (in Hjaltadalr), farm and bishop's see in Skagafjǫrðr in northern Iceland 10, 13, 37, 53, 54

Hólar, see Reykjahólar

Hólmgarðr (Novgorod), in present-day Russia 39

Hvammr, farm on Hvammsfjǫrðr off Breiðafjǫrðr 13, 36

Hvanneyrr, farm in Borgarfjǫrðr 36

Hǫfði, farm near Skálaholt in Biskupstunga 51

Hǫfn, farm in Borgarfjǫrðr 44

Hǫrgaeyrr, spit of land on Heimaey in Vestmannaeyjar 47 (see note 79)

Ingólfstell ('Ingólfr's Fell'), mountain west of Ǫlfossá in south-west Iceland 4

Ingólfshǫfði ('Ingólfr's Head'), headland in southern Iceland 4

Iceland 3, 4, 5, 7, 9, 10, 12, 14, 35, 36, 37, 38, 39, 40, 42, 45, 46, 47, 50, 51, 52, 53, 54

Icelanders 3, 13, 39, 45, 46, 47

Ireland 39

Irishmen 4, 10

Járnmeishǫfði, cliff in a bay near Hǫfn in Borgarfjǫrðr (see Kålund 1877–82: I 299) 44

Jerusalem 13, 50, 53

Jutland 38

Kálfalœkr, stream south of Hítará in western Iceland 43

Kirkjubœr, farm on Síða in south-east Iceland 41

Kjalarnes, headland north of Reykjavík in south-west Iceland 5, 39, 40

Kolsgjá ('Kolr's gorge'), north of Þingvellir (now unknown; see Kålund 1877–82: I 95) 5

Kristnes ('Christ's Headland'), farm in Eyjafjǫrðr 13

Krossaholt ('Hill of Crosses'), on Hítará in Hnappadalr 43

Krossavík (now Kirkjuból), farm north of Reyðarfjǫrðr in eastern Iceland (see *ÍF* XV 34) 49

Kœnugarðr (Kiev), in present-day Ukraine 50 (see note 91)

Landraugsholt (now Langdraugsholt?), near Hítará in Hnappadalr 43

Laugardalr, valley east of Þingvellir in south-west Iceland 8, 48, 50

Leiruvágr (coast by Starmýrarvogar?), bay in Southern Álptafjǫrðr 41

Ljósavatn, lake and farm east of Eyjafjǫrðr in northern Iceland 7

Lón, area south of Álptafjǫrðr on south-east coast of Iceland 4

Lœkjamót, farm in Víðidalr in northern Iceland 36, 38

Lœkjarbugr, farm south of Hítará in Mýrar 43

Melrakkanes, headland between Southern and Northern Álptafjǫrðr 41

Miklagarðr (Constantinople, now Istanbul) 13, 50

Minþakseyrr, spit of land west of Ingólfshǫfði on southeast coast of Iceland (unidentified; see Kålund 1877–82: I 344–5) 4 (see note 15)

Mosfell (Upper Mosfell), farm on Grímsnes in southwest Iceland 4, 7, 10, 13
Mostr, island off South Hǫrðaland in Norway 39
Mývatn, lake east of Skjálfandafljót in northern Iceland 42
Mœrr (Møre, probably Sunnmøre), area north of Hǫrðaland in western Norway 4
Mǫðruvellir, farm in Eyjafjǫrðr in northern Iceland 53, 55
Niðaróss (Trondheim), in Þrándheimr 45
Northern Quarter 7, 12, 35, 37, 42, 49, 50, 52
Northerners 7, 12, 52
Northmen 4
Norway 3, 4, 7, 9, 10, 11, 13, 38, 39, 50, 51, 52
Norwegians 4, 44
Pallteskja (Polotsk), in present-day Belorus 51 (see note 92)
Papar 4 (see note 18)
Rangá district (Rangárvellir), area between Ytri- and Eystri-Rangá (rivers) in southern Iceland 5
Rangá Quarter, see Southern Quarter
Rangá (western, now Ytri-Rangá), river in southern Iceland 45, 48
Reyðarfjǫrðr, fjord in eastern Iceland 49
Reykjahólar, farm west of Berufjǫrðr, off Breiðafjǫrðr 42, 53
Reykjaholt, farm in Borgarfjǫrðr 53
Reykjalaug, hot spring in Laugardalr 50
Reykjalaug, hot spring in Southern Reykjardalr 50
Reykjardalr, valley east of Skjálfandafljót in northern Iceland 35
Reykjardalr (Southern) (now Lundarreykjadalur), valley in Borgarfjǫrðr 50
Reykjarvík (Reykjavík), in south-west Iceland 4
Rome 52, 54
Russia 51
Saxland, eastern part of present-day Germany around Saxony 35, 38, 51

Scillies, islands off the coast of Cornwall in south-west England 39
Selvágar, bay in Northern Álptafjǫrðr 40
Seyðarfjǫrðr (Seyðisfjörður), fjord in eastern Iceland 49
Síða, a wide area along western and eastern Skaptafellssýsla in south-east Iceland 4, 7, 8, 13, 49, 53
Skagafjǫrðr, fjord and district in northern Iceland 7, 54
Skálaholt (Skálholt), farm and bishop's see in Biskupstunga in south-west Iceland 11, 12, 13, 51, 52, 53
Skarð (eastern), farm under Hekla on Rangárvellir (covered with lava 1389) 48
Skipahylr (now Skiphylur), farm south of Hítará in Mýrar 43
Skjálfandafljót, large river east of Eyjafjǫrðr in northern Iceland 42
Skógahverfi (part of Síða), area in southern Iceland 41
Skógar, farm under Eyjafjǫll in southern Iceland 35
Skrælingj(j)ar 7 (see note 57)
Southern Quarter 12, 42, 49, 50, 52
Steinsholt (now Náttmálaholt?), near Hítará in Hnappadalr 43
Svalbarð, farm on Eyjafjǫrðr in northern Iceland 37
Svǫlðr, river or island in/off Wendland 50
Swedes 3, 9, 13, 14, 53
Turks 14 (see note 111)
Upplanders, inhabitants of Upplǫnd (Oppland) in Norway 3, 14
Uppsala (Gamla Uppsala), seat of Swedish kings in eastern Sweden 9, 14
Vatsdalr, valley down from Húnafjörður in northern Iceland 35, 36
Vatsfjǫrðr, fjord off Ísafjarðardjúp in Western Fjords 54, 55
Vellankatla ('Boiling Kettle'), cove/creek on north-east side of Ǫlfossvatn 8, 48
Vendill (Vendel, Vendsyssel), in northern Jutland in Denmark (but here confused

Index of Place-Names

with Vendel in Swedish Upplǫnd) 14 (see note 117)

Vestmannaeyjar ('Islands of the Westerners' (i.e. Irishmen), Westman Islands), off the south coast of Iceland 8, 47

Vestrhóp, area south of Húnafjörður in northern Iceland 55

Víðidalr, valley west of Vatsdalr in northern Iceland 36

Vík (now Eyvík or Heyvík), farm on Grímsnes in south-west Iceland 42

Vík (inner part of Oslofjord), in eastern Norway 10, 52

Vínland 7 (see note 56), 47

Wendland, area in present-day northern Germany including Pommern, Mecklenburg and East Holstein and inhabited by Slavic peoples 39, 47

Western Fjords 48, 50

Western Quarter 12, 36, 37, 49, 52

Westerners, people from the Western Quarter 50

Ynglings, descendants of Yngvi 14

Þangbrandshróf ('Þangbrandr's Boathouse'), by Leiruvág on Southern Álptafjǫrðr 41

Þangbrandshróf ('Þangbrandr's Boathouse'), down from Skipahylr in western Iceland 43

Þangbrandslœkr ('Þangbrandr's brook', now Brandslœkr), stream by Skinnastaðir in Øxarfjǫrðr (see *ÍF* XV 134, note 1) 42

Þangbrandspollr ('Þangbrandr's pool'), by Skútustaðir near Mývatn (see *ÍF* XV 134, note 1) 42

Þingnes, headland near Hvítá in Borgarfjǫrðr, site of a regional assembly 6

Þingvǫllr ('Assembly Field'), in southwest Iceland (now usually pl. Þingvellir) 54. Cf. 'assembly field' (translation of sing. *þingvǫllr*) 8, 48

Þjórsárdalr, valley along Þjórsá (river) in southern Iceland (now uninhabited) 7, 45

Þrándheimr (Trøndelag), district in Norway 44, 45

Þváttá ('Washing River'), farm south of Southern Álptafjǫrðr in eastern Iceland 41

Ǫlfossvatn/Ǫlfusvatn (lake, now Þingvallavatn) 8, 48

Ǫlfossá (Ölfusá), river flowing from Ǫlfossvatn in southwest Iceland 4

Ǫlfus (Ǫlfoss), area in south-west Iceland 48

Ǫrnólfsdalr, farm north of Hvítá on Mýrar in western Iceland 6

Øxará, river running across Þingvellir into Ǫlfossvatn 45

Øxarfjǫrðr, fjord and district in north-east Iceland 42